14-20

THE
FLIGHT from
REASON

Library Bill of Rights

THE COUNCIL OF THE AMERICAN LIBRARY ASSOCIATION
REAFFIRMS ITS BELIEF IN THE FOLLOWING BASIC POLICIES
WHICH SHOULD GOVERN THE SERVICES OF ALL LIBRARIES.

I. As a responsibility of library service, books and other library materials selected should be chosen for values of interest, information and enlightenment of all the people of the community. In no case should library materials be excluded because of the race or nationality or the social, political, or religious views of the authors.

II. Libraries should provide books and other materials presenting all points of view concerning the problems and issues of our times; no library materials should be proscribed or removed from libraries because of partisan or doctrinal disapproval.

III. Censorship should be challenged by libraries in the maintenance of their responsibility to provide public information and enlightenment.

IV. Libraries should cooperate with all persons and groups concerned with resisting abridgment of free expression and free access to ideas.

V. The rights of an individual to the use of a library should not be denied or abridged because of his age, race, religion, national origins or social or political views.

VI. As an institution of education for democratic living, the library should welcome the use of its meeting rooms for socially useful and cultural activities and discussion of current public questions. Such meeting places should be available on equal terms to all groups in the community regardless of the beliefs and affiliations of their members, provided that the meetings be open to the public.

Adopted June 18, 1948.
Amended February 2, 1961, and June 27, 1967, by the ALA Council.

THE
FLIGHT *from*
REASON

*Essays on Intellectual Freedom
in the Academy,
the Press, and the Library*

DAVID K. BERNINGHAUSEN

American Library Association
Chicago 1975

Library of Congress Cataloging in Publication Data

Berninghausen, David K.
  The flight from reason.

  1. Censorship.   2. Libraries—Censorship.
3. Freedom of information.   I. Title.
Z657.B53   323.4'4   74-23236
ISBN 0-8389-0192-1

Contents

Foreword

The flight from reason takes many forms, both in societies and in individuals. As an illustration of such flight, witness the Soviet Union's attempts to silence creative thought by censoring its artists, a notable recent example being Alexander Solzhenitsyn. The writer of this Foreword, however, believes that in the Constitutional Republic of these United States, there can be no lasting flight from reason. The belief is premised on what we consider to be mankind's chief hope in the face of the onslaught of unreason: informed, reasonable persons in possession of the freedom to read, to see whatever they wish, and to disseminate their ideas. It is on this premise, also, that Mr. Berninghausen has undertaken his work.

Few will challenge outright the fundamental importance of this freedom, or right, that many have held to be inherent in the person. Jefferson believed that governments were instituted among men to protect such freedoms, and thus he found repugnant governmental controls on the exchange of ideas. Madison stated that "a popular government without popular information, or the means of acquiring it, is but a prologue to a farce or a tragedy." He added that "a people who mean to be their own governors must arm themselves with the power which knowledge gives." The authors of the Bill of Rights reflected the wisdom of Jefferson and Madison in drafting the First Amendment: "Congress shall make no law . . . abridging the freedom of speech and the press." This ostensibly absolute prohibition, extended to the states through the Fourteenth Amendment, forms the constitutional basis of what Mr. Berninghausen calls intellectual freedom, as well as its application to the press, the academy, and the library.

Everyone who reads a newspaper, enrolls in a class, or goes to a library benefits—or is deprived—by the extent to which intellectual freedom is a reality. As a librarian and outstanding spokesman for the practice of intellectual freedom in libraries, Mr. Berninghausen is particularly concerned for the freedoms of the librarian and the library user, freedoms the *Library Bill of Rights* was designed to foster. The principles of the *Library Bill of Rights* add a unique ingredient to librarianship in the United States. At various times and places, these principles have been explained away or criticized as something different from what their defenders hold them to be; nevertheless, they represent a commitment of the majority of librarians in the United States today.

Admittedly, intellectual freedom represents no absolute right. The limits of its applicability have long been a matter of intense debate. It is my hope that Mr. Berninghausen's reflections will provoke further discussion. This observation applies particularly to the persuasive section on library education, the cogent section on the differing concepts of librarianship, and the hopeful section on the defense of the defenders of intellectual freedom. I hope, too, that this may encourage an in-depth study of the library profession's efforts toward achieving intellectual freedom for everyone.

This book has been a long time in the writing. David Berninghausen has been a philosophical defender of the freedoms of speech and reading since the Forties, first while at Cooper Union and later as a member of the Intellectual Freedom Committee of the American Library Association and in the American Association of University Professors. He has much to say and he says it well.

DAVID H. CLIFT

September 15, 1973

Preface

It is the purpose of these essays to urge the reaffirmation of faith in reason, dialogue, and objective scholarship. The liberal approach to ideas that forms the central theme may be extended to cover art and letters also, as well as other kinds of scholarship, but the emphasis in this work is upon the need for intellectual freedom to increase one's objective understanding of the world in which one lives.

Man is not completely a rational being, and reason alone cannot be expected to bring salvation. Yet it is man's capacity to use his reason and intelligence that makes him unique among the living organisms on earth. His survival is contingent upon his ability to perceive his environment with reasonable accuracy, to investigate its mysteries without hindrance from taboos, and to communicate freely with his fellows. Ultimately, his survival depends upon his freedom to use his rational powers, limited though they be, toward resolution of the problems that confront him.

These essays are concerned with threats to intellectual freedom from both left and right. The cases described in chapter 4 illustrate attempts to suppress information by the Radical Right. The essays on intellectual freedom in the academy, the press, and the library describe the activities of the extreme Left during the 1960s and early 1970s, which seemed at times to overshadow those of the Radical Right. However, I share the view of former Senator Margaret Chase Smith, that the greatest danger to intellectual freedom in the United States was, in the period of McCarthyism, and still is, from the Radical Right.

The abuse and violence fostered by the New Left fanned the flames of extremism from the right. Within the framework suggested by the essays on the library, the press, and the academy, it would appear that the bias is to the left, and within the context of this work, this is true. But the focus of this work, as stated in the subtitle, must not obscure the more durable threat from the right.

Among the most obvious results of this threat from the left were the election of ultra-conservative government officials at various levels, the rejection of the findings of the President's Commission on Obscenity and Pornography by President Nixon and the majority of the United States senate, the appointment of four conservative members of the United States Supreme Court, and especially the June 21, 1973, decision of that court which gave individual states and localities the right to pass laws banning publications, films or plays. Thus the fanaticism of the left enabled the fanaticism of the right to capitalize on the fears of the majority, both groups gaining adherents in an attack upon the "liberal."

Whether pressures come from the left or the right, or both, it is the liberal position that suffers. During the past decade the liberal[1] was increasingly identified as the enemy. This is to be expected, for the fanatic, whether conservative or revolutionary, typically despises the liberal for being willing to tolerate the expression of "wrong and objectionable" views, because the fanatic *knows* the truth. The fanatic's absolute conviction that he knows the truth seems to him to justify his attempts to make expressions that he dislikes inacessible. Censors, whether they focus an attack upon the university, the press, or the library, try to limit access to ideas. When they succeed, the result is that everyone is handicapped in his efforts to perceive and understand his world. Hence he is handicapped in his use of reason to weigh the evidence in support of various theories or propositions.

For example, to the most convinced and intransigent opponents of abortion or pornography, free access to arguments for these evil ideas is abhorrent. Similarly, to those who oppose the use of nuclear energy, or the ROTC, or antiballistic missiles, the notion that these subjects are even debatable is intolerable. Frequently, dedicated groups mount organized campaigns advocating censorship in school, press, or library to prevent these social agencies from disseminating "false" arguments favoring such ideas.

Opposition to censorship can come only from people who advocate a "liberal" approach to ideas, those who are willing to permit the expression of all points of view, insisting that individual citizens must have access to the evidence supporting various propositions, so that they can weigh it and form their own judgments.

These essays stem from my observations of various groups of censors, especially during the period from 1948 to 1954, and again from 1967 to 1972. In the earlier period McCarthyism and the Radical Right seriously threatened the maintenance of the principle of intellectual freedom. Twenty years later, in addition to the pressures from the Right, the extreme Left brought its own attack. During both of these critical periods

1. In this context, the term "liberal" refers to a person who practices the "liberal approach to ideas," rather than one who is regarded as "left of center" on a political or social continuum. *See* "Definitions Intended" following this preface.

I was the chairman of the American Library Association's (ALA) Committee on Intellectual Freedom.

My observations of attempts to prevent free inquiry are also based on other experiences: in the early 1950s I worked with the Stop Censorship Committee of Broadway producers, actors, and directors, and with the Defense Commission of the National Education Association, helping to draft the statement: "The Public School and the American Heritage." At that time I was also a member of the Board of Directors of the New York State Civil Liberties Union. Later for seven years I was a member of the Board of the Minnesota Civil Liberties Union. As a member of the University of Minnesota's American Association of University Professors (AAUP) Committee on Academic Freedom and Tenure, I learned much about the policies and procedures of the AAUP. Later as president of the University of Minnesota chapter of AAUP, and as a member of this university's Senate Judicial Committee, I observed various aspects of the problem of maintaining academic freedom. In 1969 I served as Chairman of a Task Force of faculty and students which recommended a change from a faculty senate to a University Senate which includes students. These and other experiences have undoubtedly helped to shape my conclusions, and the reader is entitled to know of this background if he is to weigh properly the themes explored and the views expressed in these essays.

The ideas expressed in these essays are those of the author, who does not presume to speak for the University of Minnesota, nor for the library profession, nor for "the people."

Also, I state a disclaimer to any notion that this book is the last word on the subject of intellectual freedom. One of the wise men I have encountered, I. A. Richards, coauthor of *The Meaning of Meaning,* once told me: "Never be guilty of using the phrase, 'In the final analysis. . . .' It is foolish to use this expression, for you can be quite sure that yours is *not* the final analysis. There will be others."

Of course there will be other analyses. The dialogue about the nature and value of free inquiry will continue. Neither an advocacy press, nor the Radical Right's attempts to censor wrong ideas, nor the New Left's efforts to establish new, rigid patterns of orthodoxy can stop the dialogue. Perhaps, temporarily, a government *might* close some of the channels of communication, thus hindering the dialogue. What may be even more ominous is the complex problem of how to use satellites in international communications. Chapter 6 illuminates this problem by contrasting the world views of democratic states and totalitarian states on the subject of free access to information and on objectivity in the academy and the press. Apparently the United States stands alone among nations in espousing free access to programs available around the globe by satellite.

These essays, then, are presented as one part of the necessary dialogue about intellectual freedom. It is *necessary,* for, if scholars are not free to conduct honest, objective research; if teachers and students are not free to examine the evidence in support of rival propositions; if libraries are not free to collect and disseminate the reports of scholarly inquiries; or if the press is controlled by a government or by advocacy journalists, then we face a bleak future. If any of these professions were to reject the obligation to maintain a stance of neutrality on substantive issues—in their professional roles—if they were to reject the obligation to perform as objectively as is humanly possible, then decisions affecting the future will be made by those who can command the biggest weapons. Violence can so easily replace dialogue. I believe it to be the special obligation of scholars, teachers, students, journalists, and librarians to keep the channels of communication open, as an essential condition for civilization.

Acknowledgments

I am so heavily indebted to so many colleagues at the University of Minnesota and in the library profession that it is impossible to list more than a small number who have criticized early drafts of these essays.

In the field of communications, the suggestions of the following were of great value: Robert B. Hudson of the Communications Institute, East-West Center, Honolulu; and at the University of Minnesota, E. W. Ziebarth, Dean of the College of Liberal Arts and Professors J. Edward Gerald and Robert Lindsay of the School of Journalism and Communications.

In the field of librarianship, Ralph and Mary Shaw and Stanley West, University of Hawaii; Professors E. W. McDiarmid, Wesley Simonton, Edward B. Stanford, Joan H. Leigh, and Raymond Shove, University of Minnesota; Russell Bidlack, Dean of the Library School, University of Michigan; Everett Moore, University of California at Los Angeles; Grace Stevenson, former Associate Executive Secretary of the American Library Association; and Albert P. Marshall, Eastern Michigan University at Ypsilanti, these and many others, while not necessarily in agreement with the views expressed in these essays, have been especially helpful with advice and suggestions.

I am also grateful to the scores of members of the American Library Association who have expressed their appreciation for my efforts to clarify distinctions between mutually exclusive ideas: (1) The incompatibility of a concept of the ALA as a "liberal" organization, one which accepts its obligation to preserve free access to all points of view for all users of libraries, and a concept that this organization should be politicized and used to propagate worthy causes unrelated to the purposes of the library profession; (2) the incompatibility of a concept of a library as an *advocate* for a worthy cause and the concept of a publicly-supported library which recognizes its obligation to take a neutral stance on substantive, nonlibrary issues, in accordance with the Library Bill of Rights.

Definitions Intended

1. *Liberal.* This is an ambiguous term. In these essays, unless it is indicated otherwise, *liberal* is used to refer to a person who attempts to practice the liberal approach to ideas. Philosopher Morris Cohen described this approach as follows:

> This open eye for possible alternatives, each to receive the same logical treatment before we can determine which is the best grounded, is the essence of liberalism in art, morals and politics. Conservatism clings to what is established, fearing that if we let go, all the values of life will perish. The radical or revolutionary, impressed with the evil of the existing order or disorder, recklessly puts all faith in some principle without regard for the hidden dangers which it may contain, let alone the cruel hardships which readjustments must involve. The liberal views life as an adventure in which we must take risks in new situations, but in which there is no guaranty that the new will always be the good or the true. Like science, liberalism insists on a critical examination of the content of all our beliefs, principles, or initial hypotheses and on subjecting them to a continuous process of verification so that they will be progressively better founded in experience and reason.[1]

The term *liberal* is often used as an antonym for *conservative,* indicating that, on some continuum or other, a person spoken of as *liberal* is left of center, or at least left of the speaker or writer. In these essays, unless it is so indicated, the term *liberal* will not be intended to indicate a revolutionary view on a substantive issue. It is true that people who use the

1. Morris Cohen, *Faith of a Liberal* (New York: Holt, 1946), p. 8. [Quoted with permission of Harry N. Rosenfield, Administrator, Estate of Morris R. Cohen.]

liberal approach to ideas, holding them up for examination, weighing the evidence to support even the self-evident proposition against the evidence to support possible alternatives, tend to take left-of-center positions on social and political questions.

Persons who attempt to use the liberal approach to ideas are usually regarded by the revolutionary—and by the ultraconservative—as their natural enemies. "If you're not with me, you're against me!" says the fanatic. But liberals try to weigh and balance the claims of rival prophets, discounting the radical brands of revealed truth, and, as Harry S. Ashmore of the Center for the Study of Democratic Institutions says, ". . . displaying the quality that renders their breed conspicuous, and scorned, when passions run high—the capacity to entertain two opposing ideas at the same time."[2] This quality naturally produces hostility in the completely polarized fanatic.

2. *Intellectual Freedom.* In these essays this term includes three related ideas: a) academic freedom; b) freedom of the press; and c) free access to all points of view for all people through libraries.

a) *Academic Freedom:* This term refers to the freedom of a scholar to choose for himself his topic of inquiry, freedom to explore it without restrictions, freedom to reach the conclusions which seem to him to be warranted by the evidence and his analysis of it, without expectation of reward or penalty for having reached certain conclusions. This concept also includes the freedom of the teacher to describe, explain, and hold up for examination, any facts or theories pertinent to his professed field of expertise. It also includes freedom for the student to accept or reject any of these theories without penalty or reward (this definition is elaborated in chapter 5).

b) *Freedom of the Press:* In the Western democracies this term refers to the concept that reporters and editors must be free to provide honest, objective pictures of the world that surrounds man, thus helping him to perceive the world and interact with it, without fear of penalties or expectations of reward for describing events in a way that pleases or displeases some people. (Chapter 6 describes this idea in detail and contrasts the Western libertarian theory of the press and the totalitarian theory.)

c) *Intellectual Freedom in Librarianship:* In librarianship the general term *intellectual freedom* has been commonly used to designate the obligation of librarians to strive to preserve, for all users of libraries, free access to expressions of all points of view, on all controversial issues. The specific term is the same as the general term and has been, since 1940, when the American Library Association established as a standing committee The Committee on Intellectual Freedom to Safeguard the Rights of Library Users to Freedom of Inquiry.

2. Harry S. Ashmore, "Where Have All the Liberals Gone?", *Center Magazine* 2: 30 (July 1969). *Center Magazine* is a publication of the Center for the Study of Democratic Institutions.

1   *Educating Librarians for Intellectual Freedom*

I am very strongly interested that the function of the intellectual as well as his motivation and his responsibility be better understood by the public. . . . My main point is that the intellectual has a very specific function to fulfill which goes far beyond the other important functions of the citizen at large. He is the custodian of a tradition of honesty and sincerity on which the future and the honor of his country and his age depend. He has some privileges—and in order to merit these privileges he must accept a responsibility for the priesthood of truth and intellectual honor well beyond what belongs to the citizen at large.

—NORBERT WEINER[1]

In Allen Drury's *Advise and Consent* there is a scene in which the southern Senator is harassing the "intellectual" nominated for the post of Secretary of State. The Senator asks, in a nasty tone of voice: "You are an egghead, aren't you?" And instead of cringing and modestly denying any claims to intellectuality, the nominee replies: "Indeed. I am an egghead. You might say that I am an egghead in full flower, and I hope to shed a little pollen wherever I go."

Professors in library schools too should try to shed some "pollen." It is their responsibility as intellectuals to persuade their students that they have chosen a profession that commits them to the principle of intellectual freedom. Librarians, while viewed by the general public as people interested in ideas, and therefore as intellectuals, should be humble about the level of intellectuality at which they operate—but they cannot and should not attempt to escape the label or the responsibilities that go with it.

When the college graduate enters library school, he may or he may not have an appreciation of the nature and significance of free scholarship. There is much evidence in our society to indicate that many college graduates do not have this understanding. As a part of the orientation of future librarians to the world of ideas, library educators might deliber-

This essay was originally entitled "Teaching a Commitment to Intellectual Freedom." Reprinted, with revisions, from *Library Journal* 92: 3601–5 (Oct. 15, 1967). Published by R. R. Bowker Co. (a Xerox Company). Copyright © 1967, R. R. Bowker Co.

ately present twentieth-century humanity's *need* for library and information service, for its storehouse of scientific and scholarly knowledge, for every scrap of data that libraries can collect, for free scholars exercising their intelligence on the problems of human society.

Library educators cannot take it for granted that students have an appreciation of the need for, or even the possibility of, *dis*interested scholarship. Of course, the scholar is not *un*interested in his research. Naturally, he is interested in what he is doing. But he must be disinterested in the sense that he provides all the safeguards possible against bias, against sloppy or inaccurate observations, against imprecise reporting, and against the drawing of conclusions not warranted by the evidence. The scholar is, and must be, disinterested in that he reports as his findings, not what he hopes to find, not what someone else wants him to find, but what the evidence warrants. In short, the scholar requires the freedom to be honest.

Future librarians must be equipped with an understanding of the nature of free scholarship, and also an understanding of the fact that many citizens find it inconceivable that any intellectual could be disinterested. Some of the censors' attacks stem from this failure to appreciate the nature and significance of scholarship.

If library educators are to teach a commitment to intellectual freedom, what shall be its content? It would be possible, of course, to present here a long list of references to writers such as John Milton, Zechariah Chafee, Thomas Jefferson, John Stuart Mill, among others.

But have library school students read, for example, *On Liberty?* Library education standards require a four-year degree for admission, and while it is probably safe to assume that students are interested in ideas, it is not a justifiable assumption that they have read the classic writers on freedom of speech and thought. Indeed, of 150 students to enter the library school at Minnesota in one year, only 14 had read *On Liberty*.

When we assign this small book as required reading in our library school, discussion reveals a rather common reaction to it, as follows: "Well, most of this squares with what I think, myself; however. . . ." And the rest of the comment points to difficulties which Mill failed to clear up. Mill's ideas on freedom of thought have been absorbed into our cultural consciousness, even though our students have not read Mill, and most seem to feel they can accept his three chief contentions:

1. Suppression of opinion may blot out truth; no one is infallible and an unconventional opinion may turn out to be true.
2. Even though an opinion is false, truth is served by refuting error; beliefs not founded on reasoned conviction are not held firmly enough to guide human conduct.
3. No opinion is completely true or false; an unconventional opinion may be useful because it contains some particle of truth. Freedom of thought and opinion should not be curbed by collective authority.[2]

Regardless of the degree of acceptance of Mill's ideas, students who have read *On Liberty* have knowledge of his ideas in common, and this is useful for critical and pointed discussion of actual cases. Cases, of course, serve only as illustrations, as guides to the nature of the problem, but they can and should be a part of the program of instruction in library schools which attempt to teach a commitment to intellectual freedom.

From the large number of possible cases I have chosen for illustration here the amendment to the New York State Education Law of 1950. On August 11 of that year, Lewis Wilson, Commissioner of Education, sent to public schools a directive which said: "Subject to rules and regulations of the Board of Regents, a pupil may be excused from such study of health and hygiene as conflicts with the religion of his parents or guardian. Such conflict must be certified by a proper representative of their religions as defined by Section 2 of the religious corporations law."

The Commissioner's directive stated that he approved the exemption of the children of parents or guardians of the Christian Science faith from instruction in the units of Disease Prevention and Control and three other specified areas.

As a result of this directive, the New York Teachers Guild, the Association of Biology Teachers, and the New York State Civil Liberties Union prepared briefs *amicus curiae* on the issue, presenting these arguments:

The law is impractical and discriminatory and it also imposes a censorship on education
The law establishes a precedent for further control by special groups
The law establishes an intolerable iron curtain over ideas which are now part of our common heritage.

The Christian Science leaders argued:

> We are not asking for exemption from the teaching of the germ theory of disease nor from any teaching which affects the prevention and control of communicable disease. All we ask is exemption from compulsory study of the symptoms and processes of diseases and the medical treatment of them. We do not wish any alteration in Regents' examinations. As a minority group, we are willing to make any sacrifice for the good of the majority other than the sacrifice of our religious rights.[3]

At first glance it appears to many students that, in this case, John Stuart Mill's emphasis upon freedom of religious choice collides with his ideas on freedom of thought, and library school classes usually have a lively discussion. Questions that are discussed include: How can a school administrator carry out the provisions of this law and avoid embarrassment of any pupil? Does the principal take a religious census of his pupils? If he does, isn't that a violation of the law against discrimination? Does the school send the minority group to the library whenever germs are mentioned? Is this a proper use of the library? Does the librarian have a responsibility to keep away from Christian Scientists books which mention germs?

Also, most library school students have little or no understanding of the fact that legislatures make laws which affect the operations of libraries. The case illuminates this aspect of librarianship, creating a problem for the librarian. Will he be violating the law if he buys books or magazines or films that treat of the germ theory of disease? If this law passed in New York is followed to the letter, is education possible? And a major question raised is: How do we in schools and libraries resolve a conflict between these two cherished principles: religious freedom for the individual; and freedom of thought in education?

Unless we are willing to accept as valid the contention that *education* and *indoctrination* are synonymous, this conflict is more apparent than actual. A pupil belonging to the Church of Christ, Scientist, who studies the history of the Panama Canal and learns that yellow fever was controlled by killing off the mosquitoes, thereby enabling the laborers to build the canal, is still entirely free to believe in and practice his religion. His history teacher cannot coerce him to a belief which he is determined to reject. His freedom to choose and practice his religion has not been taken away from him.

This case also provides an opportunity for the library school student to learn that the American Library Association has allies in its efforts to preserve the freedom to read in our society. Item 4 in the Library Bill of Rights, which urges librarians to cooperate with other individuals and groups, is thus illustrated.

It is relatively easy to organize the forces *for* censorship, for the appeal can be made in simplistic terms, for example, "Join the Citizens for Decent Literature and Stamp Out Juvenile Delinquency." Frequently, this slogan is supplemented with another, such as, "Obscenity Is Communist-Inspired, Let's Stamp It Out." Such slogans are appealing. They are also deceptively simple, and they seem to suggest that here is a formula which will bring quick salvation. They are appealing because there is in every one of us a desire for the blessed security that comes from absolute assurance that we know how to rid our society of juvenile delinquency.

It is more difficult to organize forces *against* censorship, for to be moved to action on behalf of freedom to read, one must recognize that the relationship between reading and behavior is a complex, rather than a simple, matter. One must be sophisticated enough to resist the natural wish to find the one, single cause of evils of this world. One must be able to distinguish between single, or one-to-one causal relationships and multiple causation.

In spite of the inflammatory writings of Frederick Wertham, or the declarations of J. Edgar Hoover, or Congresswoman Kathryn Granahan, anyone who tries to study the "causes of delinquency" quickly finds that the one point on which almost all authorities agree is that the causes are multiple, that there is no single cause. And moreover, as one student at Minnesota discovered during an investigation of the subject, reading is almost never mentioned as a cause by the serious students of juvenile delinquency. Indeed, it is well-established by many studies that a very large majority of juvenile delinquents are nonreaders or very poor readers.

Here, then, is another idea which should be included in the library school curriculum: The assumption that reading lewd literature causes delinquency is no more than an assumption. There is little or no evidence of a one-to-one causal relationship between reading pornography and juvenile delinquency.

Of course, one can hardly expect to cover the subject exhaustively in one year of library school. But professors can aim to alert all students to the realization that preserving the freedom to read is and will continue to be a responsibility for librarians. Somehow, our consideration of the subject must take it out of the realm of "academic" study. One way to do this is to refer to actual experiences of former students. For example, there was Miss S., who three months after graduation found her library adult forum program under severe public attack by right wing extremists because she had scheduled three "controversial professors" as speakers. Her head librarian and the public library board supported free speech, and finally one of the speakers won a libel suit against the critics.

Another example to consider is that of Mrs. B., a school librarian in a rural community. She gave *Catcher in the Rye* to an English teacher to read, with the result that the teacher complained to the superintendent. In this instance, the superintendent and the school board were persuaded to study and adopt the Library Bill of Rights and the School Library Bill of Rights as school board policy. Later the English teacher began to read much more widely than ever before.

And, students might well flex their intellects on the case of the library school student who read Mill, Chafee, Jefferson, and various articles from library literature on censorship, but still felt committed to protect his patrons by razor-blading certain passages out of Chaucer's *Canterbury Tales*. This case creates a dilemma for the library educator. The young man's convictions must be respected. Even if it were possible to "indoctrinate" him with the lofty ideals expressed in the Library Bill of Rights, as, of course, it is not, would it be appropriate to do so? However, should he be recommended for a library position in a publicly supported institution? He is committed, not to the ideals of the library profession, but to suppress what he doesn't like.

To sharpen this point for our students, library schools should discuss the ethics of librarianship in terms of: *It is unethical for a librarian in a publicly supported library to suppress statements he doesn't like, or to exclude expressions of ideas that are objectionable to any religious or political or other organization to which he belongs. A professional librarian's first commitment must be to intellectual freedom for everyone.* It may also be instructive in this connection to assign some readings on the concept of libraries in the Soviet Union, where all librarians are required to promote only the doctrines approved by the Communist government.[4]

At the 1965 Washington Conference on Freedom of Inquiry, Lee A. Burress stated in his paper that little attention is given to intellectual freedom in the school teacher training programs, and that, in fact, there is more likely to be an emphasis upon the importance of public relations of the school than on the development of professionally competent and independent personalities. Edward R. Murrow's *See It Now* film on California librarians, showing four school librarians timidly appearing in silhouette versus Mrs. Anne Smart who was willing to state her case for censorship in full picture and voice, is a dramatic and sobering lesson for prospective librarians. Here, too, we see school officials seeking to promote smooth public relations at the expense of free inquiry.

It is also important to show students that if a climate of opinion favoring censorship, whether it is censorship of obscenity, scientific literature, or of religious, political, or social literature, becomes established, our citizen readers will not have available the necessary information for making wise decisions. As Dan Lacy has pointed out, the countries which exercise the most thorough controls over publications about sex are probably Communist China, Russia, Ireland, South Africa, and Spain. Surely it is not an accident that these countries also practice censorship in political literature.

Library school students should have the opportunity to learn that censorship is contagious—that it tends to spread from one kind of literature to others—and that if we accept the Postmaster General, with his thousands of volunteer helpers, as our literary critics, it is not going to be easy to maintain our traditional freedom of information.

The library school curriculum should alert students to the distinction between "approved" and "recommended" lists of books. The Daughters of the American Revolution, or the National Organization for Decent Literature, or the Citizens for Decent Literature publish and distribute lists of approved and unapproved books. Librarians must avoid any issuance of a list of "approved" titles, for this inevitably suggests that any titles not listed are "unapproved." Libraries may *recommend* books, but it is a violation of the principle of intellectual freedom for a library or librarian to *approve* books.

For example, in 1958 the DAR prepared a master list of textbooks, classifying them as "satisfactory" or "unsatisfactory." This organization, like any other in the United States, has every right to take positions on issues. They may and have opposed the United Nations and participation in the United Nations by the United States. They have every right to oppose foreign aid and fluoridation. Perhaps it will not be a major disaster if they protest against the Tarzan books, though, as Harry Golden writes:

> Some of the DAR ladies took time out from their fight against the United Nations and fluoridation to demand the elimination of the Tarzan books from the libraries. The DAR suspects Tarzan and Jane are living together without benefit of clergy, openly and happily if athletically.
> But as with fluoridation, the ladies are wrong. Jane and Tarzan were indeed married by Edgar Rice Burroughs in the second Tarzan book and sometime later Boy floated down from an airplane, which solved the obstacle of illegitimacy and at the same time gave Boy an advantage in not being related to Jane and Tarzan and therefore not as neurotic as they. . . .[5]

But when the DAR presumes to dictate to our school teachers, declaring that here is a list of 50 satisfactory books and here are 165 unsatisfactory books now in use in our schools, they go too far. They create a dangerous climate of censorship. The list of unsatisfactory authors on the DAR list includes Henry Steele Commanger, Allan Nevins, Harold Laski, Morris Ernst, Carl Carmer, Vera M. Dean, George Counts, Harold Lasswell, and Zechariah Chafee, all of whom are highly respected authorities in their fields.

In 1960 the Mississippi legislature—by a vote of 82 to 44—gave Governor Ross Barnett the power to select all of the state's textbooks. Authors Jack London, Arthur Miller, Carl Sandburg, and Archibald MacLeish were deemed subversive by some Mississippians and the governor urged: "Clean up our textbooks. Our children must be properly informed of the Southern and true American way of life."

Probably very few of the good people who join volunteer censor groups have read the books of Commager, Chafee, or MacLeish. These are just names—names of authors that someone has put on a list of "unsatisfactory" books. Well-intentioned people who join organizations to control obscenity are seldom aware of the contagious character of censorship, and library schools have an obligation to reveal to their students that wherever a society has a weakness or a blind spot, it tends to feel that censorship is necessary. Once it adopts the practice in one field, it seems necessary in other fields, as illustrated by historian James Silver in his book *Mississippi, the Closed Society.* Censorship is contagious.

And speaking of blind spots, since library education must accept the responsibility for teaching documentation, some documentalists have a curious notion that they do not need to know anything about the problems of censorship in libraries—that this is a problem for public and school libraries only. This is not so. Witness the banning of the *Bulletin of Atomic Scientists* in various libraries. For a specific illustration, consider the story of Dr. Edward U. Condon, driven out of his job as director of the U.S. Bureau of Standards because people less well informed than he thought his interest in Russian scientific literature grounds for suspicion.

Dr. Condon's contributions to scholarship were very considerable. His record was scrutinized in three full-scale loyalty investigations, and in each he received full clearance. Library educators must be sure that they teach an understanding by documentalists that the director of the U.S. Bureau of Standards, our scientists, and our librarians are failing to do their jobs if they are *not* interested in securing and distributing Russian scientific literature.

Documentalists, and all other librarians, must learn that censorship is contagious, and that the Library Bill of Rights applies to all media collected or distributed by libraries. Although written for a public library, the present policy of the Palisades Free Library, New York, is pertinent:

> [The responsibility of the Library] . . . is to serve all the community, not to promote—and above all, not to censor—any particular political, moral, philosophical, or religious convictions or opinions. It is not the purpose of the Library to stimulate or to cater to trivial, antisocial, prurient, or immoral interests. But no one, least of all a free public library, has the right to judge what another may or may not read or hear.
>
> If a member of the Library wishes to find out for himself whether a certain publication is worthless, tasteless, vicious, or inaccurate, it is the function of the Library to give him an opportunity to do so. Furthermore, history shows that many books which have been most controversial or objectionable to some persons or groups have in due course been recognized to be among those books which most, rather than least, belong in public libraries. If an idea is truly dangerous or evil, the best protection against it is a public which has been exposed to it and has rejected it; the worst protection is a public which has been shielded from exposure to it by official or self-appointed guardians.
>
> Therefore, in the event that anyone in or out of the community should object to the Library's acquisition or retention of a certain publication on moral, political, religious, or philosophical grounds, the objection should be recognized as an indication that the publication in question may well be of more than routine interest and may be likely to be requested by members of the community who wish to judge its merits and demerits for themselves.

This policy statement illuminates what was (before its 1967 revision) an unfortunate aspect of the otherwise very valuable policy statement of the ALA, the Library Bill of Rights. Before 1967 the statement had said that books "of sound factual authority" should not be proscribed or removed from libraries. In the 1948 revision of the Library's Bill of Rights, when it became the Library Bill of Rights, this point had been debated, and it was decided then to leave the phrase in the policy. However, by 1967 it had become evident that there are many documents which some people would judge to be *not* "of sound factual authority" which should be and must be in libraries.

In Belleville, Illinois, Robert B. Kirchgraber, the public librarian, who is a Roman Catholic, refused to place in the library the periodical *Church and State,* an unsolicited gift subscription. He believed that this publication, the official organ of Protestants and Other Americans United for Separation of Church and State, was disqualified because it was not "of sound factual authority." As Kirchgraber pointed out, his argument for exclusion was based upon the Library Bill of Rights (as it then read).

This case provides a fine opportunity for library science students to gain a sense of participation in the ongoing process of librarianship. The ALA statement against prejudicial labeling, or the Freedom to Read statement, were once current, undecided questions. For the beginning library student, however, they may very well be merely "of historical interest." Current issues in librarianship always exist and should be included in library school curricula. Old issues, such as those presented in chapter 4, can illuminate basic principles.

Outbreaks of censorship are likely to occur when nonreaders discover the world of books and ideas. As has been pointed out elsewhere, it is a predictable result of the expansion of library services through federal aid to libraries, that there will be even more attempts at censorship. As a school system is staffed with better prepared teachers, teachers who stimulate the intellectual processes of their students by introducing books such as *1984,* or *Catcher in the Rye,* instead of sticking to "safe," noncontroversial textbooks, there will be further attempts at censorship.

Library school students, our future librarians, need this kind of perspective. They also need to learn that the censors who frequently try to impose their own prejudices and their own limitations upon everyone else are frequently very few in number, representing a tiny fraction of our society, which, even though it has not read Mill's *On Liberty,* basically believes in the value of freedom of thought. Also, they need to learn that publicity can be an effective weapon against the censor.

Finally, in any consideration of teaching a commitment to intellectual freedom, some attention should be given to the nature of truth and scholarship. This is, of course, a large subject and actually should be the outcome expected of any liberal education (*see* chapter 2).

For nearly forty years, library education in America has been based upon an assumption that students who have been awarded a Bachelor's degree have acquired the appropriate prerequisite for a year of graduate library education. As we have shown in this essay, and will demonstrate in chapter 5, "The Flight from Reason," the liberal arts college has not always succeeded in providing its graduates with the necessary liberal education.

All college graduates who apply for admission to library schools may not have achieved an appreciation of the values of a liberal education, which depends especially upon acceptance of two propositions:

1. The best approach to any theory or idea advanced is to hold it up for examination, asking what evidence exists to persuade the examiner to prefer this theory to one of the possible alternatives, and

2. Tolerance for free expression of any proposition advanced is essential for the advancement of man's knowledge of his universe.

Unless librarians understand and accept both of these propositions, they cannot expect to preserve intellectual freedom for the users of libraries. Librarians who lack this understanding may fall victim to those who seek to use the American Library Association and the American public library to propagate their personal biases and convictions.[6]

Library educators should note the findings by Remmers and Radler, that teenagers believed, by a majority of 60 percent to 27 percent, that "Police and other groups have sometimes banned or censored certain books and movies in their cities, and that they should have the power to do this."[7] It would be foolish to hope that when these young people reach library school they will have relinquished this attitude. Library educators should provide students with the perspective for understanding the meaning and significance of intellectual freedom, declaring positively that: "We believe that what people read is deeply important; that ideas can be dangerous; but that the suppression of ideas is fatal to a democratic society. Freedom itself is a dangerous way of life, but it is ours."

2 *Intellectual Freedom and the Communication Process*

There is an island in the ocean where in 1914 a few Englishmen, Frenchmen, and Germans lived. No cable reaches that island, and the British mail steamer comes but once in sixty days. In September it had not yet come, and the islanders were still talking about the latest newspaper which told about the approaching trial of Madame Caillaux for the shooting of Gaston Calmette. It was, therefore, with more than usual eagerness that the whole colony assembled at the quay on a day in mid-September to hear from the captain what the verdict had been. They learned that for over six weeks now those of them who were English and those of them who were French had been fighting in behalf of the sanction of treaties against those of them who were German. For six strange weeks they had acted as if they were friends, when in fact they were enemies. . . .

—WALTER LIPPMANN[1]

Fifty years after Mr. Lippmann published this story it is obvious that man's world has undergone great changes. Moreover, as Alvin Toffler dramatically tells us in *Future Shock,* the rate of change continues to accelerate. Travellers to remote areas of this planet have noted that today, in almost every tiny village, at least the chief has a radio, and that, to some extent, news of the whole family of man is available to all.

Walter Lippmann's story, "The World Outside and the Pictures in Our Heads," reminds us that man reacts to and interacts with the external world according to the pictures of reality which he holds in his head. If we assume that ideas have consequences, then these pictures should approximate the reality. If they do not, the individual may act inappropriately and fail to survive. Even a whole species, if it holds a false picture of the external world, may fail to survive.

Scholars, teachers, journalists, and librarians, by their choice of profession, are forced to give special attention to the process of communication. This process begins with perception through our senses. Perception is followed by the effort of the perceiver to organize his perceptions in a way that has meaning to *him*. The process includes the reflection which leads to the formulation of ideas; then comes the attempt to put these ideas into words and sentences (with all the attendant semantic difficulties). Members of these professions must also become acutely aware

11

of how selectivity, both by the originator of a message and by the receiver, tends to impede successful communication. At every step along the way, errors may be, and often are made.

Scholars and teachers are very much concerned with that kind of intellectual freedom called "academic freedom." Journalists constantly urge their publics to recognize the importance of "freedom of the press." Librarians accept a special responsibility for preserving free access to expressions of all points of view, on all subjects, for all people. All these professional groups share a special concern for intellectual freedom. (These three kinds of intellectual freedom are defined in some detail in the Definitions following the author's acknowledgments.)

Perception

Through his perceptions, man, like other organisms, maintains contact with his environment and with his internal state or condition. Reasonably accurate perception of the external world is essential for survival of either an individual or a species.

Probably everyone will acknowledge that, at times his perception of an event is less than perfect, that is, that it fails to some degree to correspond to the reality. Perhaps it is not too much to suggest that we should question even what we have "seen with our own eyes," for even what we think we have seen or heard may be a *mis*perception, because of faulty vision or hearing, lack of our full attention, or because we got merely a quick glimpse of one small section of the world outside our heads and concluded that we had perceived enough to form a judgment as to what was really out there. Or, sometimes, we may have perceived something as if it were fixed and unchanging, when in fact, it was *in process*.

For a discussion of the process of communication and some of the difficulties in making it work, R. H. Day's definition of perception is useful as a point of departure:

> In broad terms perception can be defined as the organism's maintenance of contact with its environment, its internal state, and its own posture and motion. Two points need to be clear from the outset. First, perception involves not only keeping in touch with objects and events physically removed from the animal, but also its internal state and self-induced activity. Second, perception is not a peculiarly human activity; animals from simple unicellular organisms to highly developed vertebrates must maintain contact with events in the interests of environmental adaptations and survival. . . .[2]

The capacity of the human organism to perceive, that is, to notice energy changes, electromagnetic, mechanical, or chemical, is limited. For example, human vision does not perceive in the infrared range, as does that of a rattlesnake who can, in effect, "see in the dark," detecting a rat by means of perception in the infrared portion of the spectrum. For the human observer the *visible* spectrum composed of light waves consists of only about one-seventieth of the total (light with wavelengths extending over $301-700\mu$). The human ear is sensitive only to sounds with frequencies between about 20 and 20,000 cycles per second (cps). For the most part, only young observers with acute hearing can respond to sounds of 20,000 cps, the upper limit for a normal adult being about 12,000 to 15,000 cps.

It is important to remember that different individual human organisms have different capacities. Some of us have faulty vision due to astigmatism or myopia. Some of us hear less well than others. It cannot be expected that we will all equally perceive the world *as it is*. Unfortunately, unless we take great care, we tend to think that the world *is* the way we perceive it. (The recently popular demand, "Tell it like it is," is not merely grammatically incorrect; frequently it reveals an extreme tendency to mistake the demander's partially correct perception for reality.) Much of the time this does not matter greatly, but sometimes our individual adaptation to the environment can lead to serious difficulties, if we assume that reality matches our perception completely.

We See What We Expect to See

Although no one deliberately falsifies his environment, at least to himself, one observer's experience is never exactly that of another's. Moreover, each individual interprets his perceptual experience in terms of his previous experiences, his current mood, and his current purposes. To a significant extent, he sees what he expects to see, as the Bruner experiment with anomalous cards revealed.

Bruner and Postman[3] asked subjects to identify on short and controlled exposure a series of playing cards, most of which were normal, but some of which were anomalous; that is, there was a red six of spades and a black four of hearts. These anomalous cards were almost always identified without apparent hesitation as normal; the black four of hearts, for example, might be identified as the four of either spades or hearts. The unusual card was immediately fitted to one of the categories that the subject expected to see because it was known in his previous experience. Later, as the exposure time was increased, subjects would note that something was wrong. Finally, most subjects would identify all cards correctly.

In this experiment with the anomalous cards, there were real objects: the cards, with physical structures and characteristics that could be observed by the subjects. This *structural* reality is one of the factors governing perception. Krech and Crutchfield[4] tell us that a man's perceptions are also affected by what they call *functional factors,* those which derive primarily from the needs, moods, past experience, and memory of the individual. As he interprets the stimuli to which he chooses to respond—or, more precisely, those *particular* stimuli to which he chooses to respond—he attempts to make what he perceives fit into his own, personal frame of reference in a way meaningful *to him*. For example, a picture of a bull, seen by a Hindu, would probably be apprehended in terms of a religious frame of reference; seen by a Chinese farmer with a marriageable daughter, it might be visualized as tethered outside his gate as a symbol of prosperity to be noted by the marriage broker; whereas, seen by a Texan, it might be seen against an experience of beef production.

In observing our universe, we get many different clues as to the nature of reality. Noticing the size, the brightness, or the color of an object helps us to see what is there. Noticing that part of a tree in the distance is not visible because a house seems to blot it out tells us that the tree is farther away than the house. These clues to the nature of our environment do not actually tell us the nature of the object or its precise location; we add the clues together, draw some inferences, and then we "guess" about what is out there.

Sometimes the clues to which we respond mislead us. You may recall a certain automobile which looked much the same from the front as from the rear. Suppose you are driving along a highway and pull out to the left to pass a slow-moving car. You perceive that the left lane (you are in the United States, not Britain) is free of traffic except for one car going away from you. But as you begin to pass, a second look tells you that the car is coming at you, and just in time you fall back behind the car you intended to pass. In this instance your *point of view* is vitally important. However, if you had experienced this faulty perception from the second floor of a building, safely removed from any possible physical contact with the oncoming car, the error would not have mattered much.

Krech and Crutchfield also show how a person's perceptions are "functionally selective." The perceiver selects certain objects to which he responds, and he selects certain characteristics of these objects or events to which he gives particular attention, depending upon his needs, purposes, and mood at the time. No one pays attention to *all* the characteristics within his range.

One of the simple illustrations given by Krech and Crutchfield will help to explain the "functional" factor in perception. Let us suppose, for example, that two men are seated at a lunchroom counter looking at a menu posted on the wall. One man is very hungry, the other very thirsty but not hungry. The structural factor, that is, the menu itself, is the same for both men. But the first man will notice the hamburger and tomato-and-lettuce sandwiches, while the tea, coffee, beer items will be ignored, or barely noticed. The second man will react in the opposite manner.

And, as reporters of what they saw, the functional factor is very important. Ask both men what they "saw" on the menu, and the first will

list the food items "and other stuff," while the second will enumerate the
drink items "and other things."[5]

Each of us, as a perceiver, should be constantly aware that our needs,
purposes, or moods may be, at times, so predominant in the process of
selective perception that we slide into "wishful thinking," seeing things
that are not there at all or failing to see things that are "out there in the
world external to our heads."

It is our selection of stimuli that determines the next step in the communications process, which is to draw inferences, forming ideas, and
then, to try to find words and sentences by which we can communicate
our ideas to others.

Semantic Problems

Anatole France noted that the metaphysician has only the perfected
cry of monkeys and dogs with which to construct the system of the
world. Most of us are somewhat aware of the ambiguity of words and the
resultant difficulties in trying to get our messages received. "What a hole
is Harvard." seems to convey a negative judgment, while "What a whole
is Harvard." implies approval.

Or, if one person says, "I like swimming." and another replies, "So do
I," they may or may not be talking about the same kind of experiences.
If the first speaker grew up in a Midwestern town and has swum only in
a small creek, whereas the second speaker grew up surfing in Hawaii,
swimming, the activity referred to by each speaker (which the general
semanticists call the "referent"), is not the same thing.

Every reader can supply other examples of confusion stemming from
the ambiguities of words, and perhaps the general semanticists have
overemphasized these difficulties. However, the failures in communication that have occurred because of the structures of languages, and especially because of that ubiquitous offender, the verb *to be,* can hardly be
overstressed.

Other scholars, not necessarily only semanticists, have noted the crimes
of the verb *to be.* In *Scepticism and Animal Faith* Santayana wrote:

> The little word *is* has its tragedies; it marries and identifies differ-
> ent things with the greatest innocence; and yet no two are ever iden-
> tical, and if therein lies the charm of wedding them and calling them
> one, therein too lies the danger. Whenever I use the word *is,* except
> in sheer tautology, I deeply misuse it; and when I discover my error,
> the world seems to fall asunder and the members of my family no
> longer know one another.[6]

When used simply as an auxiliary, as in "He is reading." or as a synonym for existence, as in "I am here," the verb *to be* is usually understood

with little trouble. But, as Korzybski, Lee, and other semanticists have shown, this naughty verb is used in two other ways (in English and in other European languages) that produce major problems in communication, strong feelings, and on occasion, violence. Presumably, Santayana was referring to these two uses: (1) identification, in which the sentence implies that one thing can exist as another, and *is* equals or stands for "may be called," or "is classified as . . ."; and (2) predication of the qualities in a thing.

IS *Used as Identification*

When a speaker says, "Tom is a radical," he has used the verb "to be" in a way that abstracts or selects certain aspects of the total reality of what Tom *is* and puts a label on Tom which is supposed to indicate something. Tom undoubtedly is possessed of many qualities and characteristics. He has relationships with his family, presumably he has an occupation, certain skills which he uses to earn a living, he believes in God, or he doesn't. There are thousands of characteristics about Tom that could be perceived, yet the speaker selects a particular few of these and says, "Tom *is* a radical." By this statement the speaker has classified Tom, very probably identifying him, in relation to the speaker, as somewhat "left" of the speaker on a continuum. (In this simple statement, even the continuum is unspecified, so that the listener does not know whether the speaker refers to a religious, political, or some other continuum and frame of reference.)

Alfred Korzybski states that, if the anthropologists are correct, only a few of the primitive peoples have the verb "to be" in their languages. They do not need it because their semantic reactions and languages are practically based upon and involve literal identification. Later, in passing from the primitive stage of human society to the present slightly higher stage, the European languages introduced into the language structure the "is" of identity. In Korzybski's system:

> Identity may be defined as "absolute sameness in all respects" which, in a world of ever-changing process and a human world of indefinitely many orders of abstractions, appears as a *structural* impossibility. Identity appears, then, as a primitive "over-emotional" generalization of similarity, equality, equivalence, equipollence, and, in no case, does it appear in fact as "absolute sameness in all respects. . . ." If we use the "is" at all, and it is extremely difficult to avoid entirely this auxiliary verb when using languages which, to a large extent, depend on it, we must be particularly careful not to use "is" as an identity term.[7]

According to Korzybski and other general semanticists, this act of abstracting a few characterists from an infinite number of possibilities, in which all human beings engage, is especially dangerous if it is done without the *consciousness* that it is being done. When we say about another person, "He is a racist," we tend to assume that we have perceived all that it is necessary to perceive about him, and we dismiss him by classifying him under a label indicating our judgment of him. Such an identification can never be entirely reliable, for it is inevitably, to some degree, false to the facts about the object so classified.

IS *Used to Predicate a Quality*

The second way in which the verb "to be" causes great difficulties in communication can be illustrated by such statements as "Snow is white," "The water is hot," and "This is a good book." Although setting up a relation of equivalence, the copulative verb elucidates but a single aspect of the subject. This aspect is of value to the communicator and may or may not have the same value for the receiver of the message. Used in this way, "is" really serves as a synonym for "appears to me to be." In making such statements, especially if we are unconscious of the fact that we have projected our evaluations of an object or an event perceived, the verb can cause distressing results, if we insist that our projections *are* reality.

Scholars, teachers, journalists, and librarians concerned with their roles as disseminators of information and preservers of intellectual freedom might profitably reflect on the use of "is" with a predicate adjective in the sentence, "The water is hot," in the following context: suppose we have before us a table on which are three buckets of water, one at a temperature of 40 degrees, one at 80 degrees, and one at 120 degrees. You hold your left hand in the 40 degree water and your right hand in the 120 degree water for one minute, and then you put both hands into the 80 degree water. How, in a sentence, do you describe the water temperature? Reacting to the sensation perceived through your left hand, do you say, "The water in the middle bucket is hot"? Or, do you verbalize as a reaction to the sensations deriving from your right hand? Of course, in the English language there is a way to express your perceptions accurately. Avoid the verb "to be" and say: "To my left hand the water in the middle bucket feels warm, to my right hand it feels cold."

Suppose there is only one bucket of water, at a temperature of 80 degrees, and Mr. A and Mr. B each puts one hand into the water. Mr. A says the water is hot, and Mr. B says, "No, it is cold." An argument ensues, perhaps ending in a physical fight over what its temperature "is."

And when reader A dips into *Catcher in the Rye* he may say, after reading only a page or two: "This is a bad book. Ban it!" Reader B, however, may say: "This is a good book." Both readers are reacting to the stimuli provided by the book in terms of their past experiences, their purposes, their moods, their mind sets, their possibly differing degrees of sophistication as readers.

Educators who have studied the process of communication are better prepared to understand the reactions of Readers A and B. In addition to what has been, perhaps, an overemotional aversion to "censorship," librarians with a knowledge and understanding of the process of communication and attitudes of readers may be assured that there are solid reasons for resisting reader A's attempts to force libraries to protect library patrons by banning materials that A finds objectionable.

The Process of Communication

Wilbur Schramm tells us that when we communicate we are trying to establish a "commonness" with someone. That is, we are trying to share information, an idea, or an attitude. Communication requires at least three elements—the source, the message, and the destination.

> Now what happens when the source tries to build up this "commonness" with his intended receiver? First, the source encodes his message. That is, he takes the information or feeling he wants to share and puts it into a form that can be transmitted. The "pictures in our heads" can't be transmitted until they are coded. When they are coded into spoken words, they can be transmitted easily and effectively, but they can't travel very far unless radio carries them. If they are coded into written words, they go more slowly than spoken words, but they go farther and last longer. Indeed, some messages long outlive their senders—the *Iliad,* for instance; the Gettysburg address; Chartres cathedral. Once coded and sent, a message is quite free of its sender, and what it does is beyond the power of the sender to change. Every writer feels a sense of helplessness when he finally commits his story or his poem to print; you doubtless feel the same way when you mail an important letter. Will it reach the right person? Will he understand it as you intend him to? Will he respond as you want him to? For in order to complete the act of communication the message must be decoded. And there is good reason . . . for the sender to wonder whether his receiver will really be in tune with him, whether the message will be interpreted without distortion, whether the "picture in the head" of the receiver will bear any resemblance to that in the head of the sender.[8]

Wendell Johnson's schematic diagram giving a stage-by-stage summary of what goes on when Mr. A talks to Mr. B, which is reproduced on the next page, may be useful.[9]

Earlier it was suggested that words themselves may influence our perception of an event, and in an attempt to communicate how this may occur, it seemed desirable to postpone this aspect of the problem until we had looked at semantic difficulties and the process of communication. It appears that there are interactions between language structures,

What Goes on When Mr. A Talks to Mr. B: The Process of Communication

1 An event occurs

2 which stimulates Mr. A through eyes, ears, or other sensor organs, and the resulting

3 nervous impulses travel to Mr. A's brain, and from there to his muscles and glands, producing tensions, preverbal feelings, etc,

4 which Mr. A then begins to translate into words, according to his accustomed patterns, and out of all the words he "thinks of"

5 he "selects," or abstracts, certain ones which he arranges in some fashion and then

Mr. A speaks to Mr. B

by means of *sound waves*

and light waves

6 whose ears and eyes are stimulated by the sound waves and light waves, respectively, and the resulting

7 nervous impulses travel to Mr. B's brain, and from there to his muscles and glands producing tensions, preverbal "feeling," etc.

8 which Mr. B then begins to translate into words, according to *his* accustomed verbal patterns, and out of all the words *he* "thinks of"

9 he "selects," or abstracts certain ones, which he arranges in some fashion and then

etc Mr. B speaks, or acts, accordingly, thereby stimulating Mr. A—or somebody else—and so the process of communication goes on, and on—with complications. . . .

words, and patterns of thought which may influence perceptions from the beginning. For example, if the Navaho Indian has in his language words corresponding roughly to "red" or "white," but he has only one word that includes all blues and greens, he may not be so alert to perceiving distinctions in this part of the color spectrum as the normal American or European. Probably it is not that the Navaho is colorblind, but rather that his vocabulary tends to let him ignore some of the distinctions which a European is forced, by his language, to make.[10] For that reason, the Navaho's perception, and his following attempt to communicate by his spoken language, will be different because he has not abstracted, or selected in the same manner as a European would, *because of the structure of his language.*

Assuming that the perception of an event is the beginning of the communication process, the Wintu language, spoken by Indians of the Sacramento valley, illustrates another way in which language may influence the choice of stimuli that the Wintu observer notices and, even more significantly, forces him to express something which the English language does not require English speakers to express. It is easy for someone who speaks English to make a statement without considering the evidence for it, but a Wintu might be expected to be more perceptive and more careful to express his "message" because of the structure of his language, which requires him to indicate by a suffix the evidence on which his statement is based.

> *He* (the Wintu) cannot say simply *the salmon is good.* That part of *is good* which implies the tense (now) and the person (it) further has to contain one of the following implications: (the salmon is good) I see, I taste (or know through some sense other than sight), I infer, I judge, I am told.[11]

Paul Henle and his coauthors of *Language, Thought and Culture*, to avoid overemphasis, hedge their view by stating:

> The contention of this section, then, is that language is one of the factors influencing perception and the general organization of experience. This influence need not be primary or unique or compelling, but neither is it negligible.[12]

The Nature of Truth

After having called attention to how misleading the verb *to be* may be, it would be not only pretentious, but contrary to the whole analysis here presented, to say what truth *is.* Instead, let us consider a way of viewing truth.

Most truths are stated in sentences, made of combinations of words, formed to communicate ideas from speaker or writer to listener or reader.

There is a natural tendency in all of us to underestimate, or to forget the difficulties described earlier, difficulties which begin with the originator's perception of the world outside his head, a perception which never includes *all* and may be even more of a misperception than it is an approximation to reality.

Various observers see what they choose to see, depending upon their experiences and their purposes, and when they "code" their messages, it is to be expected that their words may possess the quality of correspondence with reality to a greater or lesser degree. Words are never precise, nor will they ever be decoded and understood in the same way by all the receivers of the messages.

This is not to claim that the facts, as such, do not exist in the external world. But when they are described in sentences or in films or in other media, selectivity has played an important role in the process. Usually there is an incitement to believe or to doubt or obey. The proposition also tends to "freeze" what are ongoing processes into static entities. Sometimes it identifies, or classifies one thing as another. A proposition almost never says *all* about an object or an event.

John Hospers in his *Introduction to Philosophical Analysis* discusses the concept of a true proposition:

> Let us first introduce the concept of *states of affairs.* . . . These states of affairs occur or exist in the world even if no one reports their occurrence in language. Their existence is independent of language, but we can describe them by means of language.
>
> It would seem that we can now define "truth" quite easily. A true proposition describes a state of affairs that occurs; or, in the case of a proposition about the past, a state of affairs that did occur; or in the case of the future, that will occur.[13]

But Hospers warns that specifications of time and place must be clearly stated. Careful, honest communicators are wary of stating as "truth" general propositions without many qualifications explaining in what context, under what conditions, upon what evidence this or that proposition may be considered to "correspond with reality." Thus, if truth is viewed as a quality of a proposition, possessed by the proposition to some degree, though not in an absolute sense, it will be clearer why the demands for suppression of certain expressions in school, press, and library should be resisted.

It is not easy to continuously remind ourselves that our perceptions are only partially accurate. Often we lose awareness that others will see things differently. But professional librarians who are conscious of how the communications process operates will hesitate to deny to *any* library user the opportunity to entertain *any* expression of "truth," by *any* observer, from *any* point of view.

Ordinary Language and Neutral Language

It may be useful to distinguish between the languages of science and common, everyday forms of speech. One of the major factors in the success of physical and biological scientists in operating within their environment is their invention of a neutral, nonmoral vocabulary. This vocabulary permits and encourages the practice of suspended judgment, for it leaves the scientist free to observe what is before him without undue influence from moral attitudes accepted before he begins his observations.

In contrast to this neutral speech, our normal speech or writing is loaded with moral judgments: our names for objects have emotional aspects which indicate how we should act toward these objects. Unquestionably, a journalist, teacher, or librarian is an individual, entitled to hold a point of view and, unavoidably, have a mental set and a moral attitude on many issues which he would hope to see spread and accepted by everyone. However, in his professional role he is, and should be, under pressure from his professional organization to avoid attempting to dictate the morals and beliefs of students or readers. His professional organization has an obligation to persuade him to maintain a neutral stance on substantive issues whenever he is active in his college, newspaper, or library, regardless of his activities as a private citizen. He should understand why an act to suppress information contrary to his personal convictions will destroy the integrity of his institution and his profession. It should be an objective of professional education to provide future practitioners with an understanding of the liberal approach to ideas described in definitions following the preface to these essays, and of why it is essential.

3 The Threat to Liberal Values in the Communications Institutions

Dr. Anatol Rapoport tells us that man has a unique ability to transmit experience by means of symbols, interacting with his ancestors and descendants over periods of time. Whereas plants live by "binding energy," and animals, in addition to being energy binders are "space-binders," able to move about, man not only has both of these capacities, but also is a "time-binder." By transmitting his culture through written and recorded symbols, man can become even more a master of his environment and of himself, *if* the experience transmitted is organized into true-to-fact orientations. However, if the experience transmitted is organized into false-to-fact orientations, man becomes a slave of his neuro-linguistic reactions and a menace to himself.

> All existing cultures are based partly on true-to-fact orientations and partly on false-to-fact orientations. A tribe may have highly efficient fishing and canoe-building techniques, but its notions of health and disease may be organized into a body of superstition, which renders it helpless in an epidemic. Our own culture has attained a high level of true-to-fact orientation with regard to technology and hygiene, but our social organization is such that technology threatens to blast us out of existence, and a great deal of our knowledge of health (especially mental health) cannot be applied.[1]

The inventions of writing and printing extend man's capacity to perceive his environment. He can record and preserve descriptions of events and ideas. Modern techniques of scholarship enable him to inquire into many of the unknown areas of the universe. Modern technology in the news media helps him to learn of events all around the planet, (today, even a part of outer space), within hours or minutes. Journalism plays a vital role in extending man's perception of his world.

Libraries which collect, organize, retrieve, preserve, and disseminate information add two dimensions to man's opportunity to perceive and maintain contact with his environment. One dimension is the possibility for in-depth exploration of a subject through study of current, scholarly, scientific reports by specialists who have attempted to discover truth about various aspects of man's environment through controlled experiments, aided by neutral, scientific, nonemotive language. In-depth study requires more than the one-minute newscast and more than the somewhat longer description of an event provided by newspapers, though these serve to alert many people to new discoveries. The full reports, written in scientific, neutral language, published in scholarly journals and made available in libraries, are essential for the advancement of man's knowledge.

The second dimension added by librarianship is time-binding. This is the ability of man to look back in time, comparing reports of how man tried in earlier times to resolve his problems. Only man has the advantages stemming from his ability to record, preserve, and reexamine data. (It is worth noting, however, that in a totalitarian society this advantage is reduced when politicians issue decrees stating, for example, what shall be the orthodox theories in genetics or philology, forbidding scholars to report evidence and findings contrary to official doctrines.)

While the missions of scholars, teachers, journalists, and librarians are not identical, all these groups are naturally much concerned about intellectual freedom in their professional activities. In fact, they usually exert much effort to inform and persuade society in general that, unless these professionals can work in the condition called "intellectual freedom," their work is not worth much as an aid to man in perceiving his world.

Practitioners in these fields work with perceptions, words, and ideas. All engage in selection. From the infinite number of events that occur each day that might be reported, journalists select an infinitesimal few. They then code their descriptions of these events into words, sentences, paragraphs, then put them into ink or sound waves, and send them out to their publics as grist for their thinking processes.

Librarians, too, select, from the thousands of books, films, journals newspapers, tapes, and pictures encoded and published, not only by journalists but by artists and scholars in all fields of inquiry. These are selected, acquired, and organized into library collections for retrieval, preservation, and dissemination.

At any stage in the process of communication it is easily possible, by unrepresentative selectivity, whether deliberate or accidental, for these professional groups to present a picture of the world which does not closely approximate the real world. Forces which intentionally distort the process, or prevent it from operating, should be regarded as anti-intellectual freedom and potentially very harmful to all men.

In the 1940s and 1950s, during the period of American history frequently labeled the McCarthy period, academic freedom and the freedom to read were seriously threatened from the Right, as we will see from the library censorship problems described in chapter 4.

Liberal values were still under attack from the Right during the 1960s and 1970s, but now what was called the "New Left" also took up the cudgel. In response to the latter, various groups expressed their conviction that this is the worst of all times, in the worst of all nations, the United States, and thereby manifested a "guilt syndrome." American institutions, especially universities, were adjudged guilty of not having found complete, perfect solutions to economic, social, and environmental problems. American society as a whole was condemned as evil and corrupt and without value. There was a general rejection of the liberal approach to ideas (defined earlier in the section following the preface). An "activism" expressed through demonstrations, seizures of university buildings, and nonnegotiable demands became a kind of religious frenzy. Unable to find an outlet through organized religion, frustrated by failures to correct obvious illnesses in society, the activists twisted their fantasies into a moral absolutism which threatened intellectual freedom in all democratic institutions. The total conviction of their total righteousness led to admiration of the virtues of dictatorship in such undeveloped countries as Cuba and China. In their revulsion from civilization itself, rejecting the possibility of free, honest scholarship and refusing to study pertinent evidence on specific problems, the activists entered the political arena.

Although it is not the intent of this writer to analyze the political scene in the United States, the consequences to intellectual freedom in our institutions were marked and dangerous. Probably fortunately, the attempts to impose a particular religious view of society and a particular simplistic view of how to resolve its problems were not unified and directed toward one end. (It did appear that the various groups of "cause" people were determined to pull down the "rotten establishment" that had failed to build the perfect society.) But whatever issue seemed of prime importance to a group, the question raised was not, "What are the facts and how can the evil be reduced?" Instead, the question was always, "Who is guilty?"

Political scientist Adam Ulam[2] emphasizes that many of the most prevalent clichés and slogans used in the 1968 and 1972 political campaigns had a religious symbolism. For example, when a university or a corporation is called upon to acknowledge that it is elitist, or racist, or sexist, or whatever, it is put under pressure to confess that it is in a state of sin, and that only after such an admission can penance begin. And Ulam notes that to a nineteenth-century liberal it would have appeared to be the height of absurdity to postulate that an *institution* can have moral attributes. But, instead of pursuing the proper task of the university, learning, or of the press, to present descriptive reports of news events, or of the library, to disseminate information on all sides of all issues, professionals in these fields became intimidated by rhetoric and platitudes and the demands that these institutions must become advocates of specific causes. Too few scholars, journalists, or librarians dared to ask "But what does this slogan mean?" or "How would it work in practice?" For, says Ulam, asking such pertinent questions would bare the speaker's ignorance, lack of sophistication, or selfishness.

The "liberal" notion that democratic institutions must be free from both government control and the moralistic passions of the day in order to give men the opportunity to expand and acquire knowledge and apply it toward resolution of problems was rejected. Instead, it was argued that professors, librarians, and students should leave their classrooms, laboratories, and libraries and spend their energies debating the rights and wrongs of social and economic problems. It was not enough for members of the academy, the press, and the library to participate in the political process *as citizens;* they must commit their institutions to positions on an ever-increasing number of issues, never mind the fact that the integrity of these institutions would thus be destroyed. It is this rejection of liberal attitudes and institutions that suggests the title "The Flight from Reason."

Other observers have also described the rejection of the liberal spirit. Orin Kramer, a New York attorney, suggests that the intellectual and social life style of Puritanism, with its work ethic and strong sense of the need for order and articulated rules, has been rejected, and along with it, respect for the process, freedom of speech, majority rule, etc.:

> Under this new social order bereft of rules, whatever path the emancipated individual elects to follow should be dictated by the senses and emotions, not by reason and knowledge. . . .
>
> This distrust of rationality, institutions and conventional wisdom stems from the inability of these sources to provide the changes which the young think long overdue. Political institutions are seen as the guarantors of the perpetuation of the status quo. Once you deal rationally with established authority, according to this analysis, you are lending legitimacy to illegitimate and corrupt institutions which stand as impediments to change. The irreparably evil nature of these institutions is assumed to be beyond debate; moreover, the poison which lies within the fangs of the Establishment is so great that to join the Establishment to work for change from within is both ineffectual and personally self-destructive.[3]

Norman Podhoretz, editor of *Commentary,* notes that, once upon a time, the aim of a liberal education was to help people to develop the will and ability to overcome their normal human resistance to criticism or to a change of mind in the face of persuasive evidence or argument. But this observer presents a sobering perception of the modern university:

> The upshot is an atmosphere which is no longer conducive to fearless inquiry or even to playful speculation and which, far from

encouraging, positively obstructs the development of independence of mind and of the critical spirit. Thus do our colleges and universities continue their degenerative mutation from sanctuaries for free discussion into inquisitorial agents of a dogmatic secular faith.[4]

Daniel P. Moynihan, Ambassador to India, also has noted that we may well be on a downward slope of a cycle in the long-term trend toward loss of faith in reason:

> Attack from *within* is wholly new to (Harvard's) experience and brings forth few of the brave and honorable qualities that so characterized the university's response to attack from *without* in the 1950's. One has the sense of a somewhat overbred community that had the instinct to bring in new blood, but did not understand that in doing so it would bring in also new conditions of argument, and resentment of its very existence. In the face of ideas that intend nothing less than the destruction of what Harvard has stood for, Harvard seems to have almost no defense save good manners. . . .
>
> The fact, as I see it, is that ideological initiative at Harvard has been conceded to the extremists. Many ignore their view, but few contest them. . . . There has been of late a diminution of energy which Professor Ulam notes, but none of purpose. Mass assault has given way to "salami tactics": one professor at a time rather than one building at a time. But the institution remains trapped in its own decency, its moral authority gradually eroding, such that in the end all that will be left will be the good manners, and then it will not any longer matter.[5]

These observations of Ulam, Podhoretz, Kramer, and Moynihan are cited to focus attention upon the turning away from liberal values, from the spirit of free inquiry and reason and dialogue in our institutions. The essay, "The Flight from Reason," is an elaboration of the perception shared by these observers, analyzing the growing distrust of rationality and objectivity in the academic world and the professional associations. In succeeding essays we will examine the press and librarianship. In my opinion, in each of these professions, to the degree that the slogans of current radicalism are unexamined and gain acceptance, to that degree intellectual freedom is diminished. And, to this degree, man's capacity to perceive his environment with a reasonable approximation to reality is weakened; our present orientation to the world, in Dr. Rapoport's terms, has become "false-to-fact," and we have become slaves of our neurolinguistic reactions, a menace to ourselves.

It would be difficult to determine at any given time whether the threat to intellectual freedom and other liberal values is greater from Right or Left. Some observers felt, as early as 1970, that the pendulum was already swinging to the Right, and that, as a reaction to the extremism of the New Left, the forces of the Radical Right would gain in strength.

Perhaps the most eloquent statement placing the threats to intellectual freedom from both the Radical Left and the Radical Right in perspective, was Margaret Chase Smith's speech in the United States Senate on Monday, June 1, 1970. The Senator from Maine began:

> Mr. President, 20 years ago on this June 1 date at this same desk I spoke about the then serious national condition with a statement known as the "Declaration of Conscience." We had a national sickness then from which we recovered. We have a national sickness now from which I pray we will recover. . . .
> I said then: "Those of us who shout the loudest about Americanism in making character assassinations are all too frequently those who, by our own words and acts, ignore some of the basic principles of Americanism—
>
> > The right to criticize;
> > The right to hold unpopular beliefs;
> > The right to protest;
> > The right to independent thought.
>
> That applies today—and it includes the right to dissent against the dissenters. . . .

Senator Smith also commented on the way the press and campuses were *used,* then and now:

> I said then: "As a United States Senator, I am not proud of the way in which the Senate has been made a publicity platform for 'irresponsible sensationalism.' " Today I would add that I am not proud of the way in which our national television networks and campuses have been made publicity platforms for irresponsible sensationalism—nor am I proud of the countercriticism against the networks and campuses that has gone beyond the bounds of reasonableness and propriety and fanned, instead of drenching, the fires of division. . . .
> I spoke as I did 20 years ago because of what I considered to be the great threat from the radical right—the threat of a government of repression.
> I speak today because of what I consider to be the great threat from the radical left that advocates and practices violence and defiance of the law—again, the threat of the ultimate result of a reaction of repression. . . .
> That danger is ultimately from the political right even though it is initially spawned by the antidemocratic arrogance and nihilism from the political extreme left.
> Extremism bent upon polarization of our people is increasingly forcing upon the American people the narrow choice between anarchy and repression.
> And make no mistake about it, if that narrow choice has to be made, the American people, even if with reluctance and misgiving, will choose repression.

For an overwhelming majority of Americans believe that:

> Trespass is trespass—whether on the campus or off.
> Violence is violence—whether on the campus or off.
> Arson is arson—whether on the campus or off.
> Killing is killing—whether on the campus or off. . . .

> As was the case 20 years ago when the Senate was silenced and politically intimidated by one of its Members, so today many Americans are intimidated and made mute by the emotional violence of the extreme left. Constructive discussion on the subject is becoming increasingly difficult of attainment. . . .[6]

Republican Senator Smith had had the insight and the courage to speak against McCarthyism and for reason and conscience in 1950. Again in 1970, perceiving a threat of the same nature but from the other extreme, she again spoke for liberal values. The 1972 presidential election, along with the election of other government officials, constitutes hard evidence that Senator Smith knew what she was talking about. The absolutist, one-issue groups helped to reelect Richard M. Nixon president, in an unprecedented landslide, with the electoral votes of forty-nine of the fifty states. After this election, Frank Mankiewicz, director of Senator McGovern's campaign, although he did not use the word "blackmail," expressed clearly what he had learned: "We were always subject to this pressure from the cause people. We reacted to every threat from women, or militants, or college groups. If I had it to do all over again, I'd learn when to tell them to go to hell."[7]

Political analysts Seymour Lipset and Earl Raab, who won the Myrdal Prize for their book *The Politics of Unreason*, in their later analysis of the 1972 election said that, for a large majority of the American electorate, along with a strong desire for peace, there was strong disapproval of the militant tactics of sections of the antiwar movement. Even people under age thirty condemned student strikes against the war by an overwhelming majority. These analysts account for the landslide victory of Richard Nixon by suggesting that the Democratic convention and the McGovern campaign strategists totally misjudged the character of the electorate. Their assumption seemed to be that the electorate was divided into two large groups, one basically alienated from the American order, the other evilly dedicated to turning the clock back. Lipset and Raab conclude that there were such factions, but that they were not large and did not represent the majority of Americans.[8] The extreme left wing of the Democratic party deluded itself, failing to perceive the political situation with an approximation to the reality.

The unhappy result was that President Nixon believed he had a mandate justifying various "illiberal" activities. (And in this context we use the term "illiberal" in the political-social realm). The 1968 and 1972 elections of a president hostile to education, the press, and to libraries, as well as to civil liberties generally, seriously diminished support for the nation's liberal institutions and harmed intellectual freedom in them. For example, the four Nixon appointees to the United States Supreme Court agreed one hundred percent on cases involving obscenity, reversing a long trend of earlier, more liberal courts. In June 1973, this court rendered a decision giving local authorities the right to rule on the obscenity of films, printed materials, and plays and the impact of this decision was felt immediately. Intellectual freedom thus suffered serious wounds, resulting in part from the illiberal attacks upon the academy, the press, and the library by the New Left activists.

It is true that in 1973 riots on campuses are no longer seen daily in the television news, and the rhetoric is muted on campus as compared with the period when the bullhorns blared out on the University of Minnesota Mall: "Academic freedom is bullshit!" But even in 1973 there are few affirmations of the values of reason, free speech, dialogue, and the liberal approach to ideas. The failure of professional workers in education, the press, and the library to recognize their responsibility to maintain their objectivity and their professional neutrality on substantive issues prevents an easy optimism about the future of intellectual freedom.

Chapter 4, which follows, presents cases illustrating the censorious attacks upon libraries from the Radical Right during the McCarthy period. The reader who did not live through this era can gain perspective by which he can better judge Senator Smith's speeches in the Senate in 1950 and 1970. The reader who is familiar with the McCarthy period may wish to skip chapter 4 and go directly to the analyses of threats to liberal values from the promotion of the "advocacy institution concept" in chapter 5 (where the academy is discussed), chapter 6 (where the press is discussed), and chapter 7 (where the library is discussed).

4　Problem Cases of Library Censorship

The American Library Association adopted its first policy on intellectual freedom in 1939. That policy evolved as the present Library Bill of Rights which is reproduced as the frontispiece in this book of essays on intellectual freedom. As a consequence of this policy the ALA in 1940 established a standing committee to safeguard the intellectual freedom of the users of libraries.[1] For the first seven years this committee had little to do, because few attempts to ban books from libraries were reported to it. Since 1947 the committee has had many cases and now has a substantial knowledge of the problems of censorship. *The Newsletter on Intellectual Freedom* reports on current cases.

Librarians learned from experience that, if the principle of free access to all points of view is to be preserved, the personal convictions of librarians on controversial issues may not be permitted to govern their actions in acquisition and dissemination of information. The notion of neutrality, that a library—as an institution—must be impartial, that it does not advocate particular truths, is incomprehensible to people with strong convictions. They tend to believe that a library is hypocritical when it insists that it is neutral, i.e., that it does not advocate the contents of every idea in every book, magazine, and film in its collections. The notion that the presence of a book in a library is proof that the librarians who put it there *approve* of its contents is often very strongly held.

It seems to be a natural human trait to seek the comfort that comes from feeling that we have acquired absolute truth. When someone reaches this level of conviction on any issue, he is likely to move to the belief that because he is "right" he is justified in suppressing expressions of views contrary to his own. Librarians are human beings, no different from others in this respect, but if they suppress expressions contrary to their own by keeping them out of libraries, they become advocates for certain views or causes. If they do use their institutions to propagate their per-

31

sonal moral convictions, they can no longer insist upon the principle of intellectual freedom adopted by ALA.

From 1940 to 1971, in most cases dealt with by the Committee on Intellectual Freedom, the pressures to limit access to library materials came from conservatives on the political-social-religious continuum. In a few early cases *Oliver Twist, The Merchant of Venice, Huckleberry Finn,* or *Little Black Sambo* were the targets of censors, but not until 1971 did the ALA have to come to grips with pressures to eliminate such books as the *Caddie Woodlawn* series, *Dr. Doolittle,* or *Mary Poppins.* Pressure for the "reevaluation" of these children's books came from librarians who probably considered themselves *liberals* (on the social continuum), but their justification for censorship was identical with that of the conservatives who more frequently attempt to impose their personal moral values upon everyone. Librarians rallied under the slogan "social responsibility," enjoying a warm glow of self-approval for their idealism, ignoring what they had learned about preserving intellectual freedom, and refusing to consider the question: What does "social responsibility" mean? (Chapter 7 analyzes the social responsibility concept of librarianship and elaborates on what this means.)

The California Association of Children's Librarians in 1971 recommended a reevaluation of children's books with an eye toward racist and sexist incidents and expressions. And in 1972 ALA's Children's Services Division adopted a policy statement on the reevaluation of children's books based upon the rationale that *some things are right and some things are wrong.* It was argued that it is the social responsibility of librarians to make value judgments of library materials "in the light of current knowledge or beliefs."

Drawing on his considerable experience as former Assistant Director of the ALA Office for Intellectual Freedom, James A. Harvey observes about this moral value philosophy of book selection that it is a traditional tool of the censor. He notes that this reevaluation syndrome prompted children's librarians in Caldwell Parish, Louisiana, to paint tempera diapers on the naked hero of *In the Night Kitchen,* and, says Harvey:

> Where the "some things are right and some things are wrong" school stumbles in pursuing this purpose is in the imposition of personal definitions of "information and knowledge" upon the library collections. They would do well to recall that, at one time, some librarians believed that wisdom could not be derived from any fiction; fiction was fodder for the idle mind. Ergo, fiction collecting was ignored. Further, we have just come through a decade when to be a political and social conservative was seemingly lacking in wisdom and understanding. As a result, many library collections contain little material to aid the conservative's intellectual pursuits. If the November [1972] election was any indication, we seem to be entering a period when to be a political and social liberal or radical

will be viewed as unwise, (i.e., outside the scope of "contemporary thought and social climate"). Will future collections reflect this shift? With apologies to Keats, wisdom, like beauty, is in the mind of the beholder, not just in the value judgments of librarians. This is a principle which, like it or not, applies to children as well as adults. . . .[2]

Although the proponents of reevaluation, including the editor of the *School Library Journal*,[3] may deny that it was their intent to censor, their term "reevaluation" must be considered a euphemism for censorship. In contrast to this view, stands the interpretation of the Library Bill of Rights called "Free Access to Libraries for Minors," recommended by ALA's Committee on Intellectual Freedom and officially adopted by the ALA Council on June 30, 1972. This statement reminds librarians that Article 5 of the Library Bill of Rights reflects the belief that young people are entitled to the same access to library materials that adults have. This policy, which probably is not accepted by some librarians and some citizens, states:

> In today's world, children are exposed to adult life much earlier than in the past. They read materials and view a variety of media on the adult level at home and elsewhere. Current emphasis upon early childhood education has also increased opportunities for young people to learn and to have access to materials, and has decreased the validity of using chronological age as an index to the use of libraries. The period of time during which children are interested in reading materials specifically designed for them grows steadily shorter, and librarians must recognize and adjust to this change if they wish to maintain the patronage of young people.[4]

On this point even "liberal" or left-of-center librarians may be divided. Some elevate the principle of protection of young and impressionable minds from expressions judged to be demeaning, while others may stand behind the principle of intellectual freedom for children.

As James Harvey suggests, it must be recognized that the moral value philosophy as a basis for censoring children's books can also be—and often is—used as the basis for censorship of adult informational materials. The censor of materials at any level finds it easy to justify suppression of materials he personally considers objectionable. The developments detailed in Case A, Censorship of Films in Peoria, illustrates the point.

Some proponents of the "social responsibility concept of librarianship" even hope to achieve prepublication censorship by pressures upon publishers to persuade them to publish what are, in their moral judgment, good books and to stop publishing bad books. It is typical of this kind of censor that he overlooks the fact that if he can do this, those who hold moral values contradictory to his have an equal right to enter the propaganda field, attempting to influence publishers.

Censorship is contagious. When a society or a community has a blind spot, or when, by unspoken agreement, certain subjects are taboo, censorship follows. It spreads both geographically, as the second case, that of the banning of *The Nation* illustrates, and from one type of publication to others. Although to some extent aimed continuously at literature of the social sciences, obscenity, blasphemy, and subversive publications, censorship may also follow a cyclical pattern, at one time focusing on a particular kind of publication.

In the late 1940s and early 1950s, Senator Joseph R. McCarthy used a U.S. Senate committee as his instrument for conducting a witch hunt for Communists, stimulating censorship of allegedly subversive literature. It is difficult today to recapture the feeling of repression felt by most liberals during the McCarthy period. And here the term *liberal* includes those on the left side of the political-social continuum as well as those who try to practice the liberal approach to ideas. (*See* the definitions following the preface for definitions of *liberal*). Even a July 1973 showing of Edward R. Murrow's "See It Now" criticism of McCarthy's methods somehow failed to reveal why many people were afraid to say what they thought and why some professors advised their students not to be seen reading certain publications. The climate of repression of the period between 1950 and 1954 is almost unimaginable today. (But note the similar attacks upon investigators of the genetic factor in individual differences in chapter 5).

As more and more cases were reported to the Committee on Intellectual Freedom through the late 1940s and early 1950s, ALA wrestled with the problems of applying the principles of intellectual freedom in specific cases. Careful study of the Bartlesville, Oklahoma, case, where the *New Republic* and the *United Nations Bulletin* were banned and the librarian was fired, helped librarians to understand that it is difficult to get the facts about a case. When the Sons of the American Revolution in New Jersey urged libraries to warn readers against subversive literature by labeling all "communist" literature, the Committee on Intellectual Freedom recommended a policy against prejudicial labeling.

In 1948 a California State Senate Investigating Committee on Education condemned *Building America*, the National Education Association's series of social science instructional materials, as controversial and unfit for use in the schools. The state superintendent of schools stated that he would stake his professional reputation upon the proposition that these books were not subversive. The California Parent Teacher Association judged the books in the series to be well prepared and factual in approach, neither subversive nor communistic. The state board of education unanimously adopted the books for use early in 1947. Yet the legislature held up appropriations and appointed a Senate Investigating Committee in April 1947. That committee split four to four on the question of whether *Building America* was subversive.

American librarians learned from this case that the Radical Right can sometimes succeed in limiting students to only those views which they consider sound by banning points of view they find objectionable. One of the earliest educational projects of the ALA's Committee on Intellectual Freedom was the publication of the pamphlet "The Right to Find Out," prepared for the California Committee on Intellectual Freedom by the staff of the San Bernardino County Library. Frederick Melcher, at the time president of R. R. Bowker & Company, printed the pamphlet, which I had edited for the ALA Committee on Intellectual Freedom. The pamphlet was circulated widely by the Committee to librarians, who thus had an opportunity to study the allegations against *Building America*, volume by volume, contrasting the charges with the critical estimates of the San Bernardino County Library Staff. For example, regarding volume 30, entitled "Seeing America," the California State Senate Investigating Committee said:

> "being the last & certainly one of the worst books of the series. . . . a picture of a dejected-looking middle aged man clad in overalls & leaning against a vacant building. Caption: 'As motionless as a cigar-store Indian of old, the despairing figure of a jobless man leans against a vacant store. This might be Any Town, U.S.A.' where unemployment is still a problem."[5]

The librarians' analysis pointed out that this volume had been published in 1937 when the nation was emerging from an economic depression, and that the purpose of the book was to discuss the different problems facing our people in each region and the ways some of these problems are being solved.

The State Senate Investigating Committee report on volume 30 further complained that

> the nation is shown to a theoretical young couple by way of view of the seamy side, with nowhere a picture of a beautiful park, other abundant examples of healthful, happy life. And so the young people have seen America. They have seen its slums, its shanties, its expropriated farms & drouth victims, its hot dog stands, & the shanties of the miners & steel-workers. They have seen its mules, its jack-asses, & its jobless.[6]

This criticism the librarians challenged by citing page references to attractive pictures, emphasizing that the theme of the volume was the tracing of the history of regions and pointing out that progress in solving our social ills was being made. The librarians' analysis concluded that the purpose of the volume—to present various points of view of our nation's problems—had been achieved in an objective manner.

Other volumes discussed in the pamphlet were "Community Planning,"

"Conservation," "Civil Liberties," "Our Minority Groups," "America's Outposts," "Russia," and "China," showing in parallel columns the criticisms leveled by the censors and the librarians' countering analysis. The contrast helps to depict the temper of the times during the McCarthy period, enabling librarians to see how censorship can occur here, for *Building America* was banned and forced to cease publication.

The following four cases illustrate other issues of intellectual freedom with which American librarians have had to deal.

CASE A. *Film Censorship in Peoria.* In the history of library censorship this case is important because it raises questions about access to films that seemed not to reflect "current knowledge and beliefs" about the United Nations and human brotherhood; it is especially so because it raised a major question of whether the Library Bill of Rights covered nonprint media. To the American Legion and to one local newspaper human brotherhood was considered a part of Communist ideology. As do extremists of both Left and Right today, Senator Joseph R. McCarthy consistently declared that anyone who did not agree with him and approve of his crusade must be a dangerous character. McCarthy's point of view was an extreme illustration of the "some things are right and some things are wrong" philosophy, and librarians who disseminated films or books which he and his supporters considered subversive were intimidated.

CASE B. *The Case of the* Nation. In 1948 the New York City Schools banned the *Nation* magazine from their libraries because of the allegedly antireligious articles by Paul Blanshard. These articles criticized secular practices of the Roman Catholic Church. In one sense, this is a landmark case, for it was the first time that national publicity was drawn to a case of censorship in a library. It is instructive also in that it illustrates the contagious nature of censorship, for, after the banning in New York, school administrators in Newark, New Jersey, and other cities, and even a few colleges considered banning the magazine. Helen R. Sattley, Director of School Libraries in New York City brings the story up to date with her letter to me which appears in the discussion of this case. Her "Statement on Book Selection," with reference to *Down These Mean Streets* by Piri Thomas which follows her letter is especially valuable.[7]

CASE C. *Wrenshall Bans Orwell's* 1984. This antitotalitarian novel has been a target for censors in many places. In 1960 in Wrenshall, Minnesota, the school board banned *1984* and fired the teacher who had assigned it to his students. This analysis highlights several points about censorship of instructional materials, individual reading levels of students, and the freedom to read. It also introduces the question of a teacher's—and his students'—academic freedom. In this case, the final outcome was the lifting of the ban and the return of the teacher to his position.

CASE D. *The* Report *of the Commission on Obscenity and Pornography.* This is not a case of an attack upon freedom to read in a library, but it illuminates the temptation felt by some librarians to endorse the majority report by urging ALA to give it its stamp of approval. Librarians committed to the advocacy concept of librarianship argued for endorsement. The essay also analyzes the "categorical rejection" of the majority report by the President of the United States and all but five members of the U.S. Senate.

CASE A: *Film Censorship in Peoria*

Human brotherhood, universal human rights, Communist propaganda, and the suggestion that the library profession harbored "fellow travelers" were among the issues raised by the Peoria case in 1950–1951. The Peoria Public Librarian's decision to ban three films, at the dictation of the local American Legion, and his justification of the ban on the grounds that the Library Bill of Rights did not include films, caused librarians to give special attention to this question. The result was a footnote to the Library Bill of Rights, adopted in 1951: "The Library Bill of Rights shall be interpreted as applying to all materials and media of communication used or collected by libraries."

This footnote is now included in the text of the Library Bill of Rights, as revised in 1967.

The Peoria case was especially memorable as an illustration of the problems of a librarian who tried to preserve intellectual freedom during the McCarthy period of American history. Censorship attempts tend to go in cycles, and in the early 1950s the fear of Communism whipped up by the House of Representatives' Un-American Activities Committee and by Wisconsin's Senator Joseph R. McCarthy made it certain that the chief target of the library censor would be "subversive materials." (This does not suggest that obscenity and blasphemy and advanced theories on social welfare were not also always likely targets, but the major thrust at the time was against "subversive" literature.) For example, consider the tortured logic used to prove that the United Nations was a Communist organization and that the film *Of Human Rights* was "Communist propaganda." This film is an illustration of the United Nations' Declaration of Universal Human Rights, which, in fact, incorporated much more Anglo-American ideology than it does Soviet Russian ideas. But the Peoria *Star* of Thursday, November 29, 1951, carried the following story:

A Lesson in the Techniques of Communist
Propaganda

A United Nations film, "Of Human Rights" was obtained by the audio-visual department of the Peoria public library about a year ago. It has been used a great deal to spark discussion in groups that gather to talk about public affairs. The film is easily recognizable as United Nations propaganda in behalf of its universal declaration of human rights, and we are told that it often led discussion groups into penetrating and adverse criticism of that document.

But how many of these earnest people had the slightest suspicion that what appeared to be a United Nations propaganda film was really a clever Communist propaganda film?

The Americanism committee of Peoria Post No. 2, American Legion, viewed the film Monday night and listened to an analysis of the Red propaganda techniques used in it. The analyst was Dr. Nicholas Nyaradi, former Minister of Finance of Hungary and now a member of the faculty of Bradley University. He described the film as Communist propaganda of the most dangerous kind.

The first test of its effectiveness as propaganda is that its purposes are cunningly concealed. Most people, on seeing "Of Human Rights" would not only fail to observe the propaganda aspect of it (Communist propaganda, that is) but would emphatically deny that it contained such propaganda if they were told that it did. A few persons who have grown accustomed to recognizing propaganda would see it. Still fewer persons, who understand the Red propaganda techniques would be able to explain how the film accomplishes the deeper purposes intended.

And then, said the *Star,* in a comment that must rank as one of the most amazing illustrations of illogic of all times:

Some months ago, during a public controversy over a Communist propaganda film, an East Peoria clergyman conceived the idea of showing the film in his church and deciding by the vote of the audience whether it was Red propaganda. If that were tried with "Of Human Rights" there would be an overwhelming vote, declaring that it was not Red propaganda.

Thus by the first test, it would prove to be clever propaganda. People do not recognize it as such, and refuse to believe so even when told. . . .

In the early 1950s the Radical Right, supremely confident that it had a monopoly on *the* truth, took off on flights from reason in much the same way that the New Left did in the late 1960s.

To follow up the story quoted above, the *Star* carried a piece on December 1, 1951, entitled "Propaganda Films and Adult Education." In this it was stated that a library offering films to the public ought to make sure that there is no infiltration of subversive propaganda in its offerings. Library board members should have some means of obtaining expert appraisal of doubtful films, but, said the *Star:*

Our local library cannot turn to the American Library Association for help, for that body has approved Communist propaganda films. It has also approved dubious principles contained in the National Education Association statement, "The Public School and the American Heritage," a document which was discussed in this column not long ago.

Neither can the library board rely upon the judgment of its librarian, under whose administration four Communist propaganda films turned up in the audio-visual department within a period of a few months. It was only four months after the public controversy over the films "Brotherhood of Man," "Boundary Lines," and "Peoples of the U.S.S.R." that he bought "Of Human Rights," a Communist propaganda film that has had wide circulation in Peoria in the last year. It seems to us that extra precautions should have been taken after the dispute about the three films to prevent the repetition of that sorry occurrence. As these incidents multiply, it begins to appear that they are more than unhappy coincidence. . . .

The Free Public Library in Peoria had been proud of its film program that was providing information to its public in the belief that informed people are the best citizens. At some time before July 1950, the Americanism Committee of the Peoria American Legion, Post 2, protested the circulation of the three films mentioned in the foregoing editorial.

The *Brotherhood of Man* is an animated film, in color, on the subject of race relations. It is based on *The Races of Mankind,* a Public Affairs Pamphlet by Dr. Ruth Benedict and Dr. Gene Weltfish. (As was true in Birmingham, Alabama, where *Senior Scholastic* Magazine was banned because of a special issue on Brotherhood Week, the concept of human brotherhood, including all races, was considered a Communist bit of ideology and should not be available in Peoria.)

The film *Boundary Lines* is a plea to eliminate the arbitrary boundaries which divide people from each other as individuals and as nations. It was awarded the bronze medal at the Brussels Film Festival of 1947. *Brotherhood of Man* and this film both had been starred for first purchase in the ALA Audio-Visual Board's 1950 list.

Peoples of the USSR, produced by Julien Bryan and depicting the variety of peoples living in the Soviet Union, is a geographical travel film rather than a political film. In 1950 it had been banned in the Soviet Union but had been used widely in the orientation of U.S. troops to acquaint them with the Russian peoples. This film had also been on the ALA Audio-Visual Board's recommended list, but had recently been removed from it.

At a special meeting of the Peoria library board in June 1950, it had been decided that there was no subversive material in these films, and that they should not be withdrawn from circulation. But in September the board reconsidered and finally decided that the films were to be restricted to use in audiovisual screening rooms at the library.

The newspaper kept the controversy going with its column "Straws in the Wind," by Editor Gomer Bath, January 9, 1952:

Peoria in Lewis Column

News is getting around the country that Peoria, the first city to put Paul Robeson in his place, is the first city to recognize and expose the nature of the UN propaganda film, "Of Human Rights." This is the film that Librarian Xenophon Smith bought, after failing to get the recommendation of a library preview committee, and even now defends, on the ground that for anyone to object to his purchases of library materials constitutes "censorship."

The story has gotten to Washington, D.C. Fulton Lewis, Jr., devoted a whole column to it last week.

After writing about a dozen paragraphs on the United Nations Covenant on Human Rights (an analysis in all details like the summary of it in The Peoria Star), Mr. Lewis continued:

> To help propagandize the declaration, the UN has spread around the nation a film labeled "Of Human Rights." It was not until this shill for world government hit Peoria that there was much of an outcry against it.
>
> The Peoria post of the American Legion took one look at the one-world version of super-government and hit the sawdust trail. The Legion, supported by two local newspapers, The Peoria Star and the Peoria Journal, has labeled the film's propaganda dangerous. . . .
>
> As a result, the American Legion is urging a counter-constitutional amendment, which states specifically that no international treaty or agreement can now or ever interfere with the constitutional liberties now enjoyed in America.
>
> Write your senator about this amendment, instead of the UN declaration, if you want to strike a blow for liberty as it exists here.

Mr. Lewis had better be careful or he will have the American Library Association Committee on Intellectual Freedom growling at him.

The *Star* had hinted at subversion in the library profession in its editorial of December 28, 1951, under the heading, "Confused Thinking About Propaganda," which stated that the whole Committee on Intellectual Freedom appeared confused. The editor felt that, if the committee is representative of the library profession, one of the great dangers of the day lay in the fact that people in key positions have not yet learned what propaganda is. He then went on more bluntly:

> But there is an alternative conclusion, the importance of which should not be underrated. There may be fellow travelers in the library profession, as there have been in government, labor unions, movies and education. Such persons would understand very well

the nature of film propaganda and the natural outlet for it through public libraries. This cannot be regarded as a fantastic possibility. It has happened in every other field of communications. Why should we assume that public libraries have not been infiltrated?

This attack by the newspaper and the American Legion on the Peoria Library film program did not go unopposed, whether nationally or locally. The *NEA Journal* of January 1952 reported that the executive committee of the U.S. National Commission for UNESCO had struck back at groups responsible for attacks on educators who teach about UNESCO and the UN. This resolution read:

> It is well known that UNESCO seeks to impress on youth the importance of international understanding and cooperation as a path to peace. We resent the attacks on our educators who teach about UNESCO and the United Nations. These attacks often emanate from groups which hide their identity under titles deceptively like those of honorable organizations. The attacks distort the purposes of UNESCO, and sometimes they are directed toward control of courses of study and of contents of textbooks, the end in view being to diminish opportunities to learn the true aims of UNESCO and the United Nations.
>
> Such offenders are, in many cases, the notorious supporters of totalitarianism and of rowdy attacks on racial and religious groups. They carry on falsely in the name of patriotism.
>
> The U.S. National Commission for UNESCO warns against this device of hiding behind the flag, while, at the same time, seeking to destroy freedom. The Commission calls on public groups and the press to continue to expose those who assail the integrity of teachers because of their interest in the United Nations.

Locally, the other Peoria newspaper, the *Journal*, finally began to give some support to the concept of intellectual freedom. On January 7, 1952, the *Journal* reported that a group of some 25 clergymen had sent a letter to the library board denouncing censorship and urging the board to resist all outside efforts to limit the range of its offerings. The ministers said their attitude toward the films did not constitute endorsement of their contents, but reflected their belief that all citizens ought to have free and equal access to them that they may arrive at their own decisions. The ministers expressed their concern that no policy of labeling be adopted, for labeling itself becomes a means of censorship.

The *Journal*, unlike the *Star*, editorialized on December 16, 1951, to the effect that Americans have been free to seek information where they please and to make up their own minds on any subject, including theories of government. This paper warned against the risk of imposing a totalitarian censorship upon what the people of this country can read and see and talk about. On February 9, 1952, an editorial in the *Journal* criticized the Legion's proposal that the library label propaganda films as such and that it discontinue their purchase and unrestricted circulation. Said the *Journal:*

> . . . The Constitution is deliberately broad on this point (freedom of information, speech and press). . . . Because the UN Declaration of Human Rights is not nearly so broad, setting up certain restrictions on freedoms of speech and information, many Americans including the Legion and this newspaper, are opposed to its adoption by the United States. . . .
>
> The Legion is performing a valuable service to the people of this community in fighting against adoption of the UN Covenant. It likewise is performing a service in calling attention to what it considers propaganda in the UN motion picture promoting the Declaration and Covenant of Human Rights. But it is assailing the very rights it seeks to defend when it endeavors to prevent other persons from seeing the film and making up their own minds about its message. . . .

Under the libertarian theory of the press, a newspaper has the obligation to report the news as objectively as possible, but it also claims the privilege of editorializing with the intent of shaping public opinion. Editorially, both the *Star* and the *Journal* were critical of the UN Covenant, but on the issue of censorship of the film *Of Human Rights* the papers parted company. (It is necessary to distinguish between a newspaper's editorial privilege and a publicly supported library or university, which is obligated to preserve its institutional neutrality on substantive issues, if it is to preserve intellectual freedom for its patrons.)

In this case, the *Star* editor was so certain that the American Legion (locally) and he were "right" that he insisted upon removal of any contrary expressions from the public library. The *Journal* editor, while he rejected the idea in the UN Covenant, also rejected the idea that the people of Peoria should be "protected" from wrong expressions.

From the beginning of the controversy, the *Star* assumed that the fact that a film was in the Library meant that the Library approved of the ideas in the film.

The *Star,* failing to distinguish between an "approved list" of films and a list recommended for purchase, criticized the Audio-Visual Board of ALA. As early as July 25, 1950, the *Star* editorialized to the effect that the important point was that the Audio-Visual Board did not see anything subversive or propagandistic in the film *Peoples of the USSR.* Since the board could see no Communist propaganda in the film, they were obviously not qualified and their "approved list" was worth nothing at all.

Such a conclusion was hardly warranted by the fact that the ALA

Audio-Visual Board had rejected a political test as a criterion, in accordance with the ALA Library Bill of Rights. The board had used its tentative standards for evaluating films: (a) validity of contents; (b) importance and/or timeliness of contents; (c) organization of material presented; (d) aesthetic quality (composition, dramatic unity); (e) technical excellence (sound, color, music, print quality); and (f) usefulness in the community. The Peoria Legion and the *Star* insisted that unless there had also been applied a political test for propaganda, the judgment of the board was worthless. For the record, it should be noted that Raynard C. Swank, Chairman of the Audio-Visual Board stated on this point:

> ... *Peoples of the USSR* was omitted [from the list] only because it was judged to be inferior and out of date. In line with the Library Bill of Rights, no materials were either included or excluded because of race, nationality, political or religious views.
>
> With films, as with books, we must stand firmly on the principle of free access to ideas and information, and on the conviction that censorship is incompatible with our responsibility to the American people.[8]

In most communities there are some groups and individuals who feel it to be their duty to censor the ideas that are contrary to their personal convictions. The idea that educators and other librarians have an obligation to inform all people on all sides of all issues, giving them the opportunity to develop their own powers of critical judgment and reach their own conclusions, was as distasteful to the Legion and the *Star* editor as the New Left today finds the idea of academic freedom on university campuses. But if *any* group of volunteer arbiters of morals or political opinion is ever permitted to establish a coercive, orthodox concept of Americanism, insisting that only its point of view can be freely circulated, then intellectual freedom has been lost.

The proper approach to ideas for the liberal university—and the liberal library—is to make accessible a variety of viewpoints so that all citizens may examine and criticize, modify, approve, or reject them as guides to action, but never to ban them. This does not suggest that educators or librarians are free to use their official positions, their public institutions, or their professional associations to establish official orthodoxies advocating Communism, Mohammedanism, or the banning of DDT as the solution to environmental problems. The fact that books by Marx, Hitler, Mao, or Winston Churchill are in libraries does not indicate that their contents are "approved" or "advocated" by libraries, or by librarians, in their official, professional roles. If libraries are to defend successfully the presence of books or films expressing unorthodox and unpopular ideas, the tenable position for a library is to insist that the principle of intellectual freedom is paramount; that, in the Peoria case, the library will stock the expressions by the American Legion, the Peoria *Star* and *Journal,* the ministers of Peoria, and the films of Julien Bryan and the United Nations.

This controversy was partially resolved by the Library Board as indicated by a statement by Xenophon P. Smith, Librarian of Peoria, May 9, 1952:

> For your information . . . I want to say that under the circumstances as they exist, I feel our Library Board has achieved a fair and thoroughly democratic solution to our film controversy in its present rulings. Analyzing these you will see there are technically no special restrictions on our purchasing policies for films. After purchase, and before circulation, films in the areas of international, national, political, economic, social and religious issues must be presented at a public preview. Following this preview, groups are encouraged to submit any comments concerning the film in question which they wish to make. These comments pro or con are then gathered together in a separate notebook-type file binder for each film. This is processed with a book card and prepared for circulation in the normal fashion for library materials. When a borrower subsequently takes out that particular film, attention is called to the availability of this file of material about the film. The borrower is not in any sense required, however, to take the file of comments. Under these circumstances it seems to me that our procedures have now become quite consistent with general library practices.
>
> One added point needs to be remembered in connection with these present rulings. Because it was felt that a limit of 25 words from any organization for each film was insufficient, the present method was adopted without any limitation as to number of words. The earlier restriction was a purely practical one when it was required by our first ruling that all comments "should be permanently attached to the film container." Under the present ruling the film or the film container is not labeled in any manner. Another specific point of the present ruling is that the three films which had previously been restricted as to circulation were removed from that category and now all of our films circulate freely without any restriction, and so far only four of them have these special file binders with comments.[9]

This solution, cumbersome though it certainly is, helps us in the present to review the necessity for the library profession now, as in 1951, to affirm the concept of institutional neutrality on substantive issues. During the McCarthy period[10] librarians recognized as never before, and possibly as they do not today, that, as representatives of the whole, general public, library trustees and librarians have a professional obligation to resist all pressures by any one segment of the community, or any one segment of the library profession, to establish its own views as "correct."

CASE B: *The Case of the* Nation

The banning of the *Nation* from New York City public school libraries in 1948 was the first case of library censorship to receive national—and even world-wide—publicity. Several aspects of the situation were unprecedented; hence ALA's actions were especially important as they set precedents.

The publicity resulted in part from the first exhibit booth of the Committee on Intellectual Freedom at the ALA conference in Atlantic City. Both Benjamin Fine of the New York *Times* and Fred Hechinger of the New York *Herald Tribune* featured the case in their reporting of the ALA conference. Even the Hindi *Times* in New Delhi covered the story.

As chairman of the ALA Committee on Intellectual Freedom, I spoke at several hearings of the New York Board of Education, thus raising the question of whether an ALA officer was authorized to speak for ALA. (At first it was held that he could not do so, nor could he commit ALA to join with other organizations in opposing the ban.) Later, under the urging of ALA President E. W. McDiarmid, both ALA and I were permitted to join the Ad Hoc Committee to Lift the Ban on the *Nation*, and I was appointed by its chairman, Archibald MacLeish, to serve on a small executive committee along with Dean Ernest Melby of the College of Education of New York University and Mrs. Eleanor Roosevelt. By the time this Ad Hoc Committee had developed a brief opposing the ban, ALA was ready to be included among the civic, religious, and professional organizations opposing the ban and endorsing the brief.

Hiram Haydn, then editor of the *American Scholar,* invited me to write the following essay[11] on the subject; to accomplish this, the *Nation's* files on the case were made available to me.

The Case of the *Nation*

DAVID K. BERNINGHAUSEN

The Nation, *one of the oldest liberal magazines in America, was banned from the New York City public school libraries on June 8, 1948. The superintendents admit that this is censorship, but, they feel, defensible censorship because of Paul Blanshard's articles describing and criticizing the official position of the Catholic Church in certain secular matters. Despite the efforts of the Ad Hoc Committee to Lift the Ban on the* Nation, *headed by Archibald MacLeish, the ban was renewed for a second year in June, 1949.*

The issue involved in the *Nation* ban is not the study of religious beliefs, nor is it tolerance versus intolerance, as the superintendents of the New York City schools implied in their published defense of the ban. The issue is freedom of inquiry, freedom to examine alternative points of view before reaching a conclusion.

A student's freedom to examine all points of view is restricted when a central board assumes the right to decide what shall *not* be available in the high school libraries. The nine New York City superintendents require *all* library materials to be selected from their centrally approved list. Under this system no librarian or teacher is free to put non-listed materials in the library, except by special permission secured from the central office by a long and cumbersome process.

This system is not only contrary to the recommendations of professional librarians, but it is radically different from the general practice in high school libraries as revealed in a recent survey conducted by the Ad Hoc Committee to Lift the Ban on the *Nation*.

Most libraries have found it economical to centralize the *routines* of ordering materials, but it is not common practice to centralize book selection. Eighteen high schools in New York State replied to a questionnaire sent out by the Ad Hoc Committee. Not one of these schools uses any type of *permissive* list. Eleven use *advisory* lists, but these do not in any way restrict selection to an exclusive or approved list. In each of these schools, selection is done by the librarian, or by some combination of librarians, teachers and principal. Selection of periodicals is entirely unrestricted.

Thirty-four large cities throughout the country also replied to the questionnaire. Only four of these use any permissive list similar to that used by New York City; six use advisory lists; and twenty-four use no lists. Four state that they follow the recommendations of the American Library Association. Five state that for magazine selection they use the accepted guide by Laura K. Martin, a professor of Library Science at the University of Kentucky (see below).

School administrators in other cities support grass roots selection of library materials by teachers and librarians without restrictions from a central office. The First Assistant Superintendent of Schools of Chicago writes:

> For the Chicago Public High Schools no lists of magazines and periodicals are officially established, either as exclusive or recommended. Each building principal, within the appropriation set up for the purpose and with the advice and counsel of his faculty members, is free to order the magazines and periodicals which he and his teachers feel are of benefit in the teaching of the individual subject under consideration.

It is becoming common practice to delegate the authority to select library materials to a trained professional librarian in each individual school. It is an established administrative principle that only personnel who are close to the situation can adequately understand that situation and prescribe for it. Cincinnati reports:

> In Cincinnati the librarian in each school selects and requisitions periodicals. Recommendations for specific purchases are made by teachers and correlate with the curricular needs. Courses of study are constantly revised. Committees studying these revisions involve librarians as well as other staff persons.

When periodicals are used on a class set basis, these purchases are made by the individual school and are reported to the Department of Instruction.

The Superintendent of Schools in River Forest, Illinois, writes:

> All our lists of magazines and periodicals for public school library use are advisory and recommended. We have none which are permissive or exclusive.
>
> We continue to be of the opinion that magazines and periodicals of reputable publishers must stay within the reach of our public school personnel regardless of the attitudes which they express in matters of politics, religion, economics, education, and other topics of current interest. We believe that we should have both sides of the story presented on any critical issue, and welcome magazines of any publishers.

In contrast to these generally accepted policies and practices, in New York City school libraries the head librarian, whose office is at headquarters, sends the centrally approved lists to the principal of each high school. The list is then turned over to the individual school's librarian and kept in the school library. Each principal consults with the chairmen of his departments. The wishes of the teachers are made known to the chairmen. "The final decision rests with the principal who is, of course, the responsible head of the school," writes Associate Superintendent Frederic Ernst. But it is important to remember that the choices of librarians and teachers, and even the final decision of the principal, are strictly limited by the approved list.

In reply to the questionnaire, Dr. Ernst stated:

> You should know, in the first place, that all purchases of listed books and magazines are made under contracts with the publishers or jobbers. These contracts, required by the City Charter, usually make it possible for the Board of Education to get rather favorable prices. As the amount of clerical work involved in ordering is very great, we generally try to keep at a minimum requests for non-listed, that is non-contract items, because each of these items requires a special contract.

In this statement Dr. Ernst seems to be saying that permissive lists are necessary to save clerical work and to secure favorable discounts. It is clear that he has failed to distinguish between the *routines of purchasing* materials and *selection* of materials. True, most libraries have agreements with jobbers to buy large quantities of books or magazines at a favorable discount, but there is no reason to suppose that the size of this discount depends upon whether selection is made from an approved list or from the whole field of print. True, it is economical to centralize the *routines* of purchasing, but the superintendent has given no pertinent reasons for centralizing *control of selection*. It is very unlikely that any economy results from the use of a permissive list, but even if there were any point to Dr. Ernst's remarks, would it be worth the sacrifice of the

policy recommended by professional librarians, the policy of select-
ing the best and most usable materials for the specific situation, from
the whole field of print?

And what do professional librarians recommend be done with the
problem of censorship raised by the ban on the *Nation*? The Executive Board of the American Library Association has consistently
urged the President of the Association, the Executive Secretary,
and the Chairman of the Committee on Intellectual Freedom to do
everything possible to persuade the New York Board to rescind the
ban. Suppression of any point of view is in direct conflict with the
Library Bill of Rights.

The American Library Association has clearly stated its position
on censorship in the Library Bill of Rights. This official statement of
the policies which should govern all library service in America
insists upon the responsibility of the library to provide information
on all sides of all questions, without special concessions to any group.
It expressly states that no book shall be excluded because of the race
or nationality, or the political or religious views of the writer. Antici-
pating censorship like that of the *Nation,* it declares that no book
shall be removed because of doctrinal or partisan disapproval.

Most professional librarians would agree with Miss Laura K.
Martin, who edits the standard library guide, *Magazines for High
School Libraries.* Most librarians consider the whole range of maga-
zines for adults as theoretically available for high school students.
However, selection from the whole field of print is a complex task,
and Miss Martin's book provides an essential guide.

This guide lists the *Nation* as suitable for senior high school, noting the important fact that it is indexed in the *Reader's Guide to
Periodical Literature.* The author states that the open forum ideal
in the selection of weekly periodicals of news comment is more essential than in any other field. The often unique point of view presented
by the *Nation* is especially desirable in a balanced library that tries
to achieve the open forum ideal.

> *Nation* and *New Republic* continue to represent the same left-
> ist clientele, and each has its fervent adherents among the peo-
> ple who like their news edited from a frankly pro-labor, pro-
> social security, and pro-world cooperation viewpoint. A sharper
> note of criticism, biting but never carping, distinguishes part of
> the *Nation's* content, notably its reviews of books and the arts.
> . . . Its international outlook, its facility in revealing the signifi-
> cant details in situations, details which often clarify official
> silences, and the scholarly appraisals in its book reviewing col-
> umns, are contributing factors in the building of its long-stand-
> ing prestige.

Miss Martin has also commented pointedly about the too common
attitude that young minds must be protected by censorship:

> The immaturity of her clientele is the excuse often given for
> the control of reading matter. To most school librarians, the
> immaturity of their patrons is a challenge and not a limitation—
> they look upon the high school years as a precious time in which

to open doors, to show young people that difference of opinion is a normal and socially valuable phenomenon. Variety in people, ideas, and media of communication stimulates intellectual activity at any age. Wise workers with young people have less fear that in a school atmosphere their students will absorb dangerous ideas, than that too soon they will close their minds to all but a familiar pattern of traditional formulae.

The New York school administration has obviously ignored the recommendations of the American Library Association and those of the foremost professional authority in the field of magazine selection. The decision to ban the *Nation* is an unwarranted restriction of the New York student's educational opportunities. By way of illustration, let us examine the way magazines are used in libraries.

Suppose that the student goes to his school library to prepare a paper on a controversial issue. (One of the most important tools he can hope to master in school is the ability to locate information.)

He looks in the *Reader's Guide to Periodical Literature.* This student finds six references to articles on his subject in the *Nation* and six in *Life.* He reads the six in *Life.* But his teacher has warned him, as any good teacher should, that it is dangerous to rely upon only one source of information. He asks to see the six articles in the *Nation.* They are not available.

Does this student have freedom of inquiry? Does he have an opportunity to gain experience in that most important and difficult exercise—the forming of an intelligent opinion *after* examination of all the arguments?

Suppose the situation were reversed. Considering the vivid pictorial material in the June 14, 1948, issue of *Life,* it is quite conceivable that *Life* could be banned on the same grounds as the *Nation.* These pictures of the controversy between Catholics and Protestants are likely to be much more impressive to adolescent minds than the prosy style of Paul Blanshard in the *Nation.* If *Life* were banned, would the student have freedom of inquiry?

To return to the pros and cons of the specific issue, the act of banning the *Nation* from school libraries—what can be said in defense of excluding the segment of American thought represented in the *Nation?*

On October 1, 1948, the New York City Superintendent of Schools, Dr. William Jansen, published a statement of the reasons for the ban. This document is entitled "Should Religious Beliefs Be Studied and Criticized in an American Public High School?" The arguments presented are:

1. The *Nation* was not eliminated because it criticized the policies of the Catholic Church concerning political and social issues. It was removed from the list because two of the articles entitled "Roman Catholic Science, I: Relics, Saints, Miracles" (May 15, 1948), and "Roman Catholic Science, II: Apparitions and Evolution" (May 22, 1948), did *not* deal with the policies of the Roman Catholic Church with respect to public questions. "Those two articles are devoted

to a criticism of Catholic beliefs, dogmas, and religious practices. Catholic beliefs and religious practices are not only criticized but are ridiculed by innuendo."

2. The Board did not adhere to the policy of withdrawing the single articles that are objectionable because "It was obvious that with the publication of the two articles referred to, the editorial policy of the *Nation* had been modified to permit the publication of articles that are an attack on the Catholic religion."

3. The Board is of the opinion that it is contrary to the American public school tradition to bring religious controversies into the classrooms of the public schools. The Board will continue to see to it that there shall be no criticism of the religious beliefs of any groups in the schools of New York City.

As to the first argument—that the two articles on science "did not deal with the policies of the Roman Catholic Church with respect to public questions"—there can be considerable difference of opinion. Since when has science and the scientific method not been a public question? Many people consider the validity of science and the integrity of those who search for scientific truth essentially a religious matter. It is undoubtedly also a public question.

Lewis Mumford has commented that when Superintendent Jansen quotes twenty-one sentences to show that Catholic beliefs are criticized, and gives this as a defense of the ban on the *Nation,* he commits himself to the proposition that no religious belief held by any sect or creed may be discussed critically in any magazine on the approved list. This is untenable on several counts. It implies that the Board must be able to approve every idea to be found in the library, which could only mean that the library was limited to what the Board believes. If carried to its logical conclusion, this would mean that no magazine that criticized Voodooism in the West Indies could be approved for library use, lest it offend the religious beliefs of a minority. It would, finally, if rigidly followed, permit any person or group to demand the removal of any distasteful idea, for such a censor need only claim that this idea is critical of a belief he holds on faith.

In a letter to Dr. Jansen, Mr. Mumford says of these articles on relics and miracles:

> Mr. Blanshard's attitude toward miracle-working relics is no more iconoclastic than that of the head of the priory of Crammont in the Middle Ages, who implored its founder, St. Stephen of Thiern, to work no more miracles, because he was turning the monks' minds away from religion. The only question about these quotations is whether Mr. Blanshard's facts are straight. I note you do not question him on this ground.

This last sentence by Mr. Mumford emphasizes a very important principle in the American tradition of free inquiry. Traditionally, Americans have considered the proper reaction to unpleasant statements to be refutation of those statements—when and if refutation is possible. Banning "objectionable" ideas is not permissable treatment in a democratic society.

The second argument assumes a great deal on very little evidence. Professional librarians appreciate the value of *complete* sets of reference periodicals, and most of them would not approve of the policy the Board apparently sometimes follows, of withdrawing single objectionable articles. But even supposing this were a defensible policy, it has been firmly established by the courts, for example in the *Ulysses* case, that the suppression of a publication can only be justified on the basis of consideration of the publication as a whole. In suppressing all future issues of the *Nation* the Board assumed much more than can be justified by the evidence. They not only banned the *Nation* for a year, assuming that it had adopted an editorial policy of publishing attacks on the Catholic religion, but renewed the ban for a second year. The Board even refused to give any official reasons for the extension of the ban.

In regard to this second argument, Nathan Frankel of the National Lawyer's Guild wrote to Dr. Jansen: "One swallow does not make a summer. Two articles do not amount to a change in editorial policy extending consistently and continuously over a fifty year period."

Dale DeWitt, regional head of the Unitarian Ministry wrote: "To pretend that the *Nation* must, because of the Blanshard articles, frequently print anti-religious articles is an extreme decision. One is inclined to conclude that the Board is eager to find some way to eliminate the *Nation* from the school shelves."

The third and chief argument presented by the Board, that religious education and religious controversies must not be brought into the classroom, is strangely irrelevant. Religious education is not the issue. The issue is unusually clear and simple: Shall students have freedom of inquiry, freedom to examine alternative points of view, before reaching a conclusion?

Do the superintendents hold that a library is responsible for approving and advocating every argument of every author of every article in the various magazines in the library? This is obviously absurd. The virtue of a good library is that alternative points of view are available to anyone who wishes to search them out. The well balanced library is the best protection any school can have against the teacher who has committed himself to belief in one system of ideas, and who might wish to indoctrinate his students in that system.

The very title of the published statement of the reasons for the ban, "Should Religious Beliefs Be Studied and Criticized In An American Public School?" is irrelevant. It is worse than irrelevant, for it can only serve to confuse and mislead the casual reader. It is evidence of an attempt to erect a straw man to draw attention from the real threat inherent in the ban to the principles of free speech, free press, and free inquiry so fundamental to a free society.

Any comment on the New York Board's statement in defense of

the ban on the *Nation* should include the following analysis published by Mr. Archibald MacLeish and the Ad Hoc Committee to Lift the Ban on the *Nation,* under the title "An Appeal to Reason and Conscience."

The question before the Board was not the question of the suitability of the *Nation* as a text book in the City's schools. The question was whether the *Nation,* which had long been one of the periodicals available to New York City students, should continue to be available to them. In ruling that it should not, and in giving its publication of the Blanshard articles as justification, the Board in effect enunciated two propositions, both of which in our opinion are contrary to American ideas of freedom and destructive of American principles.

The first is the proposition that any published material regarded, or which could be regarded, as objectionable on grounds of faith or creed by any group in the community should be excluded from the community's schools and school libraries.

The second is the proposition that the appearance in any publication of material of this kind justifies the suppression in schools and school libraries of the publication as a whole. In the case of a periodical this means that the past publication of such material justifies the suppression of future issues regardless of the general character and record of the periodical.

The vice of the second of these two propositions is apparent upon its face. The exclusion from public institutions, by public officials, of future issues of newspapers, magazines or other periodicals, on the basis of particular material published in the past, rather than on the basis of the character of the publication as a whole, cannot be defended even as censorship. It is extra-judicial punishment pure and simple, and it involves a power of intimidation and possible blackmail in officials of government which no free society can tolerate and which a free press could not long survive. . . .

The first proposition—that any publication objectionable on grounds of faith to any group in the community should be suppressed in the schools—though more plausible on its face, is equally vicious in fact. It is a repudiation, on one side, of the principle of freedom of education; on the other, of the principle of the separation of church and state. The meaning of that latter tenet, so far as education is concerned, is that no church may use the public schools as instruments of propaganda. To give the churches of the country, or any of their members who might seek to exercise it, the power to determine by simple veto what shall *not* be available to students in the public schools; or worse, for public officials to exclude automatically anything any group might be expected to wish excluded, is to do by negative action what the Constitution and the Courts forbid by positive action. . . .

The truth is that censorship and suppression in all their forms impoverish human life and warp the human mind in an increasing and progressive sickness. Those who practice them are led by the logic of one exclusion to the tragedy of the next. If the suppression of the *Nation* for having published the Blanshard articles is allowed to stand, and if the propositions upon which it is justified are accepted, the consequences to the schools, to the press and to the vitality of American freedom may well be very serious indeed. . . .

To bar from the schools of New York future issues of one of the country's leading periodicals with a history of responsible journalism since 1865 because a past issue or issues contained paragraphs which one of the many groups which compose this country found objectionable seems to us a violation of the most fundamental principles of American equality. We believe the wrong should be righted at once, not so much in the interest of the *Nation* as in the interest of the people of the United States.

What is the philosophy of education which would justify the apparently arbitrary and stubborn disregard for the Constitution of the United States, professional library standards, and the traditional American concept of free inquiry?

It appears that these officials frown upon inclusion of controversial subjects in their curriculum and their library. If they look on textbooks and library books as authoritative sources of information, not to be questioned by teacher or pupil, once they have been placed on the permissive list, then the ban is reasonable. If they look on the whole educational process as established solely to transmit the orthodoxies of the past, then how do they decide whether the orthodoxies transmitted shall be Catholic, Jewish or Protestant? Surely, in the twentieth century, these educators cannot conceive of the pupil's task as simply to memorize the "correct" opinions placed before him. And yet, it is difficult to imagine any other view of education which would justify such characteristics as strict centralization of control over library acquisition and censorship of the *Nation*, a magazine widely recognized as desirable for school libraries.

If the New York student is required to read "the truth" in a textbook, take notes as his instructor presents the same material in a lecture, and then prove that he "knows" this truth by writing it on an examination paper, then certainly the banning of certain "incorrect" ideas is essential. But this kind of education has long been supplanted by an approach to teaching and learning that encourages the student to develop his own critical powers. Is it wise—is it even safe—to produce robots who have only "received opinions" upon which to base their actions?

If our nation's schools are built upon the authoritarian attitude which simply requires that students shall make the correct verbal responses, then the nation will be cursed with millions of new citizens able to think only in terms of black or white, dogmatic right or wrong. Educators and parents need only reflect that there are various possible interpretations of known facts, that sometimes part of the truth is suppressed, that any one man's interpretation is likely to be only a part of the truth, and that the postulates of even such a "positive" science as physics are constantly changing, to recognize the danger of continuing to produce non-thinking automatons.

The whole history of ideas indicates that knowledge is not static, that knowledge is always in a process of becoming. Alfred North Whitehead once said that we should remember that the reason certain books are called classics is that their authors exercised their creative powers to adventure beyond the established patterns of their times. The thoughts of John Wycliffe, Galileo, Paine, Emerson or Darwin were not approved by the orthodox minds of their contemporaries. Their books might even be objectionable today to some self-appointed censors. But their ideas led to new concepts of reality, and therefore changed or replaced our earlier knowledge.

The censors of the *Nation,* like all censors in America, must be reminded that the comfort of an official and exclusive doctrine is a forbidden luxury for democratic educators. True, such a doctrine would protect the educator, by making it clear what he must teach and what he must avoid. But this kind of teaching, with all its oversimplifications, will produce only immature minds, oblivious to any necessary qualifications which must accompany any carefully stated proposition. The tendency to think only in terms of black or white, and to insist that everyone must conform by believing in what appears white, and shunning what appears black, is even now too evident in our society.

But the most disturbing question raised by this unfortunate episode in American educational history has still to be considered. What do the high school students of New York think of this ban? They cannot take at face value the loud protestations of their school authorities that they are being educated for citizenship in a democracy. They can have little respect for their schools, when they have such clear and positive knowledge that they are not permitted freedom of inquiry. Can they really believe that they are being given the best possible opportunity to learn to live in a democratic society? Perhaps a good case could be presented to the effect that our youth must be disillusioned sometime, but not many educators would be comfortable in the knowledge that their students were disillusioned by their teachers' failure to live up to the American ideal of free inquiry.

Can a student accept a partial right of free inquiry and retain his faith in American freedom? It is more likely that he will find substantiation in this banning of the *Nation* for what he has already suspected: that his educators are "old pretenders" who may give lip service to the tradition of free inquiry, but in reality follow the policy stated so well by the venerable Professor of Worldly Wisdom in Samuel Butler's *Erewhon:*

> It is not our business to help students to think for themselves. ... Our duty is to ensure that they will think as we do, or at any rate, as we hold it expedient to say we do.

To learn how this case had finally been resolved, I dispatched a letter in August 1971 to Helen R. Sattley, Director of School Library Service, the City of New York, inquiring about current policies and practices. Specifically, I asked whether it is still the practice in this school system to draw up an "authorized list" of magazine titles and whether the *Nation* is now in any or all school libraries. Miss Sattley's reply,[12] which follows, is most informative and brings us up to date on this case. Her additional statement on current policies regarding book and periodical selection in New York City schools is also enlightening.

110 LIVINGSTON STREET
BROOKLYN, NEW YORK 11201

April 6, 1972

MR. DAVID K. BERNINGHAUSEN
Director, Library School
University of Minnesota
3 Walter Library
Minneapolis, Minnesota 55455

Dear Mr. Berninghausen:
I am answering your inquiry concerning *The Nation* magazine....

The Nation is on the Magazine List of the New York City Board of Education. That list, at the present time, is one of suggestions for school purchases. Schools may purchase any magazines they need, listed or unlisted. This, as you probably know, is a rather recent development and came about as we were able gradually to get funds released for junior and senior high schools to have their own checking accounts, a process held back to some extent for a number of years actually, because of the gigantic problem of central auditing for this large system, a legal necessity (for example, schools were gradually allowed 10%–45% of their funds for nonlisted materials). Individual school responsibility at all school levels was hastened by the decentralization of the school system these past two years when all schools had general checking accounts arranged for them.

To return to *The Nation;* when I came to the Board in 1953, it was not on the approved magazine list having been removed by the Board of Education in April, 1948. In 1957, our High School Standing Committee unanimously approved reinstating *The Nation*. This committee is made up of librarians, subject chairmen, teachers and Bureau staff member and meets one full day a month. The morning is spent studying those books in question which have not been sent to them for complete reading, and the afternoon is spent in group discussion. Any books questioned by even one reader are brought to this committee for study and final decisions on listing. It is also responsible for the annual revision of the magazine list.

It took us until January, 1963, to get *The Nation* reinstated on the approved list—and by this time, we had a complete new Board of Education and they were ready to right many mistakes of the former one.

We do not keep central records of the holdings of our 900 schools and so I cannot tell you if all schools subscribe to *The Nation*.

Schools have always made their own selections of books and magazines, from the Board Lists. We do have a policy statement on materials selection developed by the Board of Education, a photo copy of which I will send you. The city is also a member of the Council of the Great City Schools (1819 H Street, NW, Washington, D.C. 20006) which has an excellent 1971 pamphlet on "Designing Instructional Materials for Urban Youth: A Report on Current Practices with Recommendations for Future Publishing and Purchasing Policies."

Since policy statements are always very general, I believe you will be more interested in the lists, themselves. Therefore, I am sending to you a copy of the 1972 magazine list and, also, our senior high school book lists and supplements. From rather short lists that were considered restrictive, these book lists (a senior high school list and an elementary and junior high school list) have developed in the past 15 years into very important buying guides and bibliographies. The large lists have been revised on alternate years and there have been two supplements for each, each year.

Books on the supplements are in our materials center display for a year for librarian and teacher study and then are filed in the large Bureau collections. From 36,000–40,000 books are in these collections and also available for study and bibliographic use. They do not circulate.

My own concern at the present time is that, as local community boards—we have 31 in the city—take over the responsibility for selection of materials as well as curriculum policy there will be some districts where book selection will become narrower and more restrictive. We have fought so hard to broaden our lists and to allow schools to buy whatever they have needed, regardless of lists, that it is not easy to see these gains threatened. We have already had this happen in one Queens District last Spring with *Down These Mean Streets,* as you probably know.

I enclose the statement I prepared on this for the United Parents Association. They used it at the open Board meeting and in the Civil Liberties suit—but the CLU does not back professional decisions; they call for parent participation in selection.

I hope this gives you some answers to your questions. . . .

Sincerely yours,
(signed)

HELEN R. SATTLEY
Director, School Library Service

HRS:bf
Encl.
cc: Mrs. Minne R. Motz

In New York City, local community boards have taken over the responsibility for curriculum policy and selection of materials. The following statement[13] was prepared by Helen R. Sattley in 1971 for the United Parents Association in one Queens Borough school district. The United Parents Association adopted it and presented it as their policy on book selection at an open district board hearing on the proposed banning of *Down These Mean Streets* by Piri Thomas.

A Statement On Book Selection

by Helen R. Sattley, Director of School Libraries
Prepared at the request of the United Parents Association

Down These Mean Streets by Piri Thomas is one of the important modern autobiographies written by men whose boyhood and youth have been lived in the slums of our city and whose minds and hearts and bodies have been bruised and beaten by the experiences they have encountered. That they have been able to come through these years as men able to recognize the degradation and to hold to a belief for better times for themselves and others like them is not only an inspiration for other youths of the slums but is of great significance for those of us—adults as well as students—who are usually unaware of such conditions of living or who close our eyes to them. Thus these autobiographies, even when not especially well written, become important documents of society today. *Down These Mean Streets* was included in the Notable Books of the Year by the American Library Association for 1967.

Teachers use such books to help their students understand conditions many of their classmates are exposed to every day of their lives, so that there may be greater understanding on the part of the more fortunate students. Teachers also use them to begin discussions on what steps need to be taken to improve the conditions within the city and within society. And students read them, whether or not they are on the library or classroom shelves, because the characters and the conditions are close to them and the writing reflects a familiar style and vocabulary that is a part of their own milieu, whether adults will admit it or not.

This book was considered at two different times by our Secondary School Library Book Standing Committee after very careful reading by members of the Committee from the schools and from the Bureau. The Committee decided that it was a book that could be used in schools as librarians and faculties and principals saw the need of it, as many schools were already using it, and that it would not be recommended for general library use. Schools now have part of their allotments for direct buying of library materials and are able to purchase any materials as they need them.

The selection of materials for a school or library should always rest with the professional staffs who by training and experience in their fields of responsibility are equipped to evaluate materials of importance to their schools according to selection principles (such as those recognized by the American Library Association and the National Council of Teachers of English) and whose first hand acquaintance with their students enables them to select materials that will be meaningful to them.

Selection or exclusion of materials undertaken by groups outside the professional staff means a limiting of opportunity for students because decisions would necessarily be made by those less familiar with the breadth and depth of the subject matter and less familiar with the needs of the student body. Moreover, recommendations by a group outside the professional staff for students' use is limiting the freedom of choice of that professional staff in honestly seeking to provide for their students the kinds of materials they feel to be essential for their education and a knowledge of the world they live in.

In addition, the exclusion by any group outside the professional staff of any materials already chosen by that staff begins the chipping away of books on library shelves that a democracy must guard against: one group will object to one kind of book, another group to another kind, etc. Libraries in a democracy, however, need to have materials for all readers and cannot exclude books because one group feels it is slighted in them or finds them objectionable, for another group would then have the right to exclude other books for reasons as important to them and readers who need and want to read any of these books would be denied them. Moreover, every book needs to be judged as a whole and on the merits of what its purpose or reason for being, in its entirety, is; parts of the book taken out of context of its total contribution often distort this purpose. This is one of the fundamental principles of book selection.

The National Council of Teachers of English in its "The Students' Right to Read" statement has said:

> We want to help create a climate in which teachers are free to teach and students are free to learn, a climate conducive to open inquiry and responsible discussion of any and all questions related to the ethical and cultural welfare of mankind.

The American Library Association has stated as one of its principles in its "School Library Bill of Rights":

> To place principle above personal opinion and reason above prejudice in the selection of materials of the highest quality in order to assume a comprehensive collection appropriate for the users of the library.

These have been guiding principles for the libraries of the public schools of this city for many years. We hope and expect that they will continue to be observed as the city moves into the new structure of Decentralization.

April 12, 1971

CASE C: *Wrenshall Bans Orwell's* 1984

When parents complained about the "sex" in the novel *1984,* the school board of Wrenshall, Minnesota, banned the book and fired teacher

Richard Wyman for assigning it to eight of the twenty-two students in his senior English class. The superintendent's letter to Wyman stated that the book was not part of the English program, it was not to be used in the school, and that the library copy was to be withdrawn immediately.

The Minnesota Civil Liberties Union studied the case and issued a resolution which said:

> *1984* is important for the political education of all Americans be-
> cause it illustrates what happens in a totalitarian society. It is a very
> effective anti-Communist story and the MCLU endorses it for its
> educational value. We are surprised and concerned to learn that any
> superintendent or school board would ban it from the curriculum or
> library.

The resolution also predicted disappointment for any citizen who chose to read *1984* hoping to find obscenity or sexy passages. It also expressed a suggestion that if the board were to read the book they might decide to reverse their decision to ban this expose of totalitarian thought control.

As is often true in a censorship case, the board members had *not* read Orwell's book before they made their decision. The nation's press gave much attention to the story of this book-banning, and the mail rolled in to Wrenshall, most of it critical of the school board. The school superintendent told a Minneapolis *Tribune* reporter that the board had received letters from as far away as Japan, and said that the press throughout the country had crucified them. And one of the board members said: "We are not condemning the book. The trouble started when the teacher failed to come to us. He went right to the newspapers here. Now he's a martyr and we're Communists."

Fortunately, the school board at Wrenshall were persuaded to read the book, resulting in a decision to return the teacher to his job and the book to the library.

The Wrenshall case raises some major issues about instructional materials used in public schools. The following letter appeared in the Minneapolis *Tribune* of October 27, 1961, along with the Library Bill of Rights and the School Library Bill of Rights:

> Library Officials Defend Rights of Teachers
> in Book Assignments
>
> To the Editor: Should the Wrenshall school library include
> George Orwell's book, *1984?* We believe that this decision should be
> made locally, in Wrenshall, by the school librarian, after considera-
> tion of the facts about the book, the teaching situation, and the prin-
> ciples governing library service. We do not believe that any central
> authority should decide such a question.
>
> **About the book:** "1984" is a powerful sociological novel in which
> the author paints an almost unbearably depressing picture of what

may happen to those of us living today in what we call a free society unless we face the future with a more accurate picture of reality and with greater courage. It is an adult novel which deserves a serious reading by all thinking people. Its description of what life will be like in a thoroughly totalitarian society is a warning of what can happen. As the Minnesota Civil Liberties Union has already pointed out, it is a very effective anti-Communist story with important political educational values.

"1984" IS included in a number of lists of books recommended for secondary school libraries, such as "A Basic Book Collection for High Schools," published by the American Library Association. It is included in the "Standard Catalog for High School Libraries," a national list prepared by librarians and teachers in many libraries across the country. Both of these lists are basic book selection tools for Minnesota school libraries. It is also included in "Good Reading," a list of 1,500 titles of the most outstanding books endorsed by several educational associations.

About the teaching situation: Should all the members of the senior class be required to read "1984?" Such requirements deny all that is known about individual differences in reading ability, interest, and maturity. Also, Minnesota law states that all textbooks must be free in public schools, which means that no teacher has the right to require his students to buy even one book.

But while it would be a demonstrably ineffective teaching procedure if the teacher required all 22 seniors to read any particular book, should some of these students read "1984?" Yes, they should. In all probability only those students with sufficient maturity will do so, since the story will not have much appeal for the youngster used to a reading diet of adolescent fiction and sports stories. According to newspaper reports, in this case only eight advanced students were asked to read "1984."

ARE SENIORS in high school adults? If they aren't fully adult, and to this most people would agree, certainly they are not children. They are aware of a great many things not taught them by either parents or teachers.

How are we to educate these young people in such a way that they will be able to assume adult responsibilities? We cannot deny that the world we're giving them is full of unsolved problems, sorrow and ugliness, but we can help them to face reality and to learn to distinguish between the true and false.

We not only *can* do this, many people believe we *must* do it if civilization is to survive. And as for sex, we cannot very well deny its existence when more manifestations of it are apparent now than ever before, on television, in the daily newspapers and magazines, in the readily available sensational sex novel, and countless other places.

While there may be English teachers with so little knowledge of the learning process that they assign the same book to all members of a heterogeneous senior class, this does not appear to be the teaching situation in Wrenshall. A teacher should have the discretion and the freedom to assign a book to selected students. If he is prohibited by law from requiring such students to buy a book, then the teaching situation suggests that the book should be in the school library.

About the school library: As educators and librarians we point to the fact that one major reason for having a school library is the need to provide for individual differences among students. The notion that a single book for an entire class can provide for these differences would be hard to defend. Social promotion is a fact that cannot be ignored, and undoubtedly many high school seniors are not capable of reading a book like "1984." But should this fact suggest that therefore no student shall have access to this significant book? We think not.

The evaluation of any book for a school library must be based upon the local teaching situation, and it must also be based upon a complete reading of the book. It is grossly unfair to judge a piece of writing by taking sentences or paragraphs out of context, since this enables the reader to substitute his interpretation for that of the author.

IN ANY BOOK evaluation, it is also imperative to consider what the author is trying to say and how well he accomplishes his purpose, and whether he is sincere in his objective and competent to write on the subject. Anyone reading Orwell's book could not fail to be convinced of his sincerity, his ability, and his tremendous concern for human dignity. Since its publication in 1949, many critics have called "1984" a classic.

We hope it is apparent that in our view, the presence of "1984" in lists of outstanding books does not alone dictate to the library. Such lists are guides to recommended books; they are not lists of approved books, in the sense that only books included are suitable for purchase.

IT IS THE librarian's job to evaluate a book for possible purchase, according to the local teaching situation, as well as the other considerations. He should make the most of his selections from standard lists, as part of a planned program of buying to provide instructional materials needed by teachers and students in his school. Without doubt, some librarians will sometimes make poor choices, but as Sen. Eugene McCarthy of Minnesota writes in the last paragraph of his new book, "Frontiers in American Democracy":

"In a democracy mistakes and failures should be the consequence of too great leniency, rather than of too much restraint; the result of excessive trust, rather than of too much interference and control. Democracy, when the hard choice must be made, must run the risk of being betrayed or destroyed by its own people rather than itself become their betrayer and destroyer."

The American Library Association and the American Association of School Librarians have dealt with the problem of censorship and selection for many years. We have developed the library bill of rights and the school library bill of rights as guides to the principles of selection. We would like to see them published in your newspaper as a public service. We hope that the Wrenshall superintendent and school board will study these policy statements and eventually adopt them as local policy.

> DAVID K. BERNINGHAUSEN, *chairman*
> Minnesota Library Association
> Committee on Intellectual Freedom;
> Ruth Erstad, Minnesota School Library Supervisor,
> Minneapolis.

CASE D: *The Report of the Commission on Obscenity and Pornography*

> V. The rights of an individual to the use of a library should not be denied or abridged because of his age, race, religion, national origins or social or political views.
>
> —THE LIBRARY BILL OF RIGHTS, 1967[14]

Few presidential commissions have had the rough reception given to that on obscenity and pornography, and H. L. Mencken seems to have provided a suitable epitaph for its ill-starred report: "Human beings never welcome the news that something they have long cherished is untrue: they almost always reply to that news by reviling its promulgator." "Nevertheless," Mencken continued, "a minority of bold and energetic men keep plugging away, and as a result of their hard labors and resultant infamy, the sum of human knowledge gradually increases."[15] The majority report of the commissioners, a voice of calm and reason on the passion-provoking subject of pornography, will in time be heard with the calm and reason which it did not receive when first published.

An atmosphere of hostility to the report was created even before its publication when the commission was disowned by members of the administration, an unprecedented action. In effect the commission's report was "tried and found guilty" before official publication because it failed to confirm long-held "folk beliefs" about the "evils" of obscenity and pornography. Two years and $2 million were spent by the commission contracting studies by academic and clinical researchers on the effects of obscenity and pornography. These and earlier studies produced little evidence to suggest that exposure to pornography acts as a cause of misconduct in either youth or adults. In light of this finding, the commission recommended that adults should have free access to pornographic materials. Both the findings and recommendations of the report were rejected by President Nixon as "morally bankrupt." It was later rejected by all but five members of the Senate.

Such a rejection is a sharp reminder that the educational process that formed the biases of the senators was a sad failure in furnishing them with an appropriate attitude toward the behavioral sciences. It took centuries for people to learn to live with the notion that the earth is spherical rather than flat, and it took us several decades to "accept" the theory of evolution. When we are confronted by new theories and facts about man himself and his attempts to live with others of his kind, most of us tend to cling stubbornly to beliefs and frames of reference that should have been revised long since. Everyone demands the right to be his own expert in the social sciences. In our approach toward the findings of social scientists about the sexual nature of man, there are special obstacles in the way of reasonable attempts to evaluate a report such as that of the Commission on Obscenity and Pornography. On this subject the taboos extended so far as to persuade the President and the Senate to reject without analysis of the evidence, surely an act tantamount to censorship. Perhaps members of Congress should write their own reports if all they want to hear is politically safe confirmation of their assumptions.

The report was disowned and condemned. Yet one of its major findings is that 60 percent of adults do not believe that their access to reading and viewing materials related to sex should be restricted in any way. The musical *Hair* has been playing to full houses across the country, and legal campaigns against booksellers of sex literature fail for want of public support. It seems probable that the findings of the report will eventually lead to more freedom for people of all ages to learn about the sexual nature of the "naked ape" and that the work of the commission will be another step in the long struggle to free men's minds. In the meantime, two major challenges in the related areas of the impact of reading and the right to read face teachers and educators in teacher education programs.

First, the report indicated that there is no clear-cut evidence that reading sexually explicit material creates deviation or delinquency. Rejection of the report implies a "belief" that such material is harmful to both adults and young persons. Librarians should urge everyone to read the report, for here is a major attempt to compile what we do know about the effects of reading materials about sex. The reason that there has been so little solid research in this subject until recently is that most people are highly emotional about it, hindering enquiry; and the origins of delinquent behaviors are so complex that the isolation of any single causal factor is difficult, if not impossible. Only continued research over the years will enable us to see clearly what factors operate in this area.

The commission's report is significant, for it brings together and interprets a mass of data, thus providing a perspective not before available. It should not be neglected. We must all be concerned with more effective research and teaching as these relate to reading habits and interests and the effects of reading. Educators and librarians already have accumulated some knowledge about reading habits and interests. We know, for example, that while some sixth graders have the ability to read almost anything, others can barely read at their level of maturity or cannot read at all. We know, also, that some seventh, eighth, and ninth graders tend to read many more "adult" books than we had supposed twenty years ago. We also know that most young people will not actually read much in fields beyond their level of maturity and their interests. Such information is helpful to the school administrator, teacher, and librarian who periodically must face public attacks on the availability of many kinds of books, including classics like *1984, Catcher in the Rye,* or *The Grapes of Wrath.* Although denounced for their "sex" content, such books are, in all probability, read only by students with sufficient maturity to understand them, since their stories will not appeal to children accustomed to a reading diet of adolescent fiction and sports stories.

Second, while the report recommends that sexually implicit materials— that is, pictorial materials—should not be exhibited or sold to juveniles, it did not include verbal materials in its prohibition because the Commission believed that there was no satisfactory way to define "offensive" words in a workable, legal fashion without seriously endangering the free communication of ideas. A universally accepted definition of obscenity is impossible; any definition is highly subjective, depending on the particular attitude of the censor. We should not reduce all literature to a preconceived level deemed fit for children, especially now that the "Nixon Supreme Court" has reversed the liberal trend on obscenity issues, encouraging local definitions. We should, rather, expose children to the ready impact of the First Amendment. We cannot lock children out of the world, nor can we lock up books to keep them away from children without prohibiting access to those books to adults. We must honor the right to read.

The American Library Association has officially taken a "liberal" attitude on the freedom to read for children. In 1967 the Library Bill of Rights was revised by adding the word *age* to section 5, so that it now reads: "The rights of an individual to the use of a library should not be denied or abridged because of his age, race, religion, national origins or social or political views." In 1972 the ALA Council adopted an interpretation of the Library Bill of Rights entitled, "Free Access to Libraries for Minors." Very probably this issue will long continue to cause controversies. In my opinion, the policy is a good one.

Today there is among educators a changing concept of childhood. In a sense we are questioning whether in awarding to children a "protected" status we have not in the past run the risk of depriving them of rights and opportunities to learn to the fullest extent of their capabilities. Modular, flexible scheduling in American schools, for example, is based on the premise that a child cannot become a responsible being without the opportunity to make decisions, to experiment, and to make his own mistakes. Under such educational programs, the move is away from memorization and the "safe" textbook. The people and the materials of school and community are resources from which young people are increasingly tapping knowledge and learning to analyze what they find. A student can only develop the judgment demanded by a free society by comparing all points of view and having generous access to a wide range of materials. In addition, young people are beginning to bypass the mass media and the school textbook as authorized, establishment-type media, whose conformity and monotony frequently amounts to censorship. They are turning instead to the alternative press, to underground-produced records, cassettes, videotapes, or to homemade movies, because these seem to be free from the control of an "establishment" network or editor.

I sometimes wonder how parents can continue to hope that their children will remain "innocent" and unquestioning, always agreeing with them and accepting their beliefs and biases. Do we really want our sons and daughters to agree with us on everything? While this might be somewhat comforting, I think parents should not expect it. What I would hope is that our children will form their own beliefs and values, based on their own observations, experiences, and the facts and theories of their years on this earth, rather than accept those of their elders. And parents who hope otherwise would be well advised to anticipate that the latter will happen, regardless of their attempts to prevent it.

The burgeoning streams of communication and educational innovations are essentially part of the ongoing American effort to affirm each individual's inalienable rights. We must recognize that each of us is an individual with a distinctive personality and that our physical powers and limitations vary one from the other. We must strive to avoid regimenting every person into a single mould. But there are and probably always will be those who would seek to deny individuality, to create an "average" man. These are the would-be censors whose activities may occasionally wane but never vanish. And the greater the innovation and experiment, the greater the risk of offending the censorious.

But people in a dynamic, changing society must have information in order to make intelligent decisions. This, of course, is the essence of a free society, and it is given lip service, even by the President and the U.S. senators who rejected the report of the Commission on Obscenity.

Educators and their students, of whatever age, reading abilities, interests, and levels of maturity, cannot readily accept a categorical rejection of a major social document such as the report of this commission. If we are to make wise decisions—whether or not to smoke cigarettes, build multibillion-dollar missile systems, use phosphorus-free detergents, limit the earth's population, or whatever—we require freedom to explore the universe of which we are a part. For each of us, the picture of the world we hold in our minds determines how we react to this world around us. It is essential that this picture approximates reality as nearly as possible.

In the matter of the right to read, then, the commission's report with its ten volumes of supporting evidence deserves a full and fair hearing. The Intellectual Freedom Committee of the American Library Association proposed the following resolution which it had adopted December 2, 1970, at a special meeting held in Chicago and which was passed by the Council during its Midwinter Meeting at Los Angeles on January 20, 1971:

Resolution on the *Report* of the Commission
on Obscenity and Pornography

(Adopted January 20, 1971, by the ALA Council)

WHEREAS, The Commission on Obscenity and Pornography performed a difficult and historically significant service for the nation by initiating the first, broad scientific inquiry into the nature of obscene and pornographic materials and their effect upon users, and

WHEREAS, The Commission's efforts resulted in an important body of empirical data which should serve as the basis for sound and continuing evaluation and study of an area of social and legislative concern too long ignored, and

WHEREAS, The U.S. Senate rejected the REPORT OF THE COMMISSION ON OBSCENITY AND PORNOGRAPHY by a 60-5 vote, and the President of the United States, said, "I have evaluated that report and categorically reject its morally bankrupt conclusions and major recommendations," be it therefore

RESOLVED, That the American Library Association commends the success of the Commission on Obscenity and Pornography for amassing a significant body of empirical evidence in an area of great social concern heretofore excluded as a subject for serious scientific investigation, and be it

FURTHER RESOLVED, That the American Library Association urges the Senate and the President of the United States to reconsider their categorical rejection of this significant data and to encourage the dissemination and evaluation of these materials by the citizenry of the United States, and be it

FURTHER RESOLVED, That the American Library Association urges all libraries to provide their users with complete access to the REPORT OF THE COMMISSION ON OBSCENITY AND PORNOGRAPHY and to the important supportive volumes and critical evaluations of the REPORT and its research in consonance with the library's role in the dissemination of information vital to the communities they serve.

The foregoing resolution emphasizes that the report, with its supporting volumes, should be in every library to provide every reader with the opportunity to read it for himself, study the experiments described therein, and decide for himself as to the merits of the social science studies reported on, the findings of the commission, and their recommendations. (Some librarians and some readers, as well, undoubtedly will reject the positions taken by the majority of the commission, preferring to find more merit in the positions taken by the *minority*, and that is, of course, their privilege).

It is not surprising that the ALA resolution as well as the coalition statement in which ALA had joined with twenty-seven other professional and civic groups (*see* the list signatories appended to that document), were considered unwise by many librarians responsible for legislation and funding of federal library programs. The ALA Committee on Legislation protested to the Committee on Intellectual Freedom about the conflict of priorities. But the text of the proposed resolution was sent to ALA Councilors in advance of the meeting at which the resolution was presented, thus giving them the opportunity for advance study, and after full debate, Council approved the resolution.

It is my opinion that this resolution was timely and appropriate for one major fact reported by the Commission on Obscenity and Pornography is so relevant to the work of librarians that it deserves special attention: sixty percent of the adults in the United States hold a deep-rooted desire for freedom of information, frequently expressed, as William Lockhart, chairman of the commission[16] says, by such statements as: "I don't want anyone telling me what I can read or view!" As soon as this finding of the commission became known, the Library Bill of Rights gained support.

On the other hand, the Committee on Intellectual Freedom was also urged to propose additional action by ALA, suggesting that ALA should approve and endorse the conclusions and recommendations of the commission's report. Although librarians may be tempted to do so, if there is any one fundamental point about censorship that librarians who accept the Library Bill of Rights know with some certainty, it is that a library or a library association violates its own principles when it approves or disapproves of specific ideas. Every book has both supporters and opponents, and when librarians approve the contents of one book and reject those of another, they destroy any hope of maintaining intellectual freedom. The ALA should *never* join those associations which prepare lists of *approved* and *unapproved* publications. This association can never either approve or disapprove of the contents of a specific book, for to do so is to disavow the principle of intellectual freedom.

In this case, although ALA legitimately recommended to all libraries that the *Report* of the Commission on Obscenity and Pornography should be available and libraries may recommend to all citizens that they read it, for ALA to officially have approved its contents would have destroyed any claim that librarianship is a *scholarly* profession. Librarians frequently, and appropriately, ridicule a school board that bans a book that they have not read. ALA's resolution of 1971 implied criticism of the

U.S. Senate for rejecting a book that senators had not read. How many of the voting Councilors had read the commission report with sufficient critical judgment that they were qualified to judge its scholarship? Unless each Councilor is a competent behavioral scientist, capable of evaluating the design of the studies reported, analyzing the data, and judging the conclusions, *and,* unless each Councilor had, in fact, done so, to have voted in favor of either the majority or the minority report of the commission would have made a mockery of scholarly endeavor. It also would have made ALA vulnerable to the same criticism that ALA leveled at the U.S. Senate. What must be emphasized is that the validity of the commission's report—and its value to society—does not depend upon a vote by the ALA Council.

It is important that librarians and the friends of libraries should note that ALA did not "support" or "endorse" the findings of the majority report, in spite of the urging of the "social responsibility" advocates among its members. ALA's Committee on Intellectual Freedom which proposed the ALA resolution refused to put the association in the authoritarian role of putting its stamp of approval on the report, even though urged to do so on the floor of the Council meeting at Los Angeles, and later by the library press.

ALA's position was that libraries should make easily available to everyone the majority report, the minority report, and the supporting volumes of the Commission on Obscenity and Pornography. (As a social scientist, and one whose studies were cited by both the majority and minority, I personally do not hesitate to comment upon them nor would I feel constrained not to make a thorough evaluation of the published reports. However, I would do so as an individual scholar, never as a representative of the library profession or of the University of Minnesota. I oppose any attempt by any group of librarians to insist that ALA must officially take a position on the substance of the report. This is a matter for each individual to decide for himself.)

The joint statement deploring the kinds of criticism leveled at the commission's report which was signed by the American Library Association and twenty-six other educational and professional organizations follows.[17] In it these groups expressed a considered "concern about censorship and the need for freedom of thought and freedom of expression—freedom of choice—in all areas of human existence" and urged that the report's findings and recommendations "be tested in even-tempered dialogue." And open dialogue, whether it be even-tempered or not, is what democracy is all about!

Coalition Statement on the Report of the Commission on Obscenity and Pornography

The recently-issued report of the Federal Commission on Obscenity and Pornography, created by the Congress three years ago, was greeted with criticism based mainly on preconceived premises and personal attacks on Commission members.

The organizations which sign this statement deplore this reaction, which contravenes the process of rational discussion through which decision on public issues should be made in a democracy. We agree with the wise words of Thomas Jefferson: "If the book be false in its facts, disprove them; if false in its reasoning, refute it. But for God's sake, let us hear freely from both sides."

The Commission's Report represents two years of intensive efforts by dedicated men and women, working under a Congressional mandate which instructed them to explore facets of a social issue which disturbs various segments of the national community. They have produced a 646-page report and ten volumes of supporting factual evidence which are an exhaustive treatment of the subject. That in itself is a praiseworthy contribution to public understanding.

But the Commission's Report is not entitled to automatic acceptance simply because of its thorough study. Some of the undersigned organizations hold different views from the Commission, and may ultimately reject certain of its recommendations. But, despite our varying views on the question of obscenity, we all agree that the Report must receive a full, fair hearing; that its findings and recommendations should be tested in even-tempered dialogue; and that those who debate the Report should read it—and deal with its specific findings and recommendations.

The Report did not—as critics have erroneously charged—recommend abolition of all laws regulating obscenity. On the contrary, the Commission recommended laws to prohibit the distribution of sexually explicit pictorial material to minors, the public display of sexually explicit material, and the mailing of unsolicited advertising for such material. The Commission emphasized that adults who do not wish to receive obscene material should be protected from having it thrust upon them against their wishes. In short, the Commission did not, as some opponents suggested, recommend opening the floodgates for a wave of obscenity to engulf the public.

What the Report did recommend was the abolition of those obscenity laws which prohibit the distribution of materials to adults who choose to receive them. This is not a radical innovation. The Supreme Court has ruled that the First Amendment protects an adult's right to read and see whatever he chooses, and we believe the same constitutional principles necessarily protect the publisher or bookseller who sells these materials to consenting adults.

While others disagree with this conclusion, these differences are legitimate subjects of debate. And there should be debate also on the Commission's conclusions that obscenity statutes, because of their vagueness, suppress nonobscene works, and that scientific studies provide no evidence that obscene books or motion pictures incite adults to criminal conduct, sexual deviancy, or emotional disturbances. There should also be discussion of the Commission's proposals for a broad-scale program of sex education and for further scientific investigation.

The undersigned do not necessarily agree with each other about the issue of obscenity and its significance in American life. But we are united in our concern about censorship, and the need for freedom of thought and freedom of expression—freedom of choice—in all areas of human existence. This is why, without endorsing or opposing the Commission *Report,* we commend it for serious study and debate by legislators, courts, community leaders, and the general public. We urge that proponents and opponents of the Report participate fully and rationally in this process, a venture which can enlarge intelligent understanding of a social question that requires wise decision making.

> American Civil Liberties Union
> American Federation of Teachers
> American Jewish Committee
> American Library Association
> American Orthopsychiatric Association
> American Public Health Association
> Association of American University Presses, Inc.
> Association of American Publishers, Inc.
> Author's League of America, Inc.
> Bureau of Independent Publishers and Distributors
> *John Donovan, Executive Director, The Children's Book Council, Inc.
> *Charlton Heston, President, Screen Actors Guild
> International Reading Association
> Jewish War Veterans of the USA
> National Association of Theatre Owners, Inc.
> The National Book Committee, Inc.
> National Council for Social Studies
> National Council of Churches of Christ in the USA
> National Council of Jewish Women
> National Council of Teachers of English
> National Education Association
> National Library Week Program
> National Board, YWCA
> *Lewis I. Maddocks, Executive Director, Council for Christian Action of United Church of Christ
> *The Rev. Everett Parker, Director, Office of Communication, The United Church of Christ
> Periodicals and Book Association of America, Inc.
> P.E.N. American Center
> Sex Information and Education Council of the United States, Inc.
> Union of American Hebrew Congregations
> Women's National Book Association
> Speech Communication Association[17]

*Organization's name for identification only

5   *The Flight from Reason*

Men must use reason to weigh the truth of what rival prophets and poets have said. . . .

Unless men reason they remain sunk in blind dogmatism, clinging obstinately to questionable beliefs without the consciousness that these may be mere prejudices. "To have doubted one's own first principles," said Justice Holmes, "is the mark of a civilized man." And to refuse to do so, we may add, is the essence of fanaticism. . . .

To liberate mankind from the mass of needless restraints and superstitions that is part of the "wisdom of the past" is not an affair of pronunciamento and simple magic formula. It demands varied and accurate knowledge, critical reflection, and a constant readiness to meet with the unexpected. The honest liberal must, therefore, frequently confess that life is baffling because it outstrips knowledge; whereas the faith of the radical or conservative, if held tenaciously enough, saves its devotees from the labor of constantly examining the factual evidence, and makes it unnecessary, even disloyal, to suspend judgment until further knowledge is attainable.

—MORRIS COHEN[1]

Ideophobia, the distrust of man's powers of rationality, reached a high peak in the late 1960s and early 1970s. The Radical Right continued its attacks on intellectual freedom, and the New Left joined in the effort with attacks from the opposite direction.

In its flight from reason, that small part of the academic community so raucously demanding control over research and teaching in our universities declared that honest, objective scholarship is impossible; that the old men in the academy are phonies and hypocrites, and that there is no hope of solving problems through reason and dialogue. From Berkeley to Columbia their battle cry was heard: "We demand free speech and you shut up."

Although the missions of the scholar, the journalist, and the librarian are not identical, the functioning of these professionals is seriously affected by the current tendency to substitute "gut reactions" for rational processes. The capacity of homo sapiens to perceive his world with reasonable accuracy is thus reduced. Intellectual freedom, academic freedom, and freedom of the press are in jeopardy when emotional reactions become more than motivating forces for inquiry. This essay will include a consideration of the flight from reason in the academy and in professional associations.

When even a few students and faculty become so partisan they show a repressive intolerance for the convictions of others, then academic freedom is threatened from *within* the university. When they disrupt classes, prevent interviews with recruiters, threaten booksellers, and occupy or blow up laboratories of faculty engaged in research which they believe should be banned, academic freedom is in jeopardy.

James Q. Wilson, Professor of Government at Harvard University, reports that in 1972, even Harvard, with its long tradition of solid scholarship, was not a place where one could expect free and open discussion of certain subjects. A spokesman for South Vietnam, a critic of liberal policies in the ghettos, and a corporate executive who denied that his firm was morally responsible for the regime in South Africa were harassed and in some cases forcibly denied an opportunity to speak. In each instance the academic community was denied the opportunity to hear a discussion of *all* sides of such issues[2]

The case of Harvard Professor Richard Herrnstein is a dramatic illustration. He theorizes that our society is evolving distinct classes based upon intelligence, and that the I.Q. gap between the upper and lower classes is increasing. His findings are that intelligence is 80 per cent inheritable. The attacks upon him have been predictably vigorous, so much so that in April 1972 Harvard President Derek Bok publicly warned that the anti-Herrnstein protests had had serious effects beyond the well-being of one professor. Protests by the Students for a Democratic Society (SDS) were threatening to make scholars turn to more placid subjects. Herrnstein himself said: "The attacks on me have not bothered me personally. What bothers me is this: something has happened at Harvard this year that makes it hazardous for a professor to teach certain kinds of views."

The effect of the campaigns of violence and persecution is more insidious than is generally recognized. Some scholars have withdrawn from acknowledging their real views and opinions publicly. Fifty eminent scientists from a variety of fields have issued a resolution on scientific freedom in which they draw a parallel between our situation today and the suppression of Galileo in orthodox Italy; Darwin in Victorian England; Einstein in Hitler's Germany; and Mendelian biologists in Stalin's Russia:

> Today, a similar suppression, censure, punishment, and defamation are being applied against scientists who emphasize the role of heredity in human behavior. Published positions are often misquoted and misrepresented; emotional appeals replace scientific reasoning; arguments are directed against the man rather than against the evidence (e.g., a scientist is called "fascist," and his aruguments are ignored.). . . .

The results are seen in the present academy: it is virtually heresy to express a hereditarian view, or to recommend further study of the biological bases of behavior. A kind of orthodox environmentalism dominates the liberal academy, and strongly inhibits teachers, researchers and scholars from turning to biological explanations or efforts.[3]

Dr. H. J. Eysenck, Professor of Psychology at the University of London, reports how the "New Zealots" threatened booksellers with violence if they dared to stock or exhibit his book on *Race; Intelligence, and Education,* and broke up the classes of academics who dared even to review the book. Anyone who disagrees with the militant ideophobes, of course is a "fascist, seduced by the establishment into utter intellectual prostitution." As Dr. Eysenck states:

No attempt here to argue the case, or to deal with the facts—this would be "bourgeois objectivity" which Stalin already condemned as counter-revolutionary (and which Hitler condemned as "semitic"— he preferred to think with "blood and iron"). And, to be sure, if we *know* the truth—presumably through Marxological revelation— then the end justifies the means: burn books, boycott publishers and booksellers, break up meetings, threaten and persecute those who dare disagree with you. Force, not reason, becomes the measuring rod of truth. This was the psychology of the fascists under whose rule I grew up in Germany; it has been taken over holus-bolus by the scattered troops of the "New Left."[4]

During the past decade American colleges and universities have been caught in a cross fire from the most dogmatic radicals who demanded suppression of certain kinds of scholarship on the one hand, and from some legislators and members of the general public who would sacrifice freedom in order to get at the revolutionaries.

Undoubtedly, higher education has been in need of review and revision. It is not surprising that the Point Huron statement by students in 1962 could capture the attention of many thousands of American youth who saw many things wrong with the world and hoped to join in a movement to correct its faults. The term "activism" was perceived by many as a label for an attempt by the best educated generation in history to move our society toward practicing what it has always preached.

Motivated by an honest idealism at its beginning, the Students for a Democratic Society indicated at Point Huron that there was still a recognized value in preserving man's freedom to use his reason. SDS held that the goals of men and of society should be human dependence. It was concerned with finding a meaning of life that is personally authentic, with full, spontaneous access to present and past experiences. Men were regarded as possessed of unfulfilled capacities for reason, freedom and love. Human relationships should involve fraternity and honesty.[5]

Regardless of whether they were over or under thirty years of age, people with a liberal attitude responded favorably to these ideas expressed by SDS. *Liberals,* meaning those on the left of center on the political-social continuum, found the Point Huron statement compatible with their personal convictions. *Liberals,* in Morris Cohen's terminology, also found the statement acceptable, especially in its recognition of the value of reason, and with at least the implication that all points of view should be freely accessible, including expressions that seem to be untrue.

However, shortly after 1962, some members of SDS, including some who had signed the original statement, were attacking universities, suppressing speakers who disagreed with them, issuing nonnegotiable demands for political obedience, and engaging in deliberate terrorism. The benevolence and compassion apparent in the original document had turned to rage and hatred.

There have been many speculations about the reasons SDS, or more precisely, the most revolutionary segment of that group, moved away from the idealism of the Point Huron statement. The war in Indo-China and the apparent inability to stop it, the draft, racial and sexual inequities, pollution of the environment, all of these and other social ills, perceived under the mushroom cloud of a possible nuclear war, understandably produced extreme frustration, and not only in people under thirty. The emphasis upon youth in our culture was nothing new, but the notion that people under thirty were wiser than those over that age *was* new, and probably contributed to public disaffection with the youth cult and later political reactions.

The university was the place where youth in unprecedented numbers were gathered. And the university, like all other human institutions, was not perfect. Government influence over research, especially when it related to military objectives, government grants, and the requirement of loyalty oaths attached to them, the decreasing attention to teaching, all made the university subject to criticism. The most revolutionary SDS leaders believed it was necessary to disrupt and close down these bad, sick, irrelevant institutions which had failed to build a perfect society, and a revolution was needed to destroy the "rotten" society of the United States. From their point of view, the function of a university was not to develop critical intelligence and forward the search for truth, truth which would aid in the resolution of problems through reason; instead, the university must reject free speech and objective scholarship and enter the political arena, taking positions—as institutions—on various political and social issues. Universities must be politicized.

Although many of the criticisms mounted by SDS had some validity, the political effects noted in chapter 3 weakened the university as an institution. In 1974, the general public holds a jaundiced view of the university and is not persuaded that it deserves support. Whatever reasons SDS had for demanding politicization, our concern here is with the impact of those demands upon academic freedom in the university. David R. Goddard, former Provost of the University of Pennsylvania and Linda Koons comment cogently upon the impatience of some students and faculty who want emotionally satisfying answers to contemporary problems, rather than the accurate knowledge and critical reflection described by Morris Cohen. Rejecting the knowledge that can be produced by disciplined study, intellectual analysis, and logic as useless, these people took off on what these authors termed a "flight from reason":

> Perhaps the greatest threat to intellectual freedom within the university is the pressure being exerted to involve the university in social and political problems. Some students and faculty wish the university to go into the community to build houses, prevent pollution, combat poverty, and take political and social stands which, they think, will exert an influence on government and bring about reform . . . they would use the university as a political weapon. Here I would join them with my heart, but not my head, for surely this is the way not of social reform but of destruction of the university. Their victory would change the university into an institution no longer dedicated to intellectual virtues or to furthering of knowledge, but dedicated, instead, as Bruno Bettelheim puts it, "to the belligerent reshaping of society. . . ."
>
> If the university as a body takes official positions on controversial issues or becomes an active participant in combating community problems, it opens itself up to political attack, as well as to losing any objectivity it might have regarding issues and problems. Additionally, there is a very great danger that by taking an official position, the university would jeopardize or stifle the views of its minority, views which may contain the seeds of future social, economic, and political reform. . . .
>
> If we destroy the intellectual freedom in the universities where will it be maintained in American society?[6]

To answer this question, if our society permits the destruction of intellectual freedom in any one of the institutions with which these essays are concerned, whether it be in the academy, the press, or the library, then intellectual freedom will be destroyed in all of them and throughout our society. Intellectual freedom in all these areas of human endeavor is interdependent and inseparable.

Since 1915 the American Association of University Professors (AAUP) has worked effectively to preserve academic freedom. This organization has always emphasized that its purpose is to promote public understanding, support for academic freedom and tenure, and agreement on procedures to assure them in colleges and universities. (Often professionals in a field fail to understand the vital importance of procedures, and in the heat of a controversy over tenure would scrap all procedures which are inconvenient to their cause. Such expedient action often sets the stage for future attacks upon academic freedom.)

The AAUP has always held that colleges and universities are conducted for the common good and not to further the interests of either the individual teacher or the institution as a whole; that the common good depends upon the free search for truth and its free expression. Although the AAUP has no authority to police and control universities, its efforts based upon moral persuasion have been very effective. Its major statement defining academic freedom was issued in 1940. It has been supplemented by later elaborations. With the footnotes omitted, this is the text:

Academic Freedom

(a) The teacher is entitled to full freedom in research and in the publication of the results, subject to the adequate performance of his other academic duties; but research for pecuniary return should be based upon an understanding with the authorities of the institution.

(b) The teacher is entitled to freedom in the classroom in discussing his subject, but he should be careful not to introduce into his teaching controversial matter which has no relation to his subject. Limitations of academic freedom because of religious or other aims of the institution should be clearly stated in writing at the time of the appointment.

(c) The college or university teacher is a citizen, a member of a learned profession, and an officer of an educational institution. When he speaks or writes as a citizen, he should be free from institutional censorship or discipline, but his special position in the community imposes special obligations. As a man of learning and an educational officer, he should remember that the public may judge his profession and his institution by his utterances. Hence he should at all times be accurate, should exercise appropriate restraint, should show respect for the opinions of others, and should make every effort to indicate that he is not an institutional spokesman.[7]

The definition of academic freedom, and the procedures set up to protect learning, teaching, and research from control were adopted to counter pressures from *outside* the university.

What was truly remarkable about many of the attempts to suppress free speech on campuses and to stop the functioning of universities in the decade 1962–1972 was that the disruption came from *within* the university and was perpetrated by people who claimed to be students and teachers. Not all members of the academic community recognize their obligation to preserve the conditions under which free scholarship can be pursued. The liberalizing effects hoped for from college study are not always realized. Many campus demonstrations, regardless of the worthy aims and the sincerity of the demonstrators, became so violent and terroristic that they were counterproductive.[8] Often they resulted in a gain of influence by repressive politicians, and, inevitably, the drying up of funds from legislatures, the federal government, and private donors. While these results may have been the aim of a few people who directed the attacks on academic freedom, they were surely not intended by many who seemed to support the flight from reason.

Liberal universities, if they aim to foster research, learning, and dialogue, may not choose to stifle dissent. Even though many colleges and universities suffered severe losses in academic freedom, and later, in financial support from a society disillusioned about its academies, few denied protestors the right to demonstrate. Up to a point, this permissiveness was necessary and appropriate. Older generations need the help of critical and idealistic young people in building a better university and a better society.

My own experience in working with students on many college and university committees at the University of Minnesota has led me to respect highly the contributions students can make in governance of the institution. In 1968 and 1969 I served as chairman of that university's Task Force on Student Representation, composed of students and faculty. We affirmed our belief that it was desirable to create a *University Senate* which was to include students to replace the *Faculty Senate*. After long debate, such a University Senate was established.

In the debate I conceded that there is a risk in a senate which includes students. It is conceivable that there are extremists whose major goal is destruction of the university among most student bodies, some of whom might be elected to the senate. But this risk is inherent in any democratic institution. Based upon my experience in working with responsible and idealistic students, who have exhibited a capacity for objective and critical appraisal of the university, good judgment, and a desire to contribute constructively to its future, my conclusion is that the risk is small and worth taking.

However, in addition to critical and idealistic students, on most campuses, there have been others who were convinced that their causes were so right that the end justifies the use of any means—intransigent extremists whose declared goal was to disrupt at least ten major universities in the country, to stop them from functioning, in the belief that if such a goal could be achieved, the society itself could no longer function.

In 1967 at a conference on Students and Society held by the Center for the Study of Democratic Institutions, Stephen Saltonstall challenged anyone to point to a historical example where dialogue achieved any sort of radical reform. He suggested that disruption is the one thing our society cannot abide; that our institutions are all interrelated; and if one institution is sabotaged, the society cannot function properly as a whole. Since the institution that students are connected with is the university, disruption of this institution is desirable.[9]

Daniel Sisson, in his paper at this same conference, noted that it was held at a time when communication between youth and the adults in society was tenuous. In fact, he said, for millions of young people the dialogue had already broken down in what they regard as a society gone mad. Young people had simply turned the adults off. Sisson then gave a cogent analysis of the position of youth so alienated by what they perceived as the cant and hypocrisy of their elders:

> Disruption of constructive dialogue results in intellectual dogmatism. Students, for example, who refuse to form a coalition except on their own terms, who refuse to compromise at any level, frustrate the dialogue even while they labor under the illusion of communication. The refusal to listen, the intransigent style, the extremist position, the total conviction of one's own righteousness—all character ize the authoritarian personality and the lust for power.
>
> These are the very traits which the young find repugnant in adults. This polarization sets the scene for violence, verbal as well as physical. And violence whether it is calculated to insult or to cause bodily injury is by definition the foregoing of reasonable discussion.[10]

It is worth noting that those who engaged in attempts to destroy a university, or to keep it from functioning, were, while so engaged, definitely not students or professors, whether or not they happened to be affiliated with the university at the time. It is not characteristic of men of reason, of liberal scholars, to hold the absolute certainty that their views are the only correct views, and that those who disagree should be liquidated and their books burned. The true student is one who is dedicated to studying, to probing, to questioning, to analyzing, and to dialogue— dealing both with ideas new to him and with ideas he has tentatively, perhaps passionately, accepted.

While serving as a member of the University of Minnesota's student-faculty commission to draft a policy on demonstrations, I personally heard the arguments used by radicals totally convinced as to their infallibility and righteousness. For example, this commission was told that demonstrations stemming from opposition to the Vietnam war or the draft should be considered as different from others, and that *any* form such a demonstration took is justified. This argument must be rejected, for what a university must be concerned with—if intellectual freedom is to be maintained—is *overt behavior* which prevents the university from fulfilling its obligations to the society which supports it.

The fundamental question concerning a demonstration on campus is: Did it disrupt the university and prevent it from functioning? If the demonstration did so, it cannot be justified. The motivations of the demonstrators and the intensity with which they hold their convictions are quite irrelevant. A university has an obligation to permit dissent and demonstrations up to the point at which they impede the university's functioning, or, up to the point at which the demonstrators themselves deny freedom of expression to nondemonstrators and to counterdemonstrators, but not beyond this point.

Another argument heard by the Minnesota commission was that an act which is clearly illegal, disruptive, censurable, and punishable should be excused if its perpetrator claims that it is only a "symbolic gesture" of protest. But the university and its officers cannot be expected to distinguish between an act of disruptive nature that is inexcusable and an identical act which is to be justified on the plea that it is symbolic. This plea of the Symbol Simons cannot be taken seriously. Its foolishness could be seen easily, of course, if the situation were reversed; if the university were to justify a capricious act by claiming that it was merely symbolic.

The notion that rationality is bad and irrationality is good is frequently voiced. Many students and faculty believe that there are many injustices and social evils in our world. Apparently they also are convinced that it is the proper task of the university to correct these faults. But there are no grounds for supposing that solutions will be found through groups who reject objective scholarship and civil dialogue.

Although through logic alone absolute proof of propositions are not likely to come our way, we are not therefore forced to resort to gut reactions with their characteristic coercive acts. Reason as a process provides the capacity to discover sound principles in any field of inquiry. It includes emotion as a motivating force, as well as the intuitive making of hypotheses and the invention and use of devices to test them. Logic alone may not be able to solve problems, and it is dangerous to make it our single god, but no scholar can be effective without using logic. What is so very hazardous is that today's ideophobes have come to despise reason, dialogue, and logic and have chosen instead to deify illogic and irrationality. Instead of concurring with the credo of Descartes, "I think, hence I am," they seem to say, "I don't think, hence I am."

Dean Wayne Booth of the University of Chicago has noted that while we may disagree about the limited powers of "mere" reason, we are all aware of what unchecked emotions can lead to. Both Gandhi and Hitler were emotionally committed, and capable of converting audiences directly and personally, and Booth says in his book, *Now Don't Try to Reason with Me:*

> The direct emotional appeal of a personality and his deeply felt message seems, unfortunately, to work as well in the hands of a Hitler inciting his followers to viciousness as it does in the hands of a Gandhi leading his followers to a nonviolent revolution. . . .
> The question would seem to be, however, whether it is the main job of a college to enter into this particular kind of battle for souls. . . . A college by its very nature presupposes there is some-

thing more to men's commitments than a battle of personalities and of propaganda devices. We might, of course, by reorganizing ourselves and hiring a new staff obtain a higher percentage of commanding personalities who could effect conversions. But conversions to *what?* . . .

The dialogue of a college differs from the dialogue of the church or the market place, important as they are, in that we are committed to exploring and clarifying the genuine reasons which make human choice meaningful rather than meaningless. All choice has emotional concomitants. All choice can be rationalized. But only *sound* choices —whether of action, thought or feeling—are reasonable. Unless we want to reduce ourselves simply to the level of being one propagandistic organization among others—the victory to go to the best propagandist or the strongest personality—we must sooner or later be willing to test our reasons. A college is first of all a testing ground of rational choice. Whatever else it is or does should be judged according to whether it assists or hinders this unique function.[11]

And news media and public libraries similarly have an obligation to assist their readers in testing their reasons for making choices by presenting all sides on all issues. When these institutions choose up sides on political and social issues, they betray their trust and become merely propagandistic organizations. As such they cannot preserve intellectual freedom.

Many graduate students who embrace irrationality are on the way to becoming college professors. The Carnegie Commission on Higher Education reported in April 1973 that the coming decade may be marked by faculty dissent as the focus shifts from student activism to faculty activism. The commission also noted that the transfer of authority from the campus to outside agencies may reverse the trend toward increasing institutional independence and self-government.[12] There is evidence to show that our institutions are in danger of losing the power to govern themselves in intellectual conduct, academic affairs, and administrative arrangements. The forces promoting politicization of universities, professional societies, and libraries help to destroy the possibility of self-government in these institutions and certainly will destroy their ability to preserve intellectual freedom for everyone.

It has been difficult for some professors to accept the fact that reason and academic freedom have been attacked from within the university. One of my colleagues, for example, denies any major significance to the incidents of suppression, "since it has happened on only thirty or forty campuses." In the past, there is no question but that this man would have been very much concerned whenever even *one* classroom was invaded or one speaker was suppressed by coercion or intimidation from the Radical Right.

Even the AAUP, with its history of effective defense of academic freedom against external attacks, was slow to recognize the threat from within the university, but by October 31, 1970, its Council issued a statement on "Freedom and Responsibility." Stressing the obligation of the university to foster dissent and to defend free inquiry, instruction, and free expression on and off campus, the AAUP stated that the expression of dissent and the attempt to produce change may not be carried out in ways which injure individuals or damage institutional facilities or disrupt classes. Speakers must not only be protected from violence, but given an opportunity to be heard. Those who seek to call attention to grievances must not do so in ways that significantly impede the functions of the university.

Whenever a student—or a nonstudent—decides to take over a classroom and prevent the scheduled instruction from taking place, the academic freedom of both students and professor has been denied. Such disruptions can be forestalled, as a philosophy professor at the University of Rochester demonstrated in 1970. He informed his class in writing that, regardless of certain circumstances that might arise in the world during the semester, his class would proceed without interruptions, inasmuch as students, or their parents, had paid for the instruction offered in this course, and that they were therefore entitled to receive it if they wanted it, regardless of whether some, most, or all other students did or did not wish them to receive it. Giving as hypothetical examples of "baneful or appalling circumstances," the presence of National Guard troops or the storing of napalm on campus, he stated: "Without implying approval of such actions, this course will proceed exactly as planned so long as there remains one student willing to continue, this being his right and my obligation." (The following year this professor was honored by undergraduates for outstanding teaching.) [13]

Academic freedom has also been violated whenever a professor used his classroom to advocate causes unrelated to the subject for which students had registered. *As a citizen,* a professor has the same right as does any other citizen to propagate and support causes in his community, to join social and political organizations, or to engage in demonstrations. But he has no right whatever to thrust his social and political views upon a captive audience of students who registered for the courses he conducts in his field of competence.

When any professor fails to distinguish between his rights as a citizen and his academic freedom, when he denies his obligation to teach in his own field of expertise, the whole academy suffers. The general public distrusts professors who abuse their position by engaging in such behavior, and, unfortunately, many are only too ready to believe that *all* professors are habitually guilty of such misconduct. This makes it difficult to maintain public faith in the value of academic freedom—and, in fact, in the value of colleges and universities.

Many citizens have always been uneasy about the idea of academic freedom. They *want* to believe that there is something of great value in higher education, but they have honest doubts about those "radical, communist" professors who are teaching their children. And there are always demagogues from the Radical Right to capitalize on these fears and doubts by charging that professors hide behind the cloak of academic freedom in order to teach subversive doctrines. Many find it difficult even to conceive of an approach to teaching and research that is *dis*interested and makes every effort possible to be objective. And the flight from reason, the rejection of objectivity in scholarship by people within the academy, reinforces such doubts, resulting in a serious deterioration of public confidence in the academy.

The public tends to view the affluent professor, and the affluent student, as overprivileged, and there is deep resentment against violent behavior by the elite. When professional groups within the university are considered to be politicizing professional associations, *and* the university, choosing sides in the general contests of the community and nation, society as a whole becomes hostile, and support for the university, both moral and financial, is withdrawn.

One school of thought in any professional field or subject discipline may become so dominant, so rigid, so tradition-bound that it is difficult for anyone to challenge its position. Such a situation is detrimental to intellectual freedom, and when it exists, the need to challenge it becomes great. For such a challenge to be fruitful, it must be made within the frame of reference of reason and objectivity, rather than by coercion, intimidation, and suppression of all views contrary to those of the challenger. To the degree that radical challengers of the "Establishment" suppress all contrary views, seeking to set up an orthodoxy to which all members of a profession are forced to conform, intellectual freedom is destroyed.

During the 1960s the distrust of reason in various disciplines was manifested by attempts by partisan misologists to seize control of professional associations, seeking to use those associations to promote specific political and social causes. Academia before 1960 had a tacit agreement with the society which supported scholars. The insistence by scholars upon freedom from control by politicians or by any segment of society was justified, for scholars have known very surely that if any governmental or other group controlled their work, it could not be honest, objective, or of any value. Society in general has agreed to these terms, trusting the scholar to keep the agreement, and, by continuous review, to keep other scholars honest.

The flight from reason in several sectors of academia has followed much the same pattern: the insistence that objective scholarship is impossible; the denunciation of existing authorities as members of an amoral, status-quo establishment afraid to make value judgments; the demand that the professional association shall take public stands on social and political issues; the identification of the "liberal" scholar, who tolerates expression of opposing opinions, as *the* enemy; and usually the implication that rationality must be replaced by irrationality.

Among psychologists, for example, those members of the American Psychological Association whose chief reason for joining was to show allegiance to a scholarly discipline, by 1970 had come to feel that they were a beleaguered minority. The revolutionaries were not content to form an organization of those psychologists who agreed upon stands to be taken on public issues; rather, they insisted that they must take control of the professional association and use it for their own purposes. Psychologist Arthur Melton of the University of Michigan, in his analysis of the attempt to politicize his association and dictate positions on political issues to which all members must conform, said:

> In my view, the gaining of knowledge and understanding is the most moral motivation of man, and a society of men devoted to that goal without any qualifications or conditions whatsoever is governed by the most enduring and humane value man can adopt. A science lives and grows by rules that forever give the advantage to the next generation of scientists, to the new insight from whomever it may come, and to the society that has reason to trust the objectivity, political neutrality, and timelessness of that science. Those who wish to use the status and reputation of a scientific organization for self-interest of individuals within it or for gaining specific political-social ends are moving to destroy the concept that knowledge is the greatest good because it alone is free to define its goals without personal, social, political or national bias. . . .[14]

In journalism also there has been a retrogression to a subjective partisan, "advocacy" which argues that objectivity is impossible. Some journalists—not only on campus or underground papers, but also in the commercial press, and incredibly, even in schools of journalism—seem to believe it justifiable to require all members of the profession to commit themselves to specific positions on controversial issues. They argue that "gut feeling" should replace the standard of factual, measurable, and verifiable descriptive reporting. Apparently they feel that the end justifies the rejection of the standard which held that *news reports* must be presented as separate from, and distinguishable from, *editorializing* which aims to shape opinion. (This subject is elaborated in chapter 6.)

In the field of history, the conflict between the New Left radicals, who deny the possibility of objective scholarship, and the moderates, including the Old Left, who view their work as requiring *dis*interested fact-finding and analysis, is succinctly described by Patrick Young:

> This need to act, to demonstrate, to force confrontation is creed among radicals. They reject the idea expressed by Carl L. Becker

in 1910 that "the state of mind best calculated to find out exactly
what happened is perhaps incompatible with a disposition to care
greatly what it is that happened."[15]

The historians of the New Left claim that the Establishment, though
it claims to be politically neutral, has actually subverted truth to its political views. Although most historians probably still seek as great a
degree of detachment and dispassion as possible in viewing the past, the
radicals insist that their professional association must collectively make
a commitment to an ideology.

When any ideology becomes an orthodoxy, and scholars seek only to
sustain its prescribed doctrines, academic freedom is threatened. The
liberal scholar is no longer free to choose his research topics and to reach
conclusions that he believes to be warranted by the evidence.

When radical members of any profession insist that all their colleagues
must commit themselves to a particular ideology, what is the effective
response? Surely it would not be to try to muzzle the radical historians.
Just as surely, it cannot be to permit them to dictate an orthodoxy for all
historians, muzzling all those who disagree. Surely it cannot be to go
along with the radicals in their demands that their associations must take
stands of commitment on controversial issues, thus denying the multi-
dimensionality of history. For liberal historians, the best response is a
reaffirmation of their allegiance to liberal, objective scholarship which
holds to the view that history is multidimensional, requiring a tolerance
for expression of a variety of theories. The liberal historian will reject
and oppose vigorously any attempt to take over the historical associations
and use them to propagate the personal convictions of any group. Radical
historians who insist that history is of a single dimension and that they
have a monopoly on its truth will be tolerated—up to the point at which
they become coercive and repressive. The liberal historian will continue
to ask: What is the evidence to support this theory? And that theory?
And that other theory?

In librarianship there has been a similar attempt to politicize the
American Library Association. The traditional neutrality of the organization on substantive political-social issues has been attacked as "unrealistic," and it is proposed that this neutrality be abandoned for an
advocacy association and advocacy libraries. In this field also it seems
to be beyond the understanding of ardent, partisan advocates of worthy
causes that politicization destroys the integrity of the profession. It is
especially harmful to the principle of intellectual freedom for the users
of libraries if a public library becomes an advocate for one side of a
dispute, rather than a provider of information on all sides. (This point
is elaborated in chapter 7.) In 1974, for example, the attempt to pass a
resolution urging the impeachment of President Nixon at the Midwinter
Meeting in January carried on the effort to politicize the ALA. The move

was unsuccessful, causing the *Library Journal* to editorialize in its typical advocacy style that the ALA Council, by refusing to enter the political arena, had committed an "atrocity."[16]

In these and other professional fields, politicization of a professional association is destructive of the right of individual conscience of every member. It is an attempt to use his interest in his profession to coerce him into a position propagating specific political-social causes. The group's prestige and the number of members are thus used for illegitimate purposes. The people who join professional associations do so because of a common interest in the problems of the field. As individuals they are free to join political and social organizations to satisfy other interests. They are also free to form groups of like-minded professionals to support specific causes, but they will destroy the integrity and credibility of their association if permitted to succeed in the effort to politicize it.

Membership in professional associations should be wide open to all qualified people, from the most extreme revolutionary to the most extreme conservative—on the political-social continuum. No member of such an association should be put into a position which forces him to be counted as endorsing the convictions of any segment of his profession on extraneous issues, whether the segment is a majority or a minority.

In various fields there seems to be a great reluctance on the part of the majority of association members to take positions differing from the new orthodoxies proclaimed by radicals. But, if liberal scholars do not assert themselves, reaffirming their faith in intellectual freedom and reason, the professions could be taken over by well-organized minorities and used for purposes unrelated to the obligations and competencies of these professionals.

And, if the professional associations of historians, psychologists, journalists, librarians, and others erect rigid, established patterns of orthodoxy, controlling scholars in their choice of research topics, marking some fields of inquiry with taboos, and dictating the conclusions to be reached, the results will be equally as harmful to man's capacity to perceive reality as would be true if the dogmas and doctrines were dictated by a government.

In each of the professions here considered, to the degree that the slogans of radicalism gain acceptance and the *idea* of liberalism is replaced by the fanaticism of the New Left or the Radical Right, to that degree intellectual freedom is diminished. And, to this degree, man's capacity to perceive his environment with a reasonable approximation to reality is destroyed.

The task of establishing a university or library is a slow and arduous process. Conversely, disrupting and destroying these institutions is much easier and far more quickly accomplished. It is often more attractive to try to "save the world" than it is to deal with the job at hand for which one is personally responsible. But permitting or participating in the destruction of intellectual freedom in our institutions, by either Right or Left, is a crime against the future of humanity, whether those who participate in that destruction understand what they are doing or not.

Perhaps a very small number of those who have fled from reason understand the significance of their acts and proceed cynically and deliberately in order to gain power for themselves. It seems probable that many more who have supported authoritarian acts inimical to academic freedom have done so on the basis of misperceptions stemming from genuine idealism. "Liberal" scholars unquestionably join those who claim to be socially responsible in their aims and hopes. However, although it is important to find ways to knock down the social barriers of the past, racial or religious, or based upon national origin or inherited wealth, it is even more important for man's future to preserve his intellectual freedom and his faith in reason.

As suggested in chapter 3, some observers feel that the threats to intellectual freedom have already swung around and will come chiefly from the Right, rather than from the Left in the 1970s. Not only political analysts Lipset and Raab, but Senators Margaret Chase Smith[17] and J. W. Fulbright have warned that, if there is any bias in our history and in the character of our society, it is not toward the Left but toward the Right. Senator Fulbright put it this way:

> Taken together, the right wing bias of our past, the intense, obsessive fear of Communism, the disruption wrought by thirty years of chronic war, the power of the military-industrial-academic complex which chronic war has spawned, and our failure to come to grips with urgent problems at home—all these collectively have posed a great strain on American democracy.
>
> Confronted with so great a concentration of forces on the other side, the extremists of the Left can have little hope of working their will on our society, but they could bring down on themselves a counterrevolution from the Right which would surely destroy their movements and possibly destroy democracy as well. I venture to predict that, if American democracy is overthrown in our generation, it will not be by radicals flying the Vietcong flag but by right-wing radicals flying the American flag.[18]

Throughout this work there is an underlying assumption that ideas have consequences; that the pictures in our minds of our institutions of press, university, and library determine their nature and the ways in which they will be operated.

It is my opinion—in spite of the attacks upon liberal values by the Right and the Left, in spite of the disaffection evident with the youth cult and the corruption of Watergate,—that American citizens still have a choice about the nature of their institutions and about whether our democratic system will survive. The channels open to us within the American political system, through campaigns, elections, and lobbying, permit individuals to bring pressures to bear upon politicians. But our choice should not be limited by the "cause people" who demand polarization on particular substantive issues and insist that our institutions must take positions on them. Our choice, on the one hand, is between a kind of absolutism that insists upon conformity of opinion regarding a *single* theory or proposition, or, on the other, a liberal approach to a variety of theories or propositions which permits and encourages examination of the evidence in support of alternatives.

As Kingman Brewster, President of Yale, asks: "If not reason, what?" Brewster emphasizes that, by its nature, a university is forced to make judgments—judgments as to who shall be admitted, who shall be graduated, who shall be granted lifetime tenure. He describes a structure called "academic due process" which has developed standards and procedures to assure that the inevitable assessments are handled with as little prejudice or cronyism as possible.[19] Such judgments obviously cannot be made with total objectivity, but academic due process sets a standard for self-consciousness and holds up a measure for the critic. Furthermore, according to Brewster, the abuse of academic power can be held in check by the requirement that reasons must be given for the opinion, reasons which "must wash" in terms of general principles and propositions embraced by the institution. The judge is disciplined by the realization that the reasons he gives in any one case would have to be applied in similar cases involving other people.[20] And Brewster's comments on the distrust of reason are especially pertinent:

> Cynical disparagement of objectivity as a "myth" seems to me both naive and irresponsible. Any claim of novelty to the observation that men are fallible at best, corruptible at worst, is naive. Its irresponsibility lies in the conclusion that, since the ideal is unattainable, it should not be held up as a standard to both practitioners and critics. . . .
>
> If we are not to slip into a dark age of irrationality, the universities must defend the ideal of objectivity. They must insist on following the dictate of evidence and reasoned argument. They must not acquiesce in the desire of the impatient to escape the moral responsibility for rational choice.
>
> If we should slip into a dark age of irrationality, far better for the universities to live meagerly, while sticking to the integrity of reason, than to prosper elegantly in the corruption of a new orthodoxy.[21]

Although intellectual freedom will always be unpopular with extremists at both ends of the social-political continuum, it is essential for the future of man, for if it is lost, the status quo, with all its inadequacies and injustices, will be most difficult to correct. Change is inevitable, but unless man uses his reason to weigh the alternatives, he has no grounds for even hoping that the change will be for the better. Without intellectual freedom and the opportunities afforded by free, objective scholarship, man's illusions and misperceptions will go uncorrected or probably even increase, and our capacity to perceive and deal with our environment will be lost.

It is essential for the inhabitant of the academic world to reaffirm his faith in the possibilities of improving man's lot through more effective exercise of his reason. He must continue to refine his devices with which he perceives his environments, to extend the range and quality of his perceptions, to record and review what other men have perceived, to carry out investigations of the unknown, and to use his intelligence and rational powers to analyze data and draw such conclusions as are warranted by the evidence. This process of objective scholarship is the instrument by which man, as a species, has survived to the present. If he is to survive another hundred, thousand, or more years, it will be because he learns to use his reason more effectively. (This is not to argue that man deserves to survive, or to predict that he will do so, or to insist that by reason alone he can solve all his problems.) Man has never been and will surely not become a completely rational being. But the notion that we need to become more irrational is truly "non sense."

Various cultures have revered the scholar and his efforts to extend human knowledge, and there have been good grounds for such respect. In the Western world, especially, during the past three hundred years, scholars have been very successful in using free scholarship as a tool with which to open up the universe to understanding for the welfare of mankind. Before the scientific revolution it was often considered the duty of the scholar to tinker with his evidence—to "cook his stuff" so as to fit his discoveries into an already established system of truth. It is still this way in an authoritarian society. And if either the Radical Right or the New Left were to win control of higher education, the instrument of scholarship would be blunted to the condition of uselessness.

It is the self-correcting method of modern scholarship that makes it possible to free ourselves from status quo attitudes, not with any guarantee that changes will be for the better, but with some hope that they may be. What the liberal scholar and the university must insist on, if they are to deserve the support of society, is the freedom to examine any question and ask: What is the evidence to support this statement and how does it compare with the evidence to support possible alternatives?

To thus elevate man's powers of perception, inquiry, and reason, claiming that his intelligence is the instrument that enables him to survive and thrive, does not suggest that by reason alone he can resolve all of his problems. Love, compassion, empathy, consideration for others, brotherhood, all these will help men to live together with other men. But man's survival and welfare are *contingent* upon his preservation of the principle of intellectual freedom. It is the *first* essential principle.

6   *Theories of the Press as Bases for Intellectual Freedom*

What is News?

News exists in the minds of men. It is not an event; it is something perceived *after* the event. It is not identical with the event; it is an attempt to reconstruct the essential framework of the event—*essential* being defined against a frame of reference which is calculated to make the event meaningful to the reader. It is an aspect of communication, and has the familiar characteristics of that process.

The first news report of an event is put together from a gestalt of eye witness accounts, second-hand accounts, tertiary comments and explanations, and the reporter's own knowledge and predispositions. The report is then coded for transmission, usually by persons who have had no connection with the actual event. It is coded by modifying its length, form, emphasis, and interpretation, to meet the mechanical demands of transmission and presentation, the anticipated needs and preferences of the audience, and the somewhat better known wishes and demands of the buyers of the news. Then the news is trusted to ink or sound waves or light waves, and ultimately comes to an audience, where it competes with the rest of the environment for favor.

A typical member of the audience selects from the mass of news offered him perhaps one-fourth of the news in a daily paper, perhaps one-half of the items in a newscast he happens to hear. These items of news are perceived by each individual as a part of another gestalt —his environment and its competing stimuli, the state of his organism at the moment, and his stored information and attitudes. Perception completed, symbol formed, the news then goes into storage with a cluster of related bits of information and attitudes, and becomes the basis for attitude change and action.

—WILBUR SCHRAMM[1]

In 1935, when fascism in Italy and national socialism in Germany were growing in strength, foreign correspondent Eugene Lyons wrote an article in which he pointed out that under a totalitarian concept of the press, propaganda was so ever-present that it produced jokes similar to the following—jokes which were told, even though to do so might bring the teller a jail sentence or execution. This is the Russian version:

> President Kalinin was making an impassioned speech in Moscow
> about the great economic progress of the Soviets. With particular
> emphasis he described the new 20-story skyscrapers on Karl Marx
> Street in Kharkov.
>
> "Comrade Kalinin," a worker in the audience rose naively to
> correct the speaker. "I live in Kharkov. Every day I walk on Karl
> Marx Street but I have never seen such skyscrapers—"
>
> "That's the trouble with workers like you," Kalinin shouted
> angrily. "You waste your time in promenading the streets, instead
> of reading the newspapers and learning what is going on in your
> country."[2]

Kalinin's response to the effect that the worker should learn what is
going on from the newspapers, rather than from his own observation, reveals the view of the role of the press in a totalitarian society. As Wilbur
Schramm has noted, the Marxist tradition has displayed, from its beginning, authoritarianism, fixedness, a tendency to make hard and sharp
distinctions between right and wrong, and an amazing confidence in explaining great areas of human behavior on the basis of a small set of
economic facts. This results in the practice of ignoring or explaining away
conflicting evidence.

Schramm contrasts the Soviet mentality (world-view) with that of
Americans:

> We are apt to think that people must and should hold different
> ideas and values, and therefore to encourage the arts of compromise
> and majority rule; the Soviet Russians are apt to think that men
> should *not* hold different viewpoints, that compromise is a sign of
> weakness, that there is one *right* position to be found in Marxist in-
> terpretation and to be defended, propagated, and enforced. To us,
> what Muller calls the "famed Russian unity" . . . seems reactionary
> and tyrannical. To the Russians, our lack of agreement, our permis-
> siveness toward argument, compromise, and criticism, seem anarchy
> or chaos.[3]

Apparently, in the Soviet view of truth every issue has only one "right"
side; a small group of party leaders controls the lens through which every
question is seen. Any other view is regarded as seen through an *unfocused*
lens. Under this totalitarian concept the press is considered an instrument for achieving unity of opinion. Editors must listen anxiously for the
"truth" and then must follow the current whims of the ruling Communist Party. The concern of the press is not with facts, but with dialectic, not with timely events, but with the Party line.

Arthur Koestler's description of what it is like to edit a paper when
one is not concerned with facts is especially revealing:

> Gradually I learned to distrust my mechanistic preoccupation with
> facts and to regard the world around me in the light of dialectic

interpretation. . . . It was a satisfactory and indeed blissful state; once you had assimilated the technique you were no longer disturbed by facts; they automatically took on the proper color and fell into their proper place. Both morally and logically the Party was infallible: Morally, because its aims were right, that is, in accord with the Dialectic of History, and these aims justified all means; logically, because the Party was the vanguard of the Proletariat, and the Proletariat the embodiment of the active principle in History.[4]

Russian editors must be very nimble and flexible—and must ignore the evidence—if they are to revise history whenever the Party takes up a new line. For example, during his regime, Stalin's legendary greatness was never challenged. After his death the legend was systematically debunked by Soviet newsmen. We have read of the smashing of his statues all over Russia and of denunciations of him as "an enemy of the people." With our very different view of the world, this seems strange to Americans. Even more incredible to us is the story of the great lengths to which it seemed necessary to go in revising historical records about Lavrentia Beria.

At one time, Beria was known to be an intimate of Stalin. In the Kremlin, in a state painting, Beria was shown at Stalin's side. He was often referred to in the press as Stalin's "comrade at arms." The major Russian encyclopedia carried a full-page portrait and a biography of Beria, listing his achievements. But when Malenkov came to power, following Stalin's death, it seemed necessary, not only to liquidate Beria, but to pretend that such a man had never existed. The problem of the state painting was easily dealt with: a painter was ordered to paint out Beria's face and paint in a new one. (He substituted the face of Khruschev.) But newspapers had frequently mentioned Beria's activities. We do not know how every existing newspaper story could be obliterated, unless, as in George Orwell's *1984,* there was a huge staff of professional distorters of history. However, it is known what was done in the *Great Soviet Encyclopedia.* Subscribers received a package directing them to remove pages 21 to 24 of volume 5 with a sharp instrument, being careful to leave enough margin so that the new pages enclosed could be pasted in. The new pages told about whaling in the Bering Sea. Thus was history rewritten.

This is not to imply that history should never be reinterpreted. However, there is a distinction between: a) this kind of *purposive control* of new interpretations and b) revisions necessary because new evidence has come to light, or because a new tool has become available. For example, in 1930 a popular world history textbook stated that the earliest known code of laws was that of Hammurabi. In the middle 1950s new clay tablets containing an earlier code, that of Ur Nammu, were discovered. Also, carbon dating, a new means for determining the age of artifacts became available. When the textbook was published in 1930 the statement about the earliest code of laws was "true." It is no longer true, for archaeologists and historians now have facts and evidence that there was an earlier code. There are legitimate reasons for rewriting history.[5] Librarians in search of a philosophy can profitably reflect upon the role of the press under totalitarian theory. Many volunteer censors in America hold a concept of the library which is closer to authoritarian theory than to libertarian theory.

In Italy under a fascist government it was similarly claimed that the "wishes of the people" governed the society. But, as Professor Hocking asks, how do you determine the "wishes of the people?"[6] Hocking suggests that no one can find out by asking the man in the street. Under totalitarian theory, the people do not, in fact, know what they want. The dictator tells them what they want. Then he does it for them. Thereupon the people's wish is fulfilled. In order to fuse the multiple ideas and desires into a policy for action, a unifying interpretation is required. Unity can come only from a single will, that of the dictator. And the press is the instrument by which the dictator "educates" the people.[7]

In 1971 Arlene Lum, a writer for the Honolulu *Star-Bulletin*, was one of the first Americans admitted to the mainland of China in many years. Her account of bookstores and libraries carried the headline: "A Bookworm Could Starve in China." She could find only translations of Marx and Lenin, the works of Mao, and "propaganda publications such as the Peking Review, China Reconstructs, China Pictorial and Chinese literature, and newspapers of the Daily Worker variety." She reported that, after spending scores of hours in dozens of bookstores in different cities, she could not find any volumes of Chinese history other than the authorized versions. In the capital city, the stores which had sold old Chinese books were closed during the Cultural Revolution of 1966–68 and never reopened.[8] This situation changed later in 1972, but the idea of "authorized versions" is especially pertinent to the problems of intellectual freedom in libraries in the United States.

As Alfred North Whitehead observed, the ideas and thought patterns, the "mentality" of a society, spring from the world-view which is dominant in the educated sections of the society.[9] This world-view, manifesting itself in various ways at every level of culture, determines the society's concept of freedom of the press, and the concept of libraries and their role as a part of the communications system. For example, in the 1930s, Germany's libraries, established under a more libertarian theory than prevailed during the Nazi regime, were considered a threat to the government and were burned by Hitler. As reported by Arlene Lum, Mao's China permits only authorized versions of history to be available. In 1948 when Russia took control of Czechoslovakia, total libraries were not burned, but they were immediately put under the supervision of librarians who had been trained in state library schools to recognize "progressive" literature, and all materials not considered "progressive" were removed.

The United Nations is well ahead of 1984 with its decision to deliberately distort reference materials in a fashion described by Orwell. In 1972, after China was admitted to the United Nations, the UN bowed to the pressure to make Taiwan a "noncountry." The *Statistical Yearbook*, published by the United Nations, twenty-third issue, 1971, listed populations, tractors produced, the number of metric tons of cement produced, for example, in both Mainland China and in Taiwan. In future editions Taiwan statistics will be eliminated.[10] One wonders what the UN will do about this noncountry in the next edition of its map of the world. Will the island be shown in outline, with no name? Will it be omitted from the map entirely? Will the map be published?

The case of the United Nation's problems with the *Statistical Yearbook* points up the contrast between the authoritarian-totalitarian theories and the libertarian-social responsibility theories of the press.

The libertarian theory of the press arose in seventeenth-century England and the United States and derives from the thinking of Milton, Locke, Mill, and others. The purposes of the libertarian press are to inform, entertain, sell, but primarily to help men to discover and know the truth through honest, objective, unrestricted inquiry and reporting, as well as to provide checks on governments.

Under all theories of the press it is the journalist's function to provide windows on the world to aid people in their efforts to maintain contact with their environments. All of us react to our surroundings according to what we perceive them to be. The survival of an individual, or a species, depends upon a perception of the world which approximates the reality. This phrase "approximates the reality" is used here to emphasize the fact that, even when we observe phenomena directly and personally, we should not expect our perceptions to be perfect. When we depend upon a journalist's report we are further handicapped by his misperceptions, plus his —and our own—semantic problems of communication. If we add to these difficulties a deliberate intent by the journalist to present only a part of reality—as in the case of the *Statistical Yearbook*—in order to shape and control the reader's picture of reality for political or social objectives, the reader's misperceptions may be so far from a reasonable approximation to reality as to have very serious consequences.

Under libertarian theory, journalists are expected to make every possible effort to present the facts, to avoid misleading their audiences by mixing the normative with the descriptive, that is, by intermixing editorial opinions and personal value judgments with their descriptions of events. They are also to avoid generalities that imply *allness,* such as: "And now for a complete summary of the news . . . ," or Walter Cronkite's familiar sign-off, "And that's the way it is." (It seems odd that so competent and sophisticated a reporter should misuse the verb *to be* in this way, implying that CBS has presented "the truth, the whole truth, and nothing but the truth," when, in fact, the Cronkite program has selected a very few of the infinite number of events that might have been reported.)

Under the libertarian theory of the press it is inevitable, understandable—and forgivable—that even when a reporter tries to present the facts honestly and objectively, there will be unintentional distortions. (A review of Schramm's description, "What Is News," at the beginning of this chapter may be helpful in understanding the journalist's problems.) Also, however, under the libertarian theory, there may sometimes be deliberate and intentional distortions of the facts.

A striking illustration of deliberate distortion of the news by clever manipulation of words was a story about the Commission on Freedom of the Press[11] which appeared in the *Chicago Tribune* of November 14, 1948. This appeared on page one, where news reports usually appeared, and with every indication that it was a news report. Although the commission consisted of eminent scholars attempting to find ways to *preserve* freedom of the press, the story systematically misled the reader as to their qualifications in so crude a way as to be almost amusing.

For example, one paragraph about Harvard Law Professor Zechariah Chafee read as follows: "Chafee has been one of the most vigorous definers of the 'Soviet view' on freedom of the press. In Russia, he has said, the Soviets 'feel that our (American) press is not free because owners and publishers can interfere with presentation of views unacceptable to them.'"[12]

Milton Mayer, who prepared a detailed, documented analysis of this *Tribune* story for *Harper's Magazine* asks: "What did the reporter intend his audience to conclude about Chafee from the term 'vigorous definer'?" (Incidentally, how did you react to those two words? Did your eye slide past them?) Mayer points out that *definer* is one who defines, and to define is to determine the essential qualities of, according to Webster. But, he emphasizes, *definer* is not a commonly used word, nor is *vigorous definer* a commonly used expression. *Defender* and *vigorous defender* however, are common expressions. (The reader's attention is called to a similar semantic ploy used in the library press in chapter 7.)

The *Tribune* did not tell its readers that Chafee was the leading authority on freedom of expression in the United States. In its systematic discrediting of each member of the Commission, it did not tell its readers that John M. Clark was a leading economist, that William E. Hocking was an eminent philosopher, or that Harold Lasswell was an expert in communication theory.

The story of a deliberate distortion of information by the *Chicago Tribune* does not properly lead to a conclusion that this is a "bad" newspaper that should be excluded from American libraries. If we consciously put dates along with the word "Tribune" we will be aware that the *Chicago Tribune* in 1974 is not the same newspaper in all respects as was the *Chicago Tribune* in 1948, and that they should not be judged as if they were identical. But, even in 1948, its propensity for distortion of the facts by semantic trickery would not have justified the exclusion from libraries of this important newspaper. According to the libertarian concept of tax-supported libraries, as expressed in the Library Bill of Rights of the American Library Association, all users of libraries need access to the widest possible variety of sources of information, including the distorted versions. The presence in a library of the *Chicago Tribune* or of an underground newspaper which makes no attempt at objectivity should never suggest to anyone that a publicly supported library endorses, supports, or approves of *any* of the ideas found in its collections. The libertarian Library Bill of Rights holds that all possible forms of expression and all points of view on all issues must be in American libraries, with all their contradictions, if the library, as one part of the communications system, is to help to expand the horizons of the people who use libraries.

In addition to distortions due to unintentional misperceptions or semantic failures, reporters have another problem. They must select events to be reported, and they do select emphases to be given to some of the facts about those events. Because of an individual observer's personal background of study and experience, he may *unintentionally* select events and write about them in a way that misleads his readers.

On the other hand, a newsman may *deliberately* commit the fallacy of accent, intentionally distorting by unrepresentative selection of events and emphases. This is frequently done by censors who select passages out of context and quote them to prove that a book is obscene or subversive.

When a reporter, editor, or producer of a radio or television news program seeks to propagandize for a cause, he tends to excuse his unrepresentative selection, or even the complete fabrication of data, on the grounds that his opinions and values are right. Thus the use of *any means* to persuade others to accept his point of view is justified.

For the consumer of the news media to perceive his world with reasonable accuracy, as shown to him by the press, it is necessary to distinguish between editorials, which are intended to shape opinions, interpretive reporting, and objective, descriptive reporting. Journalists recognize that nonspecialists lack the vocabulary to interpret the raw data of the daily news. As was noted earlier, one of the major factors essential to the success of the operations of scientists was their development of a neutral, nonemotive language. Without such a vocabulary, scientists would have been handicapped in their attempt to be *objective* in their controlled experiments and their reports about them. Emotive language is counterproductive in the scientific world. But the neutral language of science is likely to become a jargon comprehensible only to specialists; laymen are not able to understand the significance of news reports couched in the language of physicists, chemists, economists, or sociologists.

Journalists have felt it necessary to supply some interpretation of scientists' jargon for nonspecialists. Journalists also have realized that laymen lack the background information—on the geography, economics, and cultures of a rapidly shrinking planet—and the perspective to interpret the facts reported. In the 1920s, commentators began to bring to radio listeners and newspaper readers facts and opinions to explain the objective and factual news reports. Unfortunately, some commentators held their personal opinions so strongly, they were so sure of the rightness of their value judgments and moral convictions, that they failed to maintain a fair degree of objectivity. Sometimes they wrote their commentary out of whole cloth, and then sought facts or tried to create facts to support their conclusions.

A notorious example was the attempt by Paul Harvey in 1951 to sneak into an atomic research laboratory and leave a note inside the plant to be discovered by the "chagrined guards." The script of what might have been told in Harvey's radio program was found in his car, after he had been caught by the guards of the Argonne National laboratory. The exposé which had been *written before the event*, intended to show up security safeguards at the atomic laboratory, was, of course, never put on the air.[13] But despite the fact that Harvey's plot was made public, in 1971 the *Wall Street Journal* published a feature article on Harvey, stating that he was still one of the most-listened-to interpreters of the news.

It seems likely that a free society can tolerate news analysts who "interpret" the news in this fashion, assuming under libertarian theory that readers will be critical of what they read, and that there will be a variety of interpretations available to them. These assumptions are not always justified.

While our society requires a cantankerous and critical press that exposes errors and omissions of those in authority, readers are not always critical of what they read or sufficiently aware that they may be reading partial, one-sided reports. We may recall that President Nixon illustrated the common tendency to make unjustified judgments by his somewhat offhand, but *public* reference to Charles Manson as guilty of the charges against him for the Sharon Tate murders, *while the trial was in process*. Similarly, not on the basis of consideration of the total evidence presented in court, but merely on the basis of those news stories that they happened to read or see on TV, many people formed judgments about the guilt or innocence of Angela Davis or the Berrigan brothers, even before their trials began.

The problem of fair trial and free press, under libertarian theory, is so complex and difficult as to baffle almost everyone. However, it can be stated fairly that it is essential for all citizens to learn to distinguish between the partial reports and editorials appearing in news media *about* the facts in a case, and the total evidence as it is presented to the jury in court, recognizing that it is the job of the jury to decide—on the basis of all available evidence—as to the guilt or innocence of those on trial, as Appendix B indicates.[14]

The case of Joan Bodger, consultant for the Missouri State Library, illustrates how different segments of the press may present conflicting reports of what happened. Librarians who read only the library press saw one picture. Citizens of Missouri who read only local newspapers saw a different picture. This case is especially important to librarians, for it is the first such case in which the American Library Association conducted a thorough investigation of the facts by an impartial team. (*See* chapter 8 for more details and Appendix A for the full, documented report of the facts.)

Was the report by this team, which appeared in *American Libraries*, in the July–August 1970 issue, an *objective* account? The report is unquestionably more comprehensive, more carefully documented, and a better basis for judging the case than the reports of either the library press or the Missouri newspapers. It was an honest, impartial attempt to determine the facts as objectively as possible.

Can the free press in America be objective? Writing on "The Old New Journalism," John Tebbel, Professor of Journalism at Columbia University, says that the passions of the poor, the black, and the young in the 1960s produced an underground press that sneered at objectivity and seemed to return wholeheartedly to the activist, propagandist past of journalistic effort. "Objectivity" became an old man's word, as though the self-evident fact that it did not and never had existed in a pure state negated any necessity to pursue it.

Tebbel and others consider it one of the most fascinating aspects of press criticism today that the attacks from Right and Left are so similar. The reason for this, he thinks, is that both Right and Left believe that the press should be the propaganda arm of its particular movement. Tebbel emphasizes his conclusion that, should subjectivity win over objectivity in this contest, the press would be right back where it was at the beginning of the republic; "the consequences are clear from history: for in societies where the subjectivity of the press becomes too critical of strong governments, the governments move to control the press absolutely."[15]

For a comparison of a Soviet view of objectivity with what Tebbel suggests, here is what Russian journalist Kuzmichev thinks about objectivity as a standard:

> All dissertations of "objective and complete" information are liberal hypocrisy. The aim of information does not consist in commercializing news but in educating the great mass of workers, in organizing them under the exclusive direction of the Party for clearly defined tasks. This aim will never be attained by objective reports of events. Liberty, objectivity of the press, these are fictions. Information is the means of the class struggle, not a mirror to reflect events objectively.[16]

The rising generation of American journalists, and not only in the campus and the underground presses, seems to include some who are retrogressing to the "advocacy journalism" which prevailed in the early newspapers in America. Historian Charles Beard described these as "partisan sheets devoted to savage attacks upon party opponents." Some papers in the underground or alternative press today apparently operate from a belief that emotionally felt truth—"gut feeling"—should replace the slowly developed standard of factual, objective, measurable, and verifiable truth, which is, as Herbert Brucker observes, though necessarily imperfect, at least a crude portrait of the world as it is, warts, halos, significance, and all. In Brucker's words:

> To the activist-journalist what he thinks about the news is as important as the news itself. Hence the younger generation's impatience with the newspaper as mirror of the world, and its desire to transform it into a weapon with which to win the future.
>
> This is, however, a formula for getting opinions first, and thereafter looking for facts to bolster those opinions. . . . No doubt objective reporting is more difficult than the zealot's instant truth. But truth still wears as many faces as it did in the days of *Areopagitica*. Surely, it comes more nearly to him whose aim is to report both sides of an issue than to him who reverts to the ancient fallacy of believing that there is only one truth, and he has it.[17]

Sometimes interpretations come primarily from the opinions or prejudices of the reporter. Obviously, there is a kind of objectivity that takes everything at face value and lets the public be imposed upon by a demogogue such as Senator Joseph McCarthy, who waved sheets of paper in front of TV cameras, claiming that he had a list of traitors. When the press merely narrated what McCarthy had said, they unquestionably helped him in his character assassinations. More recently, as Professor Daniel Bell has pointed out, the militants at Columbia University had no difficulty whatever in getting their side of the story of alleged repression into the newspapers and onto the TV screens. The journalists who entered the barricaded buildings and listened to the students did not bother to even ask the administration if the stories were true or based on facts.[18]

Is there any difference between news interpretation and editorializing? Emeritus Professor Mitchell Charnley of the School of Journalism and Mass Communication, University of Minnesota, says it is not easy to answer this question, but some distinguishing features can be discerned:

> 1) The prime purpose of interpretive reporting, honestly used, is just what the term implies; clarification and illumination. (If it is used to lead or shape opinion, it departs from its defined purpose, and may be deceitful.) The purposes of editorials may legitimately be many: clarification and illumination, opinion-shaping, incitement to action, even entertainment.

2) The editorial is commonly institutional—the acknowledged voice of the newspaper or the broadcasting station as an institution. The interpretive news story is the voice only of its writer.

3) The editorial is anonymous (except for its institutional nature). The writer of the interpretive story is identified, and if his story presents opinion it is known to be his. It is true that any kind of news presentation may be colored by editorial purpose. As the earlier chapters of this book have made clear, permitting this to happen is considered improper practice. It occurs infrequently.[19]

Professor Charnley was writing of a period before the present evidences that the press is reverting to subjectivism. It is probably correct, as he says, that competent, honest journalists consider it "improper practice" to interlard *news reports* with their personal judgments and opinions. Maybe it occurs infrequently in the majority of daily papers in 1973. (In chapter 7 we will consider the library press which handicaps its readers by presenting only opinion coverage on professional conferences, with no straight news reporting.)

If the press in a pluralistic society is to fulfill its mission of furnishing the individual with the raw data upon which he can form his own well-founded personal judgments, ideally, the news should be presented objectively and without any warping by editorial opinion. Even though pure, complete objectivity is not possible, it should nevertheless be the goal of every newsman.

It is also possible for a news agency to fall into a trap of publishing only news that fits a preconceived pattern. George Orwell, in a preface to *Animal Farm*, which was not published with the book as he had once intended, is especially illuminating on this kind of press failure. In this preface he charged that:

> At any given moment there is an orthodoxy, a body of ideas which it is assumed all right-thinking people will accept without question. It is not exactly forbidden to say this, or that, or the other, but it was "not done" to say it, just as in mid-Victorian times it was "not done" to mention trousers in the presence of a lady. Anyone who challenges the prevailing orthodoxy finds himself silenced with surprising effectiveness. A genuinely unfashionable opinion is almost never given a fair hearing, either in the popular press or in the highbrow periodicals. . . .
>
> To exchange one orthodoxy for another is not necessarily an advance. The enemy is the gramophone mind, whether or not one agrees with the record that is being played at the moment.[20]

John Chancellor of NBC says that reporters probably tend to have a bias toward rational solutions to problems, a bias toward social action, a bias toward people who are really trying to help, a bias toward pragmatism and common sense. Newsmen learn—at first hand—that things must be done to solve problems, things that cost effort and money, and that gets them in trouble with conservatives. They learn—at first hand, in the wars and riots—that violence and radicalism seldom solve anything, and that gets them in trouble with the New Left. Most reporters, says Chancellor, are members of the extreme center—and that's a difficult place to be. Chancellor's view of the necessity for neutrality by newsmen who try to present the news objectively seems to identify him as a newsman operating under the libertarian theory of the press.[21] Such newsmen, like scholars, teachers, and librarians who try to approach ideas with a liberal view, that is, to insist that any expression or proposition should be held up for examination, weighing the evidence to support it, will be condemned by extremists at both ends of the political-social continuum.

Siebert, Peterson, and Schramm describe in their book *Four Theories of the Press* the development of the "Soviet-Totalitarian rationale" for the mass media out of earlier authoritarian theory. They also describe the "Social Responsibility rationale" deriving from the libertarian theory. The summary chart reproduced in this essay of the four rationales they identify provides a convenient reference for an analysis of the bases upon which professors can defend academic freedom and librarians can defend intellectual freedom for the users of libraries.[22]

This libertarian theory is found to be not entirely satisfactory by Theodore Peterson, by the Commission on Freedom of the Press, and by many newsmen. One defect already discussed is that presentation of the raw data with no background or clarification by the newsman does not insure that the layman will understand the significance of the news event. Another problem stems from a waning confidence in the "self-righting process" that John Milton assumed and emphasized. This is the idea that the citizen who has access to a variety of viewpoints will sort them out and reach wise conclusions. The Commission on Freedom of the Press concluded that this process does not necessarily occur. Most people tend to avoid looking at or hearing expressions with which they disagree.

The classic libertarian theory of the press also seems inadequate as a result of a change from the Miltonian view of the world as static, to the modern view of the world as constantly in process. Certainly our knowledge of the world is continuously advancing. This makes free communication of information and ideas ever more essential. If we are to benefit from our increasing knowledge, the free dissemination of it by school, press, and library becomes an ethical and social value of paramount importance. The lesser causes of advocacy scholars, journalists, or librarians, whatever their merits, must be subordinate to the principle of intellectual freedom, if we are to have the opportunity to use reason to resolve problems.

To meet the demands of a view of the world in process, a new theory

	AUTHORITARIAN	LIBERTARIAN	SOCIAL RESPONSIBILITY	SOVIET-TOTALITARIAN
Developed	in 16th and 17th century England; widely adopted and still practiced in many places	adopted by England after 1688, and in U.S.; influential elsewhere	in U.S. in the 20th century	in Soviet Union, although some of the same things were done by Nazis and Italians
Out of	philosophy of absolute power of monarch, his government, or both	writings of Milton, Locke, Mill, and general philosophy of rationalism and natural rights	writing of W. E. Hocking, Commission on Freedom of Press, and practitioners; media codes	Marxist-Leninist-Stalinist thought, with mixture of Hegel and 19th century Russian thinking
Chief purpose	to support and advance the policies of the government in power; and to service the state	to inform, entertain, sell — but chiefly to help discover truth, and to check on government	to inform, entertain, sell — but chiefly to raise conflict to the plane of discussion	to contribute to the success and continuance of the Soviet socialist system, and especially to the dictatorship of the party
Who has right to use media?	whoever gets a royal patent or similar permission	anyone with economic means to do so	everyone who has something to say	loyal and orthodox party members
How are media controlled?	government patents, guilds, licensing, sometimes censorship	by "self-righting process of truth" in "free market place of ideas," and by courts	community opinion, consumer action, professional ethics	surveillance and economic or political action of government
What forbidden?	criticism of political machinery and officials in power	defamation, obscenity, indecency, wartime sedition	serious invasion of recognized private rights and vital social interests	criticism of party objectives as distinguished from tactics
Ownership	private or public	chiefly private	private unless government has to take over to insure public service	public
Essential differences from others	instrument for effecting government policy, though not necessarily government owned	instrument for checking on government and meeting other needs of society	media must assume obligation of social responsibility; and if they do not, someone must see that they do	state-owned and closely controlled media existing solely as arm of state

of the press began to develop in the middle of the twentieth century. The Commission on Freedom of the Press termed this new theory the "social responsibility theory" (not to be confused with the social responsibility concept of advocacy libraries which developed in the 1960s and 1970s).

The major premise of the social responsibility theory of the press, according to Theodore Peterson, is that "Freedom carries concomitant obligations; and the press, which enjoys a privileged position under our government, is obliged to be responsible to society for carrying out certain essential functions of mass communication in contemporary society." Peterson sees these functions as basically the same as those comprising the libertarian theory, out of which the present social responsibility theory was derived:

> (1) servicing the political system by providing information, discussion and debate on public affairs; (2) enlightening the public so as to make it capable of self-government; (3) safeguarding the rights of the individual by serving as watchdog against government; (4) servicing the economic system, primarily by bringing together the buyers and sellers of goods and services through the medium of advertising; (5) providing entertainment; (6) maintaining its own financial self-sufficiency so as to be free from the pressures of special interests.[23]

Peterson's judgment (in 1956 when his essay was published) was that the social responsibility theory, while still chiefly a theory, was important because it suggested a direction in which thinking about freedom of the press was heading. He also indicated that, in linking rights and duties, this theory, although it derived from the libertarian theory, bore a closer resemblance to Soviet theory than to libertarian. However, under Soviet theory, the duty of the press is to the proletariat or the party in control of the government, whereas under the social responsibility theory, the duty is to the journalist's conscience. (An advocacy journalist, dedicated to a cause, is likely to interpret this as a justification for writing with whatever slant will promote his cause, ignoring some of the facts, and recognizing no obligation even to attempt to present them objectively.)

A press that is to meet its obligation to inform its readers must not lie. It must be as accurate and objective as is humanly possible. It must not mislead its readers by *failing to clearly identify fact as fact and opinion as opinion.* But when the press does mislead its audiences, the remedies suggested by the Commission on the Freedom of the Press do not seem to promise much. The commission suggested that community opinion, consumer action, and professional ethics should and could control the press. It also recommended the establishment of a nongovernmental agency for the continuous survey of press performance with respect to truth and fairness and for passing judgment on the more flagrant cases of abuse. It further suggested that individuals need not be supine when the press has lied, and that the government could issue its own corrective reports.

But how could a nongovernmental agency represent all major interests of various groups in a pluralistic society? Could any one representative on a council to guard against press abuses speak for all labor unions? For all black people? For all professors? For all business? And the leverage of such a council, at least on the national level would not be great. (Journalists and other citizens in Minnesota and Hawaii have established such agencies, and perhaps there is some hope in such state or regional councils.) It would seem that under either the libertarian or the social responsibility theories of the press, its performance will be just as good or bad as the members of the profession decide it will be.

Dr. Samuel Johnson summed up the dilemma succinctly when he said that the danger of unbounded liberty, and the danger of bounding it, have produced a problem in the science of government which human understanding seems hitherto unable to solve.

In an authoritarian or totalitarian society, as we have seen, there is no such dilemma; the press is expected to lie, to ignore the facts, to make no effort at objectivity. It merely tries to "educate" the people by painting in their minds the picture of reality and the environment seen by the men who head the Party. In a dynamic, pluralistic society, the press is not supposed to lie, but under the social responsibility theory it has an obligation to provide perspective and background to help its readers to interpret the raw data of the news. As we have also illustrated, there are unavoidable, unintentional distortions of news reports, as well as deliberate and intentional distortions. How do we prevent the press from lying? Surely it is far too dangerous to rely on, or even to permit, the government to control the press. What can reasonably be expected from government is the preservation of a climate and mentality in which the press can criticize and challenge the policies and actions of the government. Perhaps the best hope lies in the education of journalists and a code of ethics which sets up a standard of honesty, objectivity, and responsibility as a goal.

To summarize this analysis of theories of the press as bases for intellectual freedom in libraries:

> The libertarian theory of the press, from which the Library Bill of Rights derives, has some disadvantages. Nevertheless, it provides a basis for continued faith in the values of a free press and a free library as sources of information, on all sides of all issues, for all people.
>
> The social responsibility theory of the press provides some useful correctives to the pure libertarian theory, refining and strengthening it as a basis for intellectual freedom in libraries, especially by adding the notion of a world constantly in process, ever-changing. However, although advocacy journals of opinion may be valuable as one part of a free press, if they achieve a monopoly in any field, free access to all points of view on that subject disappears.

If the social responsibility theory of the press is interpreted as a justification for politicizing tax-supported libraries and/or the American
Library Association, rejecting the idea that a library and a professional association must be neutral on substantive, nonlibrary issues,
then intellectual freedom in libraries cannot exist. Operating under
the Library Bill of Rights concept, a library *has* a social responsibility to provide access to all points of view on all issues. It thus encourages and aids social changes based upon facts and reason, for no
alternative plans or arguments will be suppressed. It is essential for
the preservation of intellectual freedom in libraries to distinguish
between this Library Bill of Rights concept of libraries and the view
that libraries can be subverted into advocacy instruments to effect
specific social and political objectives.

The totalitarian theory of the press, since it denies the possibility of objective news reporting and advocates the use of both the press and
libraries as instruments for the "education" of citizens in the orthodoxies of a given moment, can never be a basis for intellectual freedom in libraries.

7 *The Social Responsibility Concept of Librarianship Versus the Library Bill of Rights Concept*

> Article I. Name: Section 1. The name of this body shall be the American Library Association.
> Article II. Object: Section 1. The object of the American Library Association shall be to promote library service and librarianship.
> —THE ALA CONSTITUTION[1]

Erosion of Purposes of the American Library Association

One might naturally assume that the first two articles of the ALA Constitution establish the common concern of librarians for the improvement of libraries and information services as the tie that binds librarians together in their professional, educational organization. Since 1876 it has been the purpose of ALA to improve the bibliographical resources, the technological devices, and the professional competencies of librarians, with the aim of providing information services to enable its members and those they serve to deal intelligently with the problems of living in a changing world. The ALA, since it first adopted the Library's Bill of Rights in 1939, also has recognized and emphasized its responsibility to provide information without censorious limitations. The ALA or a similar group seems necessary in a pluralistic society which operates in response to pressures from various groups, some of them well-organized to demand censorship of what they do not like.

Throughout the history of ALA the focus of those interested in libraries has been upon problems and programs of librarianship. In the late 1960s and early 1970s, however, an erosion of this focus occurred. Under a concept of librarianship that its proponents called "Social Responsibility," topics concerning librarianship were replaced in ALA conferences by a variety of social and political issues. This erosion has weakened the ALA, and if it continues may sever the link of common purpose which is the reason for existence of this organization.

105

The raison d'etre of the ALA is not any of the following:

1. To eradicate racial injustice and inequities and to promote human brotherhood
2. To stop the pollution of air, earth, and sea
3. To build a United Nations capable of preventing all wars
4. To promote homosexualism as a life-style
5. To advocate the lowering of the voting age to 18
6. To preserve the separation of church and state
7. To destroy—or to establish—universities
8. To judge the guilt or innocence, based on news reports, of individuals, be they Charles Manson, Angela Davis, or the Berrigan brothers, on the charges brought against them in the courts
9. To decide whether or not President Nixon should be impeached
10. To resolve hundreds of other social, scientific, or political issues, regardless of how vital they may be for the future of humanity.

The first three issues cited in the foregoing are quite possibly of such crucial importance for the future of humanity that, unless we can find ways and means to resolve the dilemmas in the areas of racial relations, pollution of the environment, and atomic wars, we may bring about our own destruction. Vital as these issues are, *it is not the purpose of ALA to take positions on how humanity must resolve them.* It is essential that librarians, in their professional activities, shall view such issues, vital though they are, as subordinate to the principle of intellectual freedom, for, unless we, as rational human beings, have access to all varieties of expression regarding the facts, theories, and alternative solutions to these problems, we will be unable to apply our powers of reason toward their resolution. There is no more likelihood that a problem like that of pollution of the environment will be solved by actions based upon "gut feeling" and ignorance of the facts than that the Nazis in Germany could build a viable society based upon their "blood-thinking."

Some of these nonlibrary problems have generated movements and organizations that are deserving of support by citizens who also happen to be librarians. Librarians who perform the library duties for which they contracted should not find that their jobs have been put in jeopardy because they devote their nonlibrary working hours to nonlibrary causes. The ALA has a legitimate concern and obligation to improve and refine its policies and procedures for protecting a librarian's job when, for example, he or she performs satisfactorily, as a librarian, but plays an active role in his community to preserve the separation of church and state. However, any "support" by ALA, if the organization is to act responsibly, requires full knowledge of the facts in a particular case and cannot properly be based upon one-sided accusations at the membership or Council meetings or in the library press.

Although there may be legitimate reasons for dissatisfaction with the American Library Association, one frequently made complaint is invalid by any standard. It is not valid to condemn the ALA for its refusal to allow itself to be used to promote the personal, social, political, or moral beliefs of any member or group of members. It is appropriate for librarians to hold different opinions on problems of librarianship, even though such differences produce controversies in the forums provided by the ALA. It is also appropriate for librarians to hold different opinions on nonlibrary problems, but it seriously weakens the organization to force divisions of opinion on out-of-scope issues. To do so diverts the ALA's attention away from those issues on which librarians have special competency and responsibility. The link of common purpose—to expand and improve library services—so essential for the unity and cohesiveness of a professional organization, has been frayed by unnecessary divisions over issues irrelevant to librarians as *librarians*.

Attempts to transform the American Library Association into a political organization for the promotion of specific causes unrelated to librarianship could destroy the viability of this library organization; already they have weakened it. It will not matter who serves as the executive director, or who is elected to the presidency, the executive board, or the Council, for unless the attention, time, energy, and resources of the ALA can be refocused upon *library* problems, the organization cannot and will not survive.

Countless librarians have worked for nearly one hundred years to build ALA as an organization to promote effective library service. That organization, with its stated purposes clearly delineated in its Constitution, has become a necessary force in our society. To help the ALA continue to focus its attention upon issues in its own field of competency, it would be useful, whenever new policies and procedures are proposed, for each member of Council to ask the following questions:

1. Does this proposal tend to increase or decrease the professional's ability to preserve free access to information for everyone?
2. Is the proposal relevant to and essential for improving the profession's personnel, technological, and bibliographical resources to provide the information needed by society?
3. Is the proposal in conflict with federal or state laws or constitutions, or with any existing ALA policies?

These questions supplement each other, and until each member of ALA's legislative assembly (the Council) has satisfied himself that he understands a proposed motion in terms of these questions, he is not prepared to vote intelligently and responsibly.

Politicization of ALA

During the years of the McCarthy Syndrome (1949–1953), the ALA's Intellectual Freedom Committee made great strides toward persuading

American librarians that public libraries and librarians are part of the political world and, as a consequence, they cannot divorce themselves from political issues that affect libraries and the freedom to read. As the Radical Right grew bolder and more insistent on censorship, librarians began to understand that the values of free inquiry, free scholarship, and free dissemination of ideas actually could be, and might be, lost. Once these values are lost, librarians would be unable to give honest reference service or circulate books freely to those who want to use the liberal approach to ideas, examining arguments on all sides of an issue.

Since 1949 the ALA has adopted resolutions on certain political issues which directly affect the capacity of librarians to perform their professional duties. To a great degree, the democratic process is carried on by pressures exerted by special interest groups, and ALA would be derelict if it ignored legislation for financial support for libraries, copyright laws, or loyalty oaths and investigations which hinder librarians from making information freely accessible to everyone. Especially, ALA must give attention to censorship laws in the federal or state governments. On the question of free access to all information by all citizens, ALA has properly played an "advocacy role." As I wrote for *Library Trends* in 1970:

> America's librarians cannot afford to be neutral about their commitment to preserve the freedom to read for everyone. At the same time, as professionals, they must remain neutral about the issues of the day, regardless of what they may do as private citizens. This truth may be even more difficult to understand and to accept as polarization around certain dogmas grows in our society. However, there are always great dangers to civilization when even a small percentage of the population become fully convinced that they and they alone have *the truth*. . . .
>
> The dogmatism of the person who knows that he alone possesses the truth is, of course, not new in this world. A clue which may help librarians to identify the extremist who feels it his duty to use any means to promote his views and exclude all other views from a library is his tendency to insist that "If you are not with me, then you are against me." Probably no group, under or over thirty, black or white, religious or anti-religious, of the political left or the political right, is without a few members who are so extreme, so rigid, so intransigent that they sincerely believe that anyone who does not view the world precisely as they do should be forced to conform or cease to exist. Librarians and the ALA are increasingly under pressure from all such superegoists when they try to control the information available through libraries.[2]

In chapter 5 I described a new kind of politicization of the academy and of professional associations which had been attempted in the 1960s, with some success. At that time some historians, psychologists, political scientists, and other professionals, strongly believed that certain political-social issues were of such importance that they were justified in taking control of their professional organizations, using them to promote their personal convictions on social and political issues. These activists thus sought to capitalize on the prestige of the association, and on the numbers of the members, to influence public opinion. It is in this frame of reference that any attempt to similarly use ALA should be considered. At the Detroit conference of ALA, for example, fifteen or more resolutions not related to the functioning of libraries were proposed.

For ALA to adopt corporate, official positions on such nonlibrary issues as the eighteen-year-old vote or desegregation by school-busing is considered by many members of ALA to be unwarranted and destructive to the professional organization. Unquestionably, the taking of stands on substantive issues unrelated to librarianship destroys the right of individual conscience of every member of ALA. Any librarian, from the most extreme conservative to the most extreme revolutionary on the social-political continuum, should be welcomed as a member of ALA. His personal convictions on political-social issues should not be considered at all in relation to his qualifications either for membership in ALA or for his employment as a librarian. The notion that a political test should govern ALA membership or employment is both dangerous and abhorrent. Although an ALA member must be free to hold his personal convictions on various issues, if he uses his professional association or the library—public, school, or academic—in which he works as a propaganda instrument for these causes, he destroys the integrity of both.

The "new" idea of librarianship promoted in the 1970s was called by its proponents "social responsibility." This new concept of librarianship might be more appropriately called the "advocacy" concept, for, as its supporters describe it, there are three facets characterizing its basic philosophy:

1. ALA should be politicized; that is, it should give up its professional character and its "traditional, conservative neutrality," becoming instead a partisan, advocacy organization.
2. Libraries should similarly be politicized. They should reject the Library Bill of Rights' concept of the library's professional responsibility to provide information on all sides of all controversial issues for all citizens. And publicly supported libraries should become "libraries of opinion."
3. The ALA and libraries have an obligation to commit themselves to strengthening and improving library services to the disadvantaged.

Unfortunately, this concept of librarianship lumps together under the name "social responsibility" one justifiable idea with two others which could only be justified in a totalitarian society.

In June 1970, at the Detroit ALA conference, a small, but well-organized segment of the library profession proposed a new policy for the profession in terms which would have ended the ALA's credibility as a defender of intellectual freedom. Aided by the library press, the Subcommittee on Social Responsibility of Action Committee on New Directions for ALA (ACONDA) rejected the principle of neutrality and intellectual freedom as stated in the Library Bill of Rights, and advocated the politicization of ALA and of publicly supported libraries. This group defined the social responsibility of the profession as follows:

> There are two conflicting definitions of Social Responsibility held by members of the ALA at present. The first is traditional, conservative, and variously phrased: "The function of a library is to have factual material on both sides of the question. The library is a reservoir for information and our business is to conserve it and wait till our users require its contents. The library is a source of ideas, not a promoter of them. A library's social responsibility is to answer the information needs of its users and to be responsible to those needs is a librarian's foremost duty, and, therefore, his chief social responsibility."
>
> The second definition of Social Responsibility is considered radical, new, activist. It can best be summed up by a definition put forth by ALA's Committee on Organization (COO): "Social responsibilities can be defined as the relationships that librarians and *libraries* have to non-library problems that relate to the social welfare of our society." It is this second definition that we will have to deal with. Events at ALA in June, 1969, and the tenor of feeling among newer librarians and many established members of the profession as well, force us to accept this latter definition of social responsibility. We believe that debate is no longer necessary. The time has come for action. The ALA has to embrace this latter definition and carry programs forward to support it.[3]

The Subcommittee on Social Responsibility of ACONDA went on to state that the neutralist position can no longer serve us because it is "unrealistic." This report also said: "The alarm reflected in the journals over our 'image,' our effectiveness, our loss of patronage, all reflect that the traditional definition of social responsibility has lost its value."

The central principle in the Library Bill of Rights is that libraries and the ALA must be impartial and neutral on substantive issues unrelated to librarianship. The argument against this principle was vigorous and persistent in the early 1970s. Although the ACONDA subcommittee stated that "debate is no longer necessary," the debate continued through 1973 over whether ALA was to be a professional or a political organization.

Fortunately, at Detroit, the parent committee, ACONDA as a whole, modified the statement which would have discarded the Library Bill of Rights by adding to its subcommittee's proposal the sentence, "It is essential to make freely available the full range of data and opinion on all aspects of such problems and to develop methods of interesting the public in learning the facts and varying points of view regarding the issues that confront us." With this addition, ACONDA was able to uphold the Library Bill of Rights concept. However, ACONDA as a whole permitted a policy recommendation to be brought before ALA's legislative body which, had it been adopted, would have changed ALA officially from a professional association to a partisan, political, advocacy organization. The recommendation of the subcommittee included the following statement:

> Additionally, ALA should be willing to take a position for the guidance and support of its members on current critical issues and should endeavor to devise means whereby libraries can become more effective instruments of social change.

This the ALA Council did not accept; instead, the proposal was modified further. Council finally adopted the statement that ALA should define the social responsibilities of ALA in terms of:

> the willingness of ALA to take a position on current critical issues with the relationship to libraries and library service clearly set forth in the position statement. . . .

The three facets comprising the social responsibility concept of librarianship need not be lumped together. It is desirable and possible to endorse that part of the ACONDA policy statment which emphasizes the obligation of ALA and of public libraries to improve library services to the disadvantaged, without also accepting that part which seeks to make these agencies advocacy institutions which deny their obligation to be neutral on substantive, nonlibrary issues. Few librarians would disagree with such statements in the ACONDA subcommittee report as:

> As a primary concern of this subcommittee, library service to the disadvantaged must not be slighted. . . .
> Library service to the disadvantaged is definitely one of the major social responsibilities that face libraries and librarians at this tme, and ALA will have to commit itself to this fact and work to help its members solve this problem. . . .[4]

The objective of strengthening library services to the disadvantaged is clearly a responsibility of libraries, librarians, and the ALA. It is directly within the scope of the library profession, according to the purposes stated in the ALA Constitution. Although the editors of *Library Journal* confused this issue by publishing an earlier draft of this essay in its November 15, 1972, issue with a misleading title, incorrectly suggesting that I was describing an antithesis between "Social Responsibility and the Library Bill of Rights," there is no such antithesis as that stated by these editors in the title that they created without my prior knowledge or consent. But there *is* an antithesis between the concept of advocacy librarianship and the Library Bill of Rights concept. In spite of the efforts of the proponents of an advocacy library and an advocacy ALA, it can be hoped that the majority of American librarians reject this concept which declares that the neutralist position of the Library Bill of Rights is "unrealistic and can no longer serve as a guiding policy for the library profession."

Councilors and members of ALA are handicapped in their efforts to determine good answers to the three fundamental questions posed earlier in this essay. With the only coverage of ALA activities that presented by an advocacy library press which denies its obligation to publish straight news reports, the credibility gap between this press and its readers has grown steadily. The "new journalism" analyzed in chapter 6 is predominant in the library press of the 1970s. Descriptive reporting of the facts is interlarded with the writer's opinions and value judgments. This practice is defended on the ground that advocacy journalism is better than old-fashioned objective journalism, which is never possible anyway. The library press seems to feel that it is providing "leadership" for the profession.

Library Journal, American Libraries, and *Wilson Library Bulletin* have served the profession badly by promoting the view that ALA must enter the arena as a partisan advocate for causes unrelated to librarianship. For example, editor John Berry of the *Library Journal* stated in that periodical's January 1, 1973, issue:

> ALA is not a library either. It is an organization that has taken stands on social legislation. It came out against the Axis in World War II and has damned Totalitarianism many times since. That is proper. We hope ALA won't be scared off or turned away from its social responsibilities because some members mistake the Library Bill of Rights for the ALA By-laws.[5]

Conceding the legitimacy of an *editorial* such as the foregoing to persuade members to change ALA from a professional to an advocate, political organization, it is the purpose of this analysis to argue against such politicization. If ALA hopes to continue as a credible champion of intellectual freedom for the users of libraries, it may not become a political organization. It may not encourage its more radical or more conservative members to try to gain control of ALA and use it to promote their personal convictions on nonlibrary issues.

Under the libertarian theory of the press, it is the privilege of a journal to *editorialize,* but two other journalistic practices common in the library press are not defensible. The library press seems to be trying to convince ALA members that the new, social responsibility concept of a politicized ALA is the wave of the future. By denying any obligation to present straight news reports of what happens at ALA conferences, and by emulating *Time* Magazine's use of the "pejorative stereotype," that is, by employing a striking phrase to depict characters and issues in a prejudicial way, this press falls far below the standards of responsible journalism.

I have already described and distinguished between editorials, interpretive reporting of the background and significance of the news, and straight, objective news reports (*see* chapter 6). Readers of the March 15, 1971, issue of *Library Journal* can find a striking illustration of advocacy journalism in editor John Berry's "report," which began:

> Despite the passage of many fine resolutions; activist frustration, postponement, and abdication were the moods of ALA Midwinter, capped by what many members labelled a . . .
>
> COUNCIL COP-OUT
> The Midwinter Meeting of the American Library Association in Los Angeles was a bum trip! Oh sure—there were *groovy* speeches and resolutions, lots of words—but by the time you got home it all boiled down to a fundamental inaction, and defeat or retreat for the forces that wanted reform in the old association. That awful combination of place, a new upsurge of state and regional chauvinism, empty resolving and rhetoric, and basic unwillingness to decide anything was just too much to overcome. The old guard, having waited out more impatient activists, and having worn down the resolve of their representatives, ganged up to choke the microphones and mimeograph machines with all that fine, almost radical, jargon in this new generation of ALA pronunciamento. But when action was proposed, they tabled, postponed or amended it to death. The most depressing aspect of it was the words, the words of activism used to fill the place with inert paper palaver. . . .
>
> *A Report of Abdication*
> Our report is, for the most part, a report of the various abdications of ALA Midwinter, 1971. Abdications by the ALA Council, the ALA Executive Board, the highly touted ACONDA, and the unnecessary ANACONDA, the members, and to a degree, even our hoped-for watchdog, the Social Responsibilities Round Table, from whom some of us at least expected the movement to reform ALA from within to come—but more about all of this later.[6]

Although Mr. Berry labels this a "report," it is typical of subjective advocacy journalism which makes no attempt to report objectively what happened, but rather, mixes some facts with the writer's value judgments. As we have seen in chapter 6, the advocacy journalist excuses this practice by signing the author's name or initials. But readers about ALA activities are left without any objective report of what happened.

In this same "nonreport," the author expressed some value judgments in praise of the ALA Committee on Intellectual Freedom. Such favorable comment was unwelcome to me, even though I was at that time chairman of this committee, for in a *news report* there should be neither praise nor blame. However, the issue of *LJ* also recognized the IFC's achievements in an *editorial,* and this I appreciated.

The earlier-mentioned article, "Council Cop-Out," illustrates the use of *Time's* "pejorative stereotype":

> The Marietta Model
> And of course there was that fine, patriotic number from Marietta Shephard. She moved, and Council voted that they deplore "the destruction of libraries, library collections and property, and the disruption of the educational process by that act, whether it be done by individuals or groups of individuals and whether it be in the name of honest dissent, the desire to control or limit thought or ideas, or for any other purpose." We all agreed!
> In truth, with few exceptions, all the resolutions of ALA Mid-winter were of the Marietta Model, nifty language expressing the ideological, racial, sexual or whatever position of the movers, and probably of those who voted for them. What few, if any of them did, and indeed, what we have never been able to do, is to put teeth in our mouthings, instead of all those confounded words. Yet words were all the Council, Membership, and the rest were able to pro-duce.[7]

American Libraries, the official publication of the ALA, similarly used *Time's* style of propagandizing. A critical reading of the coverage given the 1971 ALA conference in Los Angeles illustrates this journal's rejection of the standard of distinguishing between factual news reports and editorializing. The *news* items are so full of inaccuracies and loaded words and opinions as to mock the reader who tries to learn what happened at ALA. For example, in a story presented as *news* about (not comment on) a meeting of the Committee on Intellectual Freedom to discuss *Sylvester and the Magic Pebble,* with its illustrations of pigs in police uniforms, *American Libraries* reported that the committee met with two representatives of a policemen's organization:

> In effect, messrs. Wood and Fleming so disarmed the IFC with their gentle presence of sweet reason that the committee said they would be happy to send a representative to the July membership meeting of ICOPA [International Conference of Police Associations], and did not issue a formal statement of any kind about the book *or* the meeting. This lack of insight into what is fast becoming a serious problem for librarians across the country is regrettable, and members of ALA will have to await the IFC's Dallas meeting to see if a statement about local police agencies' attempts to remove this book from library collections will be forthcoming from the Intellectual Freedom Committee.[8]

The major point to be made about this kind of reporting is that it is illustrative of editorializing in what is supposedly a *news report*. (The distinctions between news and editorials has been discussed previously at length.) It indicates to the reader that the ALA's Committee on Intellectual Freedom had been delinquent in attending to its responsibilities and had done nothing about the attempts to ban *Sylvester*. Actually, *American Libraries* found it convenient to ignore what ALA's Office for Intellectual Freedom had already done. As early as November 1970, memoranda had been sent to many libraries, alerting them to the *Sylvester* problem. Even before ALA met in Los Angeles in January, the state committees on intellectual freedom had received a two-page letter about this book and the attempts to have it removed from libraries. In February 1971, a follow-up "Advisory Statement" on *Sylvester* had been sent to seventy city libraries. In March, the *Newsletter on Intellectual Freedom* carried a story both on the book and the meeting with Los Angeles County police. The Committee on Intellectual Freedom and the Office for Intellectual Freedom were already on record with various published statements that applied to *Sylvester*. ALA's position in favor of keeping this book in libraries could hardly be considered a secret. Yet *American Libraries,* in this editorial masquerading as a news report, was telling its readers that the CIF had done nothing.

The ALA's Publishing Board has a statement on editorial policy which says that *news* and *views* both have their place in *American Libraries*. It says that the editor must be free to analyze and interpret statements of official ALA positions conscientiously, and as his own judgment dictates, over the signature of the editor. This policy cannot, however, be legitimately used to justify the mixing of an editor's value judgments with descriptive news reporting.

As an illustration of the use of loaded words, similar to that described by Milton Mayer in "How to Read the Chicago *Tribune*," discussed in the preceding chapter, note the use of the word "cryptically" in another news report. The story was about the ALA Council vote on a proposed Program of Action for dealing with violations of the Library Bill of Rights. *American Libraries* began its report:

> The *Program of Action* was carried with a smattering of high volume "no" votes. Mr. Berninghausen then cryptically thanked Council for their votes on a "limited revised" *Program of Action*.[9]

Milton Mayer asked: "What did the [Chicago *Tribune*] reporter intend his audience to conclude about Chafee from the term 'vigorous definer' of the Soviet view?" One may also ask here: What did the *American Libraries* reporter intend to suggest to the reader by the insertion of the adverb *cryptically*? Is there really something devious about saying "Thank you" to the ALA Council for concluding its action on a proposal?

For a third illustration, even in the format adopted by *American Libraries* in 1971, giving first the news report, followed by a paragraph labeled "Comment," the editor seemed only too eager to fan the flames of dissatisfaction with the ALA staff by ignoring the facts. In reference to an SRRT resolution on the "Librarian's Bill of Rights," which had been referred to the ALA Code of Ethics Committee, the editor's "Comment" was:

> It will probably come as a surprise to Membership that the Code of Ethics Committe no longer exists. That such an important document was referred to a nonexistent committee does not speak well for staff support of Membership action. One of the first things which Membership will want to do in Dallas is to retrieve this document from this nonexistent pigeon hole.[10]

Had the editor checked the facts with Executive Director Clift or or his secretariat he would have got them right—he would have known that there was an existent Ethics Committee and had been for the past six months. But then, of course, he could not have criticized the ALA staff for its inattention to the wishes of the Membership of ALA.

Time, the weekly magazine, long ago established a reprehensible practice of mixing news reports and the value judgments they wished to promote. In the fall of 1973 it perpetrated a bad joke when it announced that "for the first time in fifty years" *Time* is going to editorialize, and then proceeded to show why President Nixon should leave his office. Although a huge majority of the citizenry may have agreed that the president should be removed from office, there must have been many wry smiles at the implication that *Time* had ever published anything that was *not* an editorial.

The *Time* style of slick epigrams which sum up a situation or cut down a person probably increases or attracts readers' attention. Yet when the three journals which report ALA activities mimic this device, and also emulate *Time* by mixing facts and opinions and by refusing to present straight news reports, there is a danger that the advocacy concept of ALA can be made to seem the new (acceptable and accepted) orthodoxy.

The editors of the library press show some signs of awareness that these practices are increasingly recognized as below the standards of responsible journalism. William Eshelman, editor of the *Wilson Library Bulletin,* in an attempt to defend what he called the advocacy press approach, admitted that "all three national journals occasionally—especially when reporting ALA conferences—exhibit its [the advocacy press's] features." Eshelman links advocacy journalism and the social responsibility concept of librarianship, describing the rationale as follows:

> The rationale for advocacy journalism is similar to the arguments for greater social responsibility on the part of librarians. Every

reporter has a point of view, the argument runs, and cannot escape some coloring of his story no matter how hard he tries to be objective. Granting that, it is therefore better to admit one's biases frankly, so that the reader is alerted and can make allowances. Truth emerges, then, from conflicting or complementary accounts of the same event. A virtue of this approach, the advocates of advocacy journalism say, is that the reader is not lulled into a false sense of having gotten the facts when, indeed, no one account can possibly present them without bias.[11]

But when are there no conflicting accounts? Eshelman's defense of the advocacy library press rests upon a premise of libertarian press theory which does not exist in the library press of 1973. The notion he expressed that "Truth emerges . . . from conflicting . . . accounts," is sound, when we look at a journal of opinion as one part of a total free press, but it cannot be a valid argument when there are no conflicting accounts. Although Eshelman has a valid point about the *difficulty* of presenting unbiased, objective news reports, many librarians would welcome an attempt to do so by the library press. As George Orwell said in his unpublished preface to *Animal Farm* (*see* note 20, chap. 6), "To exchange one orthodoxy for another is not necessarily an advance. The enemy is the gramophone mind, whether or not one agrees with the record that is being played at the moment." The library profession is severely handicapped by the fact that only opinion coverage of ALA conferences is easily accessible. Perhaps in time a new journal that presents objective news reports will fill the vacuum.

As these essays indicate, there are many parallels between librarianship and journalism. But there is a significant difference between a *journal* of opinion and a *library* of opinion. Under libertarian theory, a journal of opinion is legitimate, so long as it is only one part of a total free press. The *New Republic* or *Time* is not expected to provide information on all sides of all issues.

A partisan, advocacy *library of opinion* cannot be justified on the same grounds. In most communities there is only one publicly supported library which owes to the most conservative segment of its population the same impartiality and neutrality on substantive issues that it owes to the most revolutionary segment. It is not likely that many taxpayers will be willing to maintain a partisan library. The "leadership" toward such a concept claimed by the library press should be critically judged and repudiated.

The proponents of politicization sometimes argue that ALA is an *organization* rather than a library and therefore has no reason to be neutral on political issues. ALA, however, is an organization which has united librarians in a commitment to support the liberal approach to ideas. It serves as a spokesman for the library profession in a continuous dialogue with those who seek to limit free access to all points of view.

ALA tries to persuade the society which supports libraries that the principle of intellectual freedom deserves preservation. ALA always stresses, when an attempt at censorship occurs, that libraries do *not* slant their collections in favor of particular propositions or theories. The library, as a social agency, and the ALA as a professional organization, strive to preserve intellectual freedom for the users of libraries. The integrity of both would be destroyed, and the credibility of both would be strained to the breaking point if ALA were to accept the leadership of those who insist that it shall be politicized. Like the American Association of University Professors, if it wishes to preserve intellectual freedom, the ALA cannot become an advocate on a variety of nonlibrary issues and still expect the public to respect its arguments for free inquiry. It can be predicted with confidence that society will refuse to credit the posture and rhetoric of an organization which pretends that it is defending the liberal approach to ideas but which performs as a partisan, political, propagandistic agency.

Politicization of Publicly Supported Libraries

The same distinction should be drawn between two antithetical concepts of *libraries* that has been shown between a political ALA and the professional organization, that is, between: 1) an advocacy library, and 2) the Library Bill of Rights library.

To show why the integrity and credibility of public libraries would be destroyed under the advocacy concept, one should ask the operational question: How would librarians behave *if* they operated libraries with these two very different ideas of what a library is and what its mission in society should be? (The use of the subjunctive mood should be noted. The following analysis is a prediction of *what would happen if* the social responsibility concept of librarianship were to gain acceptance.)

In the natural sciences *what would happen if* librarians were to use their libraries to further their partisan, nonlibrary causes? At one stage the U.S. Surgeon General announced a scientific conclusion that phosphate detergents are a major villain in water pollution. Manufacturers scurried around to produce nonphosphate detergents. Later the same authority reneged, saying that phosphates were safe after all. Must librarians, following an advocacy concept of the role of libraries, seek the "guidance of the ALA" as to whether the Surgeon General was "right" the first time—or the second time—and exclude from their shelves one or the other of his reports?

For another illustration, somewhat facetious, but making its point, here is what William Gilman reports about the dangers of cholesterol:

> Common sense should have ridiculed the cholesterol panic and the resulting polyunsaturated purge conducted against milk, eggs, and

butter. Even the National Institutes of Health, government sponsor of most of the cholesterol research, has begun having self-doubts, though unofficially. At its headquarters I found in circulation an intramural, mimeographed sheet spoofing cholesterol's rise, fall, and rise over two decades:

THE MARCH OF SCIENCE: Headline Department

Pre-1946: Cholesterol is a good guy
    1947: Cholesterol found to be associated with atherosclerosis
    1948: Cholesterol seen causally related to heart disease
    1950: Cholesterol is killing you
    1954: Cholesterol is killing you, but it has help
    1958: Cholesterol, stress, and lack of exercise are killing you
    1959: Cholesterol may not be killing you, but it isn't saving you either
    1960: Cholesterol probably isn't killing you
    1962: Cholesterol isn't even helping other things kill you —much
    1963: Anything that helps make sex hormones can't be all bad
    1965: Cholesterol has been much maligned
    1966: Cholesterol is a good guy.[12]

Librarians who operate under the Library Bill of Rights concept of the role of libraries would normally acquire and keep reports on cholesterol throughout the twenty-year period, even though these reports contradict each other. Operating under the advocacy concept, librarians presumably would have to decide, year by year, which reports are "of sound, factual authority," and remove those reports which were currently "incorrect."

For yet another illustration, consider Rachel Carson's *Silent Spring*. In it she deplored the loss of birdlife and blamed pesticides, especially DDT, as the enemy threatening not only birds, but all human beings. "For the first time in the history of the world," she wrote, "every human being is now subjected to contact with dangerous chemicals, from the moment of conception until death." In spite of serious doubts about the scientific validity of her book, revealed in critical reviews when it appeared (1962), many public libraries undoubtedly bought it. Later they probably bought additional copies, for this work is still in great demand in 1974. Is *Silent Spring* a sound, factual book giving a needed perspective on ecology and pollution? Does it deserve "endorsement" and promotion by American libraries?

If librarians operate under the advocacy concept of libraries, those who are proponents of Rachel Carson's answers to the pollution problem very likely will feel that they are right *because* they are sincere in their beliefs and *because* they hold strong convictions. If they follow the logic of their concept, they would also feel that the issue must be taken to the legislative assembly at an ALA conference with the demand that this association of librarians, uninformed and incompetent as it is in this field, must take a position on DDT and *Silent Spring* and offer "guidance" to all librarians. Librarians who are not so certain that Carson had all the answers, may perceive their social responsibility quite differently. And, after the ALA Council has decided, by majority vote, which side ⟶has "the truth," those librarians in the minority, convinced as they are that *their* judgment is correct and that *their* cause is justified, will have substantial reasons to feel that they can no longer remain in an organization of librarians which has gone so badly off the track in its decision on a substantive, nonlibrary issue and which has rejected the neutral, nonpartisan role of libraries. Thus librarians will be divided over differences of opinion on a *nonlibrary,* substantive issue, in a field in which there is no reason to believe that they have special competence, and the ALA will be further weakened.

These illustrations of the consequences which would follow adoption of the advocacy concept of libraries, as defined and promoted by ACONDA's subcommittee, reveal the absurdity of this *idea* of librarianship; yet the concept has been adopted by some. The ALA's Committee on Organization, as we have seen, has defined "social responsibility" in terms which insisted that *libraries* have relationships to "non-library problems that relate to the social welfare of our society." As recently as January 1974, ALA's conference halls still were resounding with the rhetoric of those who insist upon politicizing the association.

In the examples thus far cited, the qualifications of most librarians to make evaluations of publications on substantive issues in natural science are extremely doubtful. There are, of course, social and political angles to each case which librarians *as citizens* have the right to judge for themselves, regardless of their knowledge of the subject. However, the primary qualifications needed to evaluate publications related to pollution or health are background knowledge and expertise in chemistry, physics, and biology. Very few librarians hold even undergraduate degrees in these natural sciences, and it would be presumptuous for even those few librarians to claim that they are competent to decide issues which baffle specialists in these fields.

In the more sensitive and controversial social sciences—sociology, economics, anthropology, religion, political science, or education—many laymen do not hesitate to claim expertise. In education, for example, everyone is an "expert." Regardless of their lack of knowledge of learning theories or their lack of practical experience, few people hesitate to proclaim they are more competent than professional educators.

In the especially sensitive social science field of racial relations, is it the "social responsibility" of librarians to ban the *Harvard Educational Review* because it dared to publish the Jensen study, "How Much Can We Boost IQ and Scholastic Achievement?" And shall the ban include the *Atlantic Monthly* which published an article about the study? The

Atlantic introduced the subject by highlighting the nature of the controversy:

> Berkeley professor Arthur R. Jensen's article—published in the *Harvard Educational Review* in the winter of 1969—faced head-on the possibility that blacks and whites differ in inherited intelligence. This difference, which shows up as the average difference in their I.Q.'s, may be the extra factor which gives whites a statistical advantage in economic and educational competition in certain settings. Although Jensen did not assert that this had been proved, his consideration of it provoked so violent a reaction that the earlier reactions of Moynihan and Coleman seemed polite by comparison. SDS was on the streets of Berkeley almost immediately with bullhorns blaring, "Fight racism! Fire Jensen!" Jensen's classes had to meet clandestinely to avoid disruptions by outraged activists. Some of Jensen's colleagues at the University of California tried, unsuccessfully, to have him censured. His hate mail was voluminous. In apparent panic over the vehemence of the outcry, the *Harvard Educational Review* refused to sell reprints of the article to anyone (including Jensen) until they could be bound together with a number of criticisms of Jensen's arguments.[13]

In many parts of the world, including the United States, problems related to race are unquestionably of vital importance. However, evaluations of studies such as Jensen's cannot properly be made in the streets by SDS or on the floor at ALA membership or Council meetings, for

If scholarly inquiry in this subject is taboo, then academic freedom does not exist.

If the reports of such inquiry are suppressed, intellectual freedom does not exist.

If librarians, operating under the advocacy library concept, were to ban the Jensen study and all references to it, their behavior would be not only presumptuous and in violation of the intellectual freedom of library users; such a ban, based upon a false notion of the social responsibility of librarians, would tend to prevent the correction of the social evils of racial injustices and inequities.

If men of all races are prohibited from exercising their powers of intelligence and reason upon these problems, with free access to all pertinent evidence, there can be no hope that they will be resolved.

For further illumination of the differences between library operations carried on under the advocacy concept of libraries versus the Library Bill of Rights concept, let us examine how librarians might be expected to handle the following publications:

> *Report* of the President's Commission
> on Pornography and Obscenity

Lysenko's genetic theories
Velikovsky's cosmic theories
Cleaver's *Soul on Ice*
Millett's *Sexual Politics*
Miller's *Tropic of Cancer*
Orwell's *1984*
Mao's thoughts
Hitler's *Mein Kampf*
Time Magazine
Underground newspapers
Mary Poppins
Caddie Woodlawn
Sylvester and the Magic Pebble
Little Black Sambo.

It is obvious and generally conceded that libraries have limited book budgets and cannot buy every book published. However, asking the operational question again, how will librarians actually operate under the Library Bill of Rights concept of libraries and, in contrast, under the social responsibility concept?

Operating under the Library Bill of Rights and other current policies on intellectual freedom, librarians are encouraged and expected to make accessible all of the items in the foregoing. There are no subjects or titles which are taboo, in spite of the fact that some segments of our society disapprove of the ideas in some of these publications, and would much prefer that they be inaccessible to library users. However, librarians are not compelled by the government, the American Library Association, or by anyone else, either to acquire or to ban these or other specific titles. Librarians do not claim that they have omniscience, infallibility of judgment, or a foolproof test which can meet all arguments and pressures as to which books or other media are "of sound, factual authority." (This phrase is no longer in the Library Bill of Rights since the 1967 revision of the policy.) Librarians refuse to "endorse" or "approve of" library materials, or to label documents as "authorized" or "dangerous," or in any other way that might prejudice the reader. In their *professional* work, which they consider a part of the communication system by which human beings maintain contact with the world around them, librarians maintain as high a degree of impartiality and neutrality as is humanly possible on substantive issues unrelated to librarianship and which are outside their professional field. It is the social responsibility of librarians to select library materials from all producers, from the whole world of published media, (not from any approved list), to build balanced collections representing all points of view on controversial issues, regardless of their personal convictions or moral beliefs. Librarians regard it as an abuse of their position to exclude or remove from libraries expressions of facts, theories, or opinions which present arguments against their personally cherished convictions. In their private, personal lives, librarians exercise their rights *as citizens* to play active roles as partisan proponents and supporters of social, political, or religious causes and organizations. Librarians are properly free to join the United Nations or SANE to support peace, to actively campaign for candidates for political office, to join environmental groups, or the National Association for the Advancement of Colored People, or the Daughters of the American Revolution.

(How much strife and loss of security of their jobs would be eliminated if every librarian were to follow the policy of the American Association of University Professors and that of the American Library Association, reminding his audience that he is speaking or acting *as a citizen* and not as a representative of his library or profession! No staff member should arrogate to himself the role of spokesman for his library as an institution.)

In contrast, operating under the concept of libraries as partisan advocates of various causes, librarians would probably reject the authority of the *government* to decide which are "approved" library materials and which are not. But librarians would consider it their social responsibility —*as librarians*—to make such decisions. The ALA would take partisan positions on substantive issues unrelated to librarianship and would decide which books should be in libraries and which should be banned. The publications in the aforementioned list of controversial publications would be judged as good or bad for the general public, and these and other titles would get a stamp of approval or of disapproval. ALA would take positions for "the guidance of librarians." It would be the official policy of the ALA to take such positions on nonlibrary issues in order to "educate the people." Libraries would be used by librarians as "instruments of social change" to further the convictions of librarians. Here we see even more clearly the "some things are right and some things are wrong" approach to building library collections.

To consider one specific kind of publication, it is not difficult to envision what would happen if ALA were to consider whether libraries should collect examples of the underground press. Some librarians would make the moral judgment that it is their social responsibility to ban extremist expressions from the Left which advocate the destruction of universities. Another group would feel just as strongly that they were obliged to ban extremist expressions from the Right which are "racist, anti-Semitic, or bigoted." A third group probably would hold that most of the underground press papers are biased, subjective, and propagandistic and should not be in publicly supported libraries anyway. The division of librarians over how to handle these publications would be unavoidable under the social responsibility concept of librarianship.

Under this concept of advocacy libraries and an advocacy ALA, not only would librarians be divided on nonlibrary issues, but the whole effort to preserve intellectual freedom would be without effect. Even if ALA were able to survive such unnecessary divisions, its credibility would be destroyed. If librarians use their institutions to "educate" the people as to what is true, good, or right, according to the moral value philosophy, limiting access to publications approved by librarians, then they invite every partisan individual and group in the community to try to ban what *each* finds objectionable. This concept of librarianship unnecessarily puts a weapon in the hands of any would-be censor who could then rationally justify his position by the argument that he is right and the library is wrong.

The defense of the principle of intellectual freedom for the users of libraries rests upon the concept of institutional neutrality. To reject this concept, as recommended by the social responsibility proponents, is to destroy the rationale behind the Library Bill of Rights. If this were to happen, the Committee on Intellectual Freedom and the Office for Intellectual Freedom would become inoperative and would disappear.

Whenever the Library Bill of Rights concept of librarianship is challenged, all librarians should be stimulated to reexamine ALA policies on intellectual freedom. Such reexamination is always desirable. Judith Krug and James Harvey of the ALA Office for Intellectual Freedom forcefully comment on this:

> Librarians must reexamine their own understanding of intellectual freedom as a concept separate from their individual beliefs about social, political, sexual, and religious matters. No matter how strong a librarian's personal commitment to a particular cause, it must not influence the decision to retain or remove materials from the library collection or intellectual freedom becomes merely a question of whose ox is gored.[14]

It is possible that some librarians who see themselves as generally opposed to censorship will be unable to view the principle of intellectual freedom as first in priority, and will sometimes rank another principle above it. When these librarians accept positions in *tax-supported* libraries they inevitably create for themselves an unresolved dilemma: in their selection and dissemination of library materials they must decide whether (1) to make accessible library materials presenting all sides on controversial issues, including items which they consider abhorrent, or (2) to reject the Library Bill of Rights concept and exclude from the library those views they consider harmful.

In a pluralistic society such as exists in the United States, it is legal and legitimate for privately supported libraries, controlled by those who pay for them, to operate on an authoritarian concept of the library's function in society. Groups of citizens who control such libraries may, if they choose to do so, put on the blinders of their choice and refuse to entertain ideas and expressions that they consider wrong or objectionable. They may recruit librarians of similar partisan persuasion, and order them to ban or remove certain publications from their library. They are free to reject the principle of intellectual freedom for themselves.

However, in the American society, which, by its Constitution forbids a state religion or a monolithic political organization, a *publicly supported* library cannot legally limit its information services to expressions of any party-line orthodoxy, whether that of librarians, the government, or any other segment of society.

It is also necessary for librarians to distinguish between a library's use of its resources to provide information about how citizens *themselves* may start a noninformation service—such as a day-care center, a reading-teaching program, an employment office, or training for a vocation—and promotion or funding of such services. Of course it is a proper use of library funds to supply information materials to be used by citizens in a day-care center program. But society has established many social welfare agencies. Libraries are established to provide *information services*. While *librarians* as citizens may legitimately promote creation of agencies for the alleviation of such needs, the urgency of these needs does not make them relevant to the purposes of libraries. Morris Philipson, Director of the University of Chicago Press, notes that it costs a university press about $15,000 to publish a single title. He comments:

> In a republic besieged by highminded and raucously vocal innocence, those who are ultimately responsible for the operation of a university may be unnerved by the thought that $15,000 would keep a Vietnamese village alive for one year, support cancer research, or operate a day care nursery. Should one publish *Keats and His Poetry* or *The Shape of Utopia* or *Bantu Bureaucracy* under these circumstances? No matter how painful to idealism, there is no contest. The trustees, the administration, the faculty, and the student body are not empowered to use their university's resources to save the world. They are charged with a mission to contribute to research and teaching. What they do here and now may come to make possible a better life for every family for the next 500 years.
>
> One may be appalled by gruesome social problems; but it would be worse to transform universities into agencies of social welfare than it would be to support academic scholarship and its public dissemination, because such a transformation eliminates the possibility of enhancing human life through systematic knowledge. But everything costs money; and those who are at the growing tip of something are necessarily out on a limb.[15]

Librarians have been able to unite in the effort to preserve free access to all points of view for all citizens under the Library Bill of Rights concept of libraries. It is to be hoped that they will continue to operate under this concept, and that they will find ways to meet the challenge of providing library and information services to the disadvantaged.

Although librarians have been able to unite in the support of the Library Bill of Rights, there are troublesome problems when they try to follow this ideal. One major problem arises when there is an apparent conflict between two principles of a democratic society. Does the constitutional prohibition against the establishment of a state religion justify the banning of media which criticize a religion? The New York City Public School administration argued that it did, and in 1948 and for the following fifteen years, the *Nation* magazine was banned from school libraries because it had published Paul Blanshard's allegedly anti-Catholic articles. To date the ALA has consistently held that when there is a conflict between other valued principles and the principles of intellectual freedom, professional librarians should place the latter in the highest priority and act in such a way as to preserve intellectual freedom for the users of libraries (*see* Case C in chapter 4).

Another difficulty for supporters of the Library Bill of Rights stems from a feature of the classic idea of intellecutal freedom of John Milton, frequently quoted by the Bill's defenders. This is the assumption that nature is governed by rigid laws to which all observed phenomena must conform. Since Darwin, Einstein, and especially since Heisenberg enunciated his principle of indeterminacy, natural scientists have not insisted upon the existence of such rigid laws. There seems to be an element of caprice in atomic behavior which is a part of the nature of things. The twentieth century view of the cosmos is not a

> rigid and immutable edifice where independent matter is housed in independent space and time; it is, on the contrary, an amorphous continuum, without any fixed architecture, plastic and variable, constantly subject to change and distortion.[16]

Although a library's refusal, under the Library Bill of Rights, to endorse the substantive ideas contained in any book may *seem* to suggest an indifference to the quality of books, films, or other media, this refusal to follow the authoritarian practice of giving an official stamp of approval to materials acquired does not indicate that librarians disregard the question of quality. Librarians have traditionally recognized their obligation to develop criteria and guidelines in a book selection policy designed for their particular communities and publics. However, the moral value philosophy of book selection promoted under the slogan "social responsibility" or the idea that "some things are right and some things are wrong" can only destroy intellectual freedom. If any librarian selects materials on the basis of whether the conclusions of the author agree with his own personal convictions, rather than on other criteria concerning the quality of the item, then, over a period of time, such a selection policy will result in an unbalanced, biased collection which violates the principle of "safeguarding the rights of library users to freedom of inquiry."

Summary

Under the Library Bill of Rights concept, all publicly supported libraries are expected to maintain balanced collections of facts and opinions and theories concerning all issues. Probably few except the very largest libraries manage to achieve this balance near the level of perfection, but this does not imply that the goal is unworthy and should be cast aside.

As the *idea* of a university held by society determines its nature, the *idea* of a library determines its operations. If librarians and the public were to accept the view that libraries *should* choose sides on current public issues, libraries would become "libraries of opinion," paralleling "journals of opinion." They could then no longer be expected to provide free access to all points of view, any more than does *Time* magazine or the *New Republic*. Librarians who hold strong convictions may be tempted to use their libraries to "educate the public." The concept of an advocacy library is antithetical to the concept of a library which provides information on all sides of all subjects for all citizens.

Probably the majority of American librarians still hold an idea of the ALA as a professional association, striving to promote better library services and to preserve intellectual freedom for library users. Probably the majority also still view a library as an impartial, neutral source of information, to be operated under the Library Bill of Rights concept.

But the possibility that the Library Bill of Rights concept of the library and of the ALA might be replaced by the advocacy concept poses a fundamental question for American librarians: Do the advantages of free access to all information, on all sides of all issues, for every citizen, outweigh the disadvantages? The answer that librarians give to this question will determine our future philosophy of librarianship.

8 ALA's Program to Defend Defenders of Intellectual Freedom

> The college or university teacher is a citizen, a member of a learned profession, and an officer of an educational institution. When he speaks or writes as a citizen, he should be free from institutional censorship or discipline, but his special position in the community imposes special obligations. As a man of learning and an educational officer, he should remember that the public may judge his profession and his institution by his utterances. Hence he should at all times be accurate, should exercise appropriate restraint, should show respect for the opinions of others, and should make every effort to indicate that he is not an institutonal spokesman.
>
> —FROM THE AAUP STATEMENT ON ACADEMIC FREEDOM, 1940[1]

Since 1939 when the American Library Association adopted the Library's Bill of Rights (which later evolved as the Library Bill of Rights), this organization has acted with steadily increasing effectiveness in educating its members and the public as to the nature of and significance of intellectual freedom. One index is the ever-increasing number of articles on the subject in the literature of librarianship. Another indication is the frequency with which the subject appears on the programs of state, national and regional library conferences. Since 1948, ALA inaugural addresses have emphasized the responsibility of librarians to preserve the freedom to read for all citizens. Librarians find it almost impossible to avoid thinking about these responsibilities.

ALA has reason to be proud of its long record of efforts to alert librarians and the friends of libraries to the importance of intellectual freedom. However, in the area of protecting the tenure of librarians generally, and especially those whose jobs were in jeopardy because they defended the freedom to read, until the 1970s ALA lacked the funds, the staff, and the necessary established rules of procedure by which it could be truly effective.

Naturally, the ALA looked at the policies and procedures of the American Association of University Professors as a model of how to protect job security of librarians who defended intellectual freedom. Since 1915, and especially since 1940, the AAUP has been very effective in protecting academic freedom. In 1946 ALA adopted a policy statement similar to that quoted above, linking intellectual freedom and tenure in the library profession, much as AAUP linked academic freedom and tenure in the academy.

As this 1946 ALA policy was later interpreted by some librarians, since it seemed to exclude from consideration all reasons for tenure other than intellectual freedom, the result was much misunderstanding and confusion about the definition of intellectual freedom and the nature of defense that ALA could provide. Many ALA members are not knowledgeable about AAUP policies, procedures, and practices. In addition, many librarians have misconceived its rationale and the nature of AAUP's influence upon universities.

The AAUP and the ALA policies explicitly stated that members of a library staff or a faculty may not presume to speak for their professions or their institutions. Some professionals in both fields have failed to, or have refused to see the significance of this point, and have put their own jobs and their institution's support in jeopardy by arrogating to themselves the role of spokesman for their library or college. When they do this they violate the policies of their professional organizations and forfeit the expectation that these organizations can come to their aid.

If and when a librarian arrogates to himself the right to speak for his institution on a substantive issue, he infringes upon the rights of all his colleagues, each of whom is entitled to hold his contrary personal conviction on a social or political issue. Neither the right-wing librarian nor the left-wing librarian—on the political-social continuum—has any right to commit his publicly supported library to a position on a controversial issue. The ultraconservative can work effectively alongside an extreme revolutionary—so long as both work on professional problems and observe the Library Bill of Rights. At the moment when either begins to speak for the library, attempting to use the institution as a propaganda instrument for his personal beliefs, the possibility of working in harmony with his colleagues ends.

There should be no political test of a librarian's right to work in a publicly supported library. No librarian should feel any coercion to conform to official positions imposed upon him by the chief librarian, the trustees, or his fellow workers. Under the United States Constitution, every citizen-librarian has the right to form his own private judgments on the issues of the day. If a *library* takes a position on any issue unrelated to librarianship, the librarian cannot conscientiously continue to work in the institution unless he agrees with the position. No professional librarian should thus be compelled to conform or to resign.

At least some of the incidents involving librarians who lost their jobs in the 1960s and 1970s could have been avoided if the AAUP policy quoted earlier had been understood and observed. When a librarian wishes to take his stand publicly on a local or national issue, he should preface any statement by explaining that he is speaking for himself only, not as a representative of the library or the library profession. With this simple precaution he can minimize the risks to his own job security and to future community support for his library.

The distinction between a librarian's personal intellectual freedom to act individually *as a citizen* and his professional obligation to maintain the neutrality of his publicly supported institution became blurred in the past decade. Some librarians insisted that they had the privilege of operating advocacy libraries and of making the ALA an instrument of propaganda for their personally cherished causes. The rejection of the principle of institutional neutrality thus handicapped the ALA's efforts to preserve free access to information. Many ALA members and many in the general public were willing to fight for intellectual freedom in libraries, to oppose attempts at censorship, but they were not willing to see their tax dollars used to propagate various causes through an advocacy library or a politicized library organization.

ALA members generally agree that a librarian is entitled to his personal views and should not fear the loss of his job because he expresses unpopular opinions, or engages in civil rights activities, or wears a beard. But the Library Bill of Rights was not created to protect the civil rights of librarians. The Committee on Intellectual Freedom was not established to protect the civil rights of librarians. Rather, as was explicitly stated in the original name of the committee, the purpose was to preserve free access to information for users of libraries. The original name, "The Committee on Intellectual Freedom to Safeguard the Rights of Library Users to Freedom of Inquiry," clarified the distinction between a citizen-librarian's civil rights and his professional responsibility to library users.

The AAUP provided an instructive model for librarians. However, many librarians hold misconceptions of what ALA could do for them in the way of "protection," failing to understand:

1. That AAUP has no legal authority, or any other authority by which it can order a college to give a professor back his job. Such "clout" as AAUP has depends only upon moral persuasion.
2. That AAUP, when it enters a case, aims at a fair settlement, rather than vengeance.
3. That AAUP does not implement its policies by hearing allegations of wrong doing on the floor of its national council. Complaints are made to its Committee A on Academic Freedom and Tenure, which strives to effect a settlement by mediation and arbitration. When these measures fail, an investigation of the facts, publication of a report, and in extreme cases, censure may be effective. It is recognized as a violation of due process to permit one-sided accusations on the floor of a council meeting.
4. That the sanctions of publication of a report or censure are not boycotts, for boycotts are illegal.

5. That AAUP has worked through a single committee which has had
    the authority to deal with any case of dismissal of a professor,
    whether academic freedom was involved or not, whereas, ALA has
    been, in the past, handicapped by what I call "jurisdictional fuzzi-
    ness."

To explain this fifth point, the source of much confusion, AAUP's Committee A has held jurisdiction over any case in which there is an allega-
tion that academic freedom was violated and *also* over any case in which
due process or fair employment practices were allegedly violated. Usually
it is not possible to determine precisely what happened without a lengthy
and costly investigation of the facts. AAUP, working through a single
committee, could investigate when necessary, without having other subagencies of AAUP claiming that the case fell within their jurisdictions.

In contrast, ALA, which has various subagencies and divisions, failed
to delegate to any one of these the authority necessary to pursue a complaint, until 1971, when Council created the Staff Committee on Mediation, Arbitration, and Inquiry, (SCMAI), to implement ALA's Program of Action. Librarians, looking to ALA (as an entity) for help,
could not be expected to understand how jurisdictional fuzziness delayed
or prevented action, and were naturally frustrated. As late as 1970, in
one case, three subagencies: the Committee on Intellectual Freedom, the
Committee on Tenure of the Library Administration Division, and the
Association of College and Research Libraries disputed over which had
jurisdiction. ALA, as a whole, was thus unable to act promptly and
effectively.

The inability to act produced frustrations, and it also produced a
tendency to misperceive what the Office for Intellectual Freedom could
and should do. Some librarians, finding no action for their defense forth-
coming from ALA, naturally tried to extend the concept of intellectual
freedom beyond its logical limits and viewed every case of dismissal as
an intellectual freedom case. In some cases intellectual freedom and the
Library Bill of Rights *were* involved, and in others they were *not*, but
until one agency was delegated the authority to investigate the facts in
a case, no one could determine the precise factors which led to dismissal.
We may feel that support should be provided for a librarian who is fired
because he exercised his rights as a citizen, for example, for expressing
unpopular opinions, or for engaging in civil rights demonstrations, or
for wearing a beard, but these civil rights of the librarian are not necessarily related to intellectual freedom or the Library Bill of Rights. They
do not derive from ALA at all; they are guaranteed to all citizens, including librarians, by the U.S. Constitution and the Bill of Rights and
may be preserved through the legal system and law enforcement system
of our society.

ALA's failure to resolve the question of jurisdiction helped to produce
confusion about the distinction between a) a librarian's personal intel-

lectual freedom to act politically as a citizen; and b) his responsibility to preserve free access to information on all sides of a controversy in a publicly supported library. The failure to make this distinction could become the reef on which the ALA will be destroyed and on which public libraries will break and sink. Likewise, if academic librarians cannot learn to make this distinction, free, honest scholarship and access to its findings in our colleges may be destroyed.

Unfortunately, ALA officers and councilors hold office for brief periods and frequently have insufficient knowledge of the existence of past policies. Far too often ALA's Council adopts a new policy which overlaps or negates other existing policies. Almost never do Councilors give sufficient attention to the question raised in chapter 7: Is the proposal in conflict with federal or state laws or constitutions or with any existing ALA policies? The inevitable result is that many policies on intellectual freedom conflict with others, since almost never are any policies rescinded.

In 1974 the Committee on Intellectual Freedom attempted to substitute a new, more comprehensive policy regarding job security for the 1946 ALA Statement of Principles of Intellectual Freedom and Tenure for Librarians. This required rescission of the 1946 policy, and the Committee now consciously tries to consider which old policies should be rescinded if new ones are to be adopted.

The AAUP model has been useful. Some seven hundred incidents per year are referred to its Committee A on Academic Freedom and Tenure which settles most of its cases by telephone and correspondence. AAUP's objective is always a fair settlement, rather than vengeance. A published report of the facts is one form of sanction that often brings settlement. Censure, a listing of a college which does not meet AAUP standards on academic freedom has been effective, though it is not a boycott. Professors are not urged to refuse employment in censured colleges, for a boycott is illegal. They *are* urged to inquire of AAUP to get up-to-date information as to the state of academic freedom in a college on the censured list. Similarly, librarians are now encouraged to inquire of the Staff Committee on Mediation, Arbitration, and Inquiry about a library in which they seek a job.

Librarians also should consider the following statement by Bertram Davis, General Secretary of the AAUP:

> It is an ironic consequence of the AAUP's work in academic freedom and tenure that the academic profession is more familiar with the Association's apparent failures than with its real successes. The Association, in fact, takes great pains to publicize its most significant failures. The publication in the *AAUP Bulletin* of an investigating committee's report is with rare exceptions a climactic moment in a drama of quiet but persistent confrontation during which the Association, without success, has sought the observance of its principles and the resolution of a difficulty which that observance implies.[2]

The AAUP supports its policies and its Committee A on Academic Freedom and Tenure with a Headquarters staff of fifteen. ALA, before 1967, had neither staff nor funds to deal with like problems of intellectual freedom and tenure; however, in 1967, ALA did create a new department, the Office for Intellectual Freedom, supported by a modest budget and employing a staff to implement ALA policies. Finally, in June 1971, at the Dallas conference, ALA established its Staff Committee on Mediation, Arbitration, and Inquiry, based upon the AAUP model. This committee (SCMAI) has jurisdiction over *all* cases in which it is alleged that the Library Bill of Rights has been violated, or, in which, for whatever reason, a librarian has been dismissed. The complainant is no longer tempted to claim that his intellectual freedom has been violated in order to get attention from ALA. Jurisdictional fuzziness no longer prevents action. All members are assured that a Request for Action will be given consideration, with careful attention to due process.

It would be unrealistic to assume that all professors and all librarians understand the necessity for due process,[3] and often professionals who feel that they have been dismissed without cause attempt to evade established procedures. ALA, like AAUP, has followed the adversary hearing principle of Anglo-American law, under which due process includes the following: statement of charges followed by opportunity for a fair hearing; the right of counsel, if desired; the right to present evidence and to cross-examine; a decision based on the record of the hearing; and the right to appeal a dismissal judgment.

The AAUP has shown that due process is critical in the protection of academic freedom and tenure. But librarians who have been dismissed, in the heat of indignation against what they perceive as unfair treatment, may be tempted to ignore established procedures and demand the floor of an ALA membership or Council assembly to make accusations, with no possibility of rebuttal; thus, in turn, violating the concept of due process as defined by ALA. ALA, if it is to maintain its own integrity, may not violate its own established procedures by permitting one-sided presentations of allegations against a library administration or library trustees on the floor of an assembly at an ALA conference. Demands for instant justice should never be permitted to stampede the ALA into actions or judgments which are themselves unjust to some parties.

Due process is basically a system of procedures designed to produce the best possible judgments in those personnel problems which may yield a serious adverse decision about a librarian. A clear, orderly, fair way of making a decision is the objective.

ALA established its procedures which may be used to assure due process when it adopted the ALA Program of Action. It is one part of the due process concept that a complaint by a librarian who believes that he or she has been dismissed without cause shall be assigned to the Staff Committee on Mediation, Arbitration, and Inquiry. The ALA officer presiding over a Council meeting cannot permit the Council, ALA's *legislative assembly*, to be used as a tribunal. If Council or any other subagency of ALA is tempted to usurp the authority given to SCMAI, claiming jurisdiction over complaints, the whole jurisdictional fuzziness previously described would begin all over again.[4]

The Council of ALA, its legislative, policy-making body, has as its function the final decision-making on policies recommended to it by ALA's committees. By its size, its intended function, and its time limitations, Council could never act effectively as a tribunal to hear all arguments by those who allege that they have been dismissed without cause, and all contrary arguments by library administrators or trustees who are accused by complainants. For Council to permit complainants to present their accusations before Council would be to violate every requirement in the concept of due process, as defined by ALA and by AAUP.

Yet, in June 1971, Council violated its own established procedures by permitting complaints against the Library of Congress to be presented before it. Again, in 1973, librarians dismissed from the University of Chicago were permitted to present their case, in a one-sided fashion, without all the requirements of due process required in a fair, adversary hearing. In this instance, Council did finally follow its own ALA established procedures, referring the case to SCMAI.

Again, in January 1974, some members of ALA and of the library press demanded that the University of Chicago librarians be permitted to argue their case before Council. This time Council recognized clearly that this was not its legitimate role, and, appropriately, due process was observed, and the complainants were not given the floor to present their arguments. Council acted wisely in refusing to play the role of a tribunal by recognizing that SCMAI had been assigned responsibility for investigating charges, and, when necessary, for conducting a fair hearing. Some librarians, failing to understand the significance of due process, charged ALA's officers and Council with having violated the intellectual freedom of librarians dismissed from the University of Chicago, claiming that they should have been given the floor of Council to argue their cases. It is to be hoped that, regardless of vituperative attacks upon Councilors who refuse to usurp the functions of SCMAI, Council will never again violate its own established procedures.

Naturally, the Chicago librarians were dissatisfied with the report given by SCMAI, to the effect that because the case was in litigation before the National Labor Relations Board, SCMAI could take no action. That dissatisfaction stems from a misconception of what is legally possible for ALA, and a failure to comprehend the significance of the item in the Program of Action which states that, except in extraordinary circumstances, no formal inquiry will be made into cases which are in litigation. Council has the obligation to resist all demands that it permit one-sided presentations of accusations against employers.

There is another important aspect of such cases, closely akin to the conflict usually termed "Fair Trial vs. Free Press." As noted in the essay on theories of the press, many of us tend to form judgments on the basis of limited and biased press reports and editorials. All readers of the news have an obligation to suspend judgment about an alleged violation of the Library Bill of Rights or an alleged firing without cause until adequate evidence has been produced. It is essential that librarians shall distinguish between *allegations* and *proof,* between the legitimate role played by inquiring reporters who bring facts to the surface that justify a trial, as in the Watergate case, and the role of an advocacy press which insists upon being investigator, judge, and jury. When to this kind of mixing of facts and value judgments by the press is added the prevalent human tendency to decide the guilt or innocence of the accused merely on the basis of that part of the evidence which they have happened to see in press or TV reports, the likelihood of justice is further reduced. (*See* Appendix B for statements illustrating the issue of free press and fair trial).

It is to be hoped that ALA will develop a reputation for integrity and a "clout" similar to that of the AAUP. If this is to be developed, ALA cannot afford to flout its own due process. ALA may not even *consider* censure of a library administration until there has been a full investigation of the facts in the case by SCMAI. To act responsibly, ALA's Council must refer complainants to SCMAI.

When SCMAI receives a Request for Action, alleging that the Library Bill of Rights has been violated, or that a librarian has been dismissed without cause, SCMAI must determine the facts in the case. In the case of a dismissal, was intellectual freedom an issue? Or were unfair employment practices or discrimination present? Did restrictions on the library's acquisitions program result in a lack of information on some sides of a substantive issue? Or, even though there is a wide range of materials on a subject in the library, did the librarian withhold some of the information from the library user? Determination of the answers to such questions is the responsibility of SCMAI.

In some instances SCMAI may be handicapped by a lack of funds, for such investigations are costly; the investigation of the facts in the Bodger case in Missouri cost about $2500 for expenses only. That investigation was carried out with proper care and deliberation by a team appointed by the Committee on Intellectual Freedom, and it was completed within six months. This was relatively prompt action, when viewed in perspective against the twenty-three months taken to investigate major cases by the American Association of University Professors.

ALA's first attempt to follow the AAUP model by conducting a full investigation occurred in 1969–1970. The report on the Bodger case was the first such documented report ever drafted or published. It is therefore, a "landmark" case which can and should serve as a model for future investigations. This report is presented in full in Appendix A, but a brief analysis of its significance may be instructive.

On December 7, 1969, the Office for Intellectual Freedom received a Request for Action from Mrs. Joan Bodger, formerly a children's consultant for the Missouri State Library. She alleged that the Missouri State Library, the Missouri State Library Commission, and the University of Missouri had violated various propositions of the Library Bill of Rights. Preliminary inquiries by the OIF resulted in a conclusion that there existed a possibility that the LBR had been violated. In April 1970, a team was sent to Missouri to conduct a fact-finding investigation. The extensively documented report of the facts was presented to the Committee on Intellectual Freedom in May, and to the Executive Board of ALA in June, with the recommendation that the report be published in the July-August (1970) issue of *American Libraries* as one form of sanction.

Some ALA members undoubtedly felt that mere publication of this report was not a sufficiently severe penalty. However, when the Committee on Intellectual Freedom considered appropriate action, it had to face the fact that, although it had established a policy on sanctions, it had not as yet recommended an essential part of procedures under due process; that is, it had not yet established a mechanism by which a censured administration could act to correct its practices and appeal for the removal of censure. The CIF therefore recommended only publication of the report, recognizing that this is a milder form of sanction than censure. In 1971, at the Dallas conference, procedures for the removal of censure were adopted.

With the publication of the CIF report on the Bodger case, librarians for the first time could see how the ALA procedures, based upon the AAUP model, could be operative in achieving a fair settlement of a case. It also demonstrated that librarians should recognize that stories in the library press and stories in local newspapers could be quite contradictory, resulting in very different pictures of a situation in the minds of readers. The fully documented Bodger Report presents all the evidence found by the investigating team, showing why the team, and later the Committee on Intellectual Freedom, concluded that Mrs. Bodger had courageously defended the principles of intellectual freedom.

By mounting such investigations, ALA can be assured of publicity that will contribute to its educational program on behalf of intellectual freedom. Surely Missourians learned about intellectual freedom through their local newspapers. ALA members have reason for new assurance that there are policies on intellectual freedom and tenure, that there is a staff at ALA Headquarters to implement these policies, and that due process will be observed.

This does not mean, of course, that current policies and procedures are necessarily perfect and will bring about "justice" or "fair settlement." No doubt SCMAI will, in the future, refine and improve its operations.

Also, library boards and the general public may be relatively unimpressed with such reports or even by ALA censure. As yet, it is still too early to predict the "clout" that ALA may develop; already there are indications that library trustees and administrations will try to avoid sanctions by ALA, and in time ALA's influence may even approach that of the AAUP. For illustration, this excerpt from a news item which appeared in the New York *Times* of July 17, 1969, may indicate the clout that ALA could develop in a similar situation:

> The college spokesman said that . . . the President of the College had previously agreed to support whatever the American Association of University Professors recommended in the . . . case and would resign if the board of trustees did not go along with the recommendations.[5]

Even if ALA continues to act responsibly, observing due process, conducting impartial fact-finding investigations, refusing to permit the press or complainants to use the floor of Council or membership meetings to influence ALA action, it must be remembered that ALA, like the AAUP, has no legal authority to order a library to restore a librarian to his position. Neither organization has any weapon for enforcement of its judgments other than moral persuasion.

There is a major distinction between moral persuasion, considerable though it has become in the case of the AAUP, and a court decision backed up by law enforcement officers. A college or a library *may* be influenced to restore a professor's or a librarian's position by publication of a report or by censure. When a *court of law* decides that an institution must rehire an employee who has been dismissed without due cause, that institution has no choice but to obey. This distinction is especially important, for it is very natural for a professor or librarian who has been dismissed to feel that, somehow—he may not know precisely how, but somehow—his professional organization should "support" him.

Another source of frustration is the failure to note that, under the guidelines of the ALA's Program for Action, a librarian who feels that he has been fired without cause should seek ALA's help *before* he goes to court. By its policy ALA will seldom be able to spend its limited resources for a full-scale investigation of the facts *after* the case has been put into litigation. The Program of Action states that no formal inquiry shall be made into cases which are in the process of local hearings, except in extraordinary circumstances and that no formal inquiry will be made into cases which are in litigation. One reason for this policy is that, once the case has gone into a court, attorneys on both sides have full responsibility, and as has already happened in one case, counsel may not wish ALA's help in any way. Also, as a mediator, acting *before* litigation, ALA may, before or after SCMAI's investigation and recommendation, help to effect a settlement out of court, but once the courts have been involved, ALA's influence upon a library administration is greatly reduced. After a court has *acted,* ALA's influence is nil.

It should also be noted that, under the Program of Action, complaints may be withdrawn by the complainant at any time prior to the institution of formal action, but not thereafter. When SCMAI determines that a just and equitable resolution of the problem cannot be reached through arbitration and/or mediation and that the matter warrants a formal inquiry, the Committee notifies the complainant and informs him that he has ten days to withdraw his Request for Action.

In summary, when a librarian loses his job or feels that it is in jeopardy, the first step is to write or telephone to the Office for Intellectual Freedom for advice. This office has proved itself to be effective in its first two or three years, although like the AAUP staff that serves Committee A, its unheralded, unpublicized, successful efforts at mediation tend to be obscured by difficult cases that receive more publicity.

Librarians should not expect that ALA can necessarily get their jobs back for them. It is also possible that, in some instances, investigation will result in a conclusion that the librarian *should* have been fired.

The kinds of "support" that ALA can provide for librarians are much more clearly delineated than before 1971, but "support" is an ambiguous term. Some resolutions declaring ALA's support are of doubtful value. But if SCMAI makes preliminary inquiries as a result of a Request for Action, if it then conducts a successful mediation process, resulting in a reasonably fair settlement out of court, this is one valuable kind of support. (Of course, such a result may not satisfy those for whom vengeance is the chief objective.) At the next level, if SCMAI's investigation of the facts results in publication of a fully documented report, this adds to the leverage toward fair settlement out of court, which is another form of support. In cases which result in censure, the strongest penalty available to a professional organization (but enforceable only through moral persuasion), another form of support has been made available. Still other forms of support, such as limited financial aid for legal defense, may be available through the Freedom to Read Foundation. Personal, financial hardship may be reduced through grants from the LeRoy C. Merritt Humanitarian Fund.

These various kinds of support are relatively new, and they may grow or they may die because of lack of funds. But ALA now has the policies, the procedures, the staff, and the centralization of authority and responsibility that can be counted on for more effective support of librarians who defend the principles of intellectual freedom.

A   The Bodger Report: A Landmark Case for ALA

PROCEEDINGS AND FINDINGS

Pertaining to a Request for Action Submitted by Mrs. Joan Bodger Under the Program of Action in Support of the Library Bill of Rights.

Reproduced from *American Libraries* 1, no. 7: 694–704 (July-Aug., 1970).

Findings

ON DECEMBER 7, 1969, the Office for Intellectual Freedom received a Request for Action under the *Program of Action in Support of the Library Bill of Rights* from Mrs. Joan Bodger, formerly children's consultant for the Missouri State Library. In her Request for Action Mrs. Bodger alleged that the Missouri State Library, the Missouri State Library Commission, and the University of Missouri violated various propositions of the *Library Bill of Rights*.[1] Mrs. Bodger also alleged that members of the State Library Commission, members of the administrative staff of the State Library, and units of the Missouri Library Association failed to support her actions in opposition to the alleged violations of the *Library Bill of Rights*.[2]

The Office for Intellectual Freedom staff reviewed Mrs. Bodger's complaint and concluded that, on the face of the complaint, there existed a possibility that propositions of the *Library Bill of Rights* had been violated in the situation described by Mrs. Bodger. On the basis of this finding it was recommended to Edwin Castagna, chairman of the Intellectual Freedom Committee, that the Committee accept Mrs. Bodger's Request for Action, and that it address itself to those charges involving possible violations of the *Library Bill of Rights*.

On December 22, 1969, Mr. Castagna appointed a Fact-Finding Subcommittee consisting of Homer Fletcher, Edwin Castagna, and Alex Allain, chairman, to implement Mrs. Bodger's Request for Action. Mr. Fletcher, for personal reasons, resigned from the Fact-Finding Subcommittee and was replaced by Florence DeHart.

Mrs. Bodger's Request for Action was included on the Intellectual Free-

139

dom Committee's agenda at the Midwinter Meeting, January 1970 (Chicago). Concurrent with its study of the request, the Committee notified the Missouri Library Commission of receipt of the Request for Action and of the formation of the Fact-Finding Subcommittee.[3]

On February 27, 1970, Mr. Allain requested by mail specific information in regard to Mrs. Bodger's departure from the Missouri State Library from the principal parties noted in Mrs. Bodger's Request for Action.[4]

The Fact-Finding Subcommittee met with the staff of the Office for Intellectual Freedom and ALA legal counsel, William North, on April 6, 1970, at ALA Headquarters. Mr. Castagna was unable to attend this meeting. The Subcommittee established tentative procedures to be followed in regard to acting upon Mrs. Bodger's request.[5]

On April 14 Mrs. Krug, on behalf of Mr. Allain, notified by mail the persons with whom the Subcommittee wished to speak regarding Mrs. Bodger's departure from the Missouri State Library. Members of the State Library Commission at the time of Mrs. Bodger's departure, the state librarian, the associate state librarian, the immediate past-president of the Missouri Library Association, and the current president of the Missouri Library Association were so notified.[6]

Eight other persons expressed to the Office for Intellectual Freedom their desire to offer statements regarding Mrs. Bodger's dismissal from the Missouri State Library. The Subcommittee agreed to accept first-hand information from them, and they were so notified by Mrs. Krug on behalf of Mr. Allain.

James Leathers, president of the Missouri Library Association, served as liaison between the Subcommittee and the persons with whom it wished to speak. Mr. Leathers arranged for interview rooms and scheduled times with those persons who agreed to meet with the Subcommittee.

Mrs. Jerome Duggan, Mrs. Frank Steury, Hubert Wheeler, and Rabbi Ferdinand M. Isserman (all members of the State Library Commission at the time of Mrs. Bodger's departure) for various reasons declined the Subcommittee's invitation to meet with it. John Herbst, past president of MLA, accepted the invitation but was unable to be scheduled due to a conflicting commitment.[7] Doris Bolef and Elsie Freivogel jointly submitted a written statement to the Subcommittee but did not appear before it.[8]

On Monday, April 27, 1970, the Fact-Finding Subcommittee met in the St. Louis County Public Library with Mrs. Susanna Alexander,[9] Mrs. Nina Ladof,[10] Mrs. Helen Kreigh,[11] and Mrs. Rosetta Bullard.[12]

On Tuesday, April 28, 1970, the Fact-Finding Subcommittee met in the Missouri Library Association Headquarters in Columbia with Charles O'Halloran,[13] Mrs. Bernadine Hoduski,[14] James Leathers,[15] and Mrs. Joan Goddard.[16]

On Wednesday, April 29, 1970, the Fact-Finding Subcommittee met in the Missouri Library Association Headquarters in Columbia with Ralph Parker,[17] Judge Temple Morgett,[18] and William DeJohn.[19]

Transcripts of the interviews with the above persons are confidential and are on file in the ALA Office for Intellectual Freedom.

As a result of its study of Mrs. Bodger's complaint and the interviews with the persons named above, the Fact-Finding Subcommittee has established the following events pertinent to the departure of Mrs. Bodger:

1. On February 12, 1969, members of the Students for a Democratic Society (SDS) distributed copies of *New Left Notes*, January 22, 1969, and *The Movement*, February 1969, from a booth in the University of Missouri Student

Union. Dean of Students, Jack Matthews, ordered the SDS salesmen to stop distribution of the papers which he termed "vulgar literature."

On February 19 the *Free Press Underground*—published by University of Missouri students, some of whom were SDS members—carried a cartoon from *New Left Notes* and an article from *The Movement.* The *Free Press Underground* termed these items "obscene" in additional commentary. Campus police ordered the *Free Press Underground* salesmen off the University of Missouri campus. The salesmen left the campus and began selling the newspaper on a public sidewalk adjacent to the campus. County sheriffs arrested four of the *Free Press Underground* salesmen and seized the papers.[20]

2. Over the weekend of February 22–23, Mrs. Joan Bodger, children's consultant at the Missouri State Library, drafted a letter in which she condemned what she believed was an act of censorship by the University of Missouri in regard to the removal of *New Left Notes, The Movement,* and the *Free Press Underground,* and the arrest of the students. Her intention was to publish the letter in a local newspaper, the *Columbia Tribune.*[21]

On Monday, February 24, before sending the letter to the newspaper, Mrs. Bodger showed its contents to her immediate superior, Mrs. Susanna Alexander, associate state librarian. Mrs. Alexander agreed with the content of the letter, but she suggested that Charles O'Halloran, state librarian, read the letter before Mrs. Bodger mailed it. Mrs. Alexander called Mr. O'Halloran, who was in Kansas City, and read the letter to him over the telephone. Mr. O'Halloran telephoned Mrs. Bodger and approved the publication of the letter.[22]

Both Mr. O'Halloran and Mrs. Alexander considered Mrs. Bodger's letter to be an appropriate statement of the State Library's position in regard to the removal of publications from the University of Missouri campus.[23]

Mrs. Bodger then typed the letter on stationery bearing the State Library letterhead, and signed it with her official title.

3. On February 26, 1969, Mrs. Bodger's letter was published in the *Columbia Tribune.* Following its publication, other Missouri newspapers printed editorials and letters to the editors condemning Mrs. Bodger, Mr. O'Halloran, and Mrs. Alexander. The president of the State Library Commission and the governor of Missouri received letters and telephone calls attacking Mrs. Bodger and the State Library.[24]

4. In response to the controversy, on March 11, 1969, the State Library Commission met for five hours in executive session. Present at the meeting were Rabbi Ferdinand Isserman, Judge Temple Morgett, Ralph H. Parker, Mrs. Frank Steury, Hubert Wheeler, and Mrs. Jerome Duggan, president. Mr. O'Halloran, state librarian and secretary of the Library Commission, was present for part of the meeting but was requested to withdraw when the Commission turned its attention to the incident involving Mrs. Bodger's letter.[25]

At this meeting, Mr. O'Halloran submitted to the Commission a statement defending Mrs. Bodger's actions and explaining the principles of intellectual freedom as enunciated in the *Library Bill of Rights.*[26]

Stating that "there is further information which we desire to obtain before we make any decision," the Commission adjourned and scheduled another meeting for Thursday, March 20, 1969.[27]

5. On March 20, 1969, the State Library Commission met for five hours in executive session. "All Commission members were present."[28]

Mr. O'Halloran submitted to the Commission a second statement in which he outlined the basic issues involved in the incident concerning Mrs. Bodger's letter. In this statement, he made comments which were later taken out of context by the Commission and used in the Commission's official statement to the public.²⁹ Members of the Commission considered the official statement to be a "gentle slap on the wrists" of Mr. O'Halloran.³⁰

6. After the March 20 meeting of the State Library Commission, Mr. O'Halloran requested that all State Library staff members refrain from publicly commenting on the incident involving Mrs. Bodger's letter and the *Free Press Underground*.³¹

7. On April 3, 1969, Mrs. Bodger appeared as a speaker at the Library Aide's Workshop at the St. Charles County Library Branch in O'Fallon. Approximately thirty-five persons, some representing an organization called Society to Oppose Pornography (STOP), picketed the library branch. The picket signs attacked Mrs. Bodger, Mr. O'Halloran, and others involved in the *Free Press Underground* incident.³² William Orthwein, a reporter from the St. Louis *Globe-Democrat*, attempted several times to question Mrs. Bodger. Mrs. Bodger explained that she had been asked not to speak about the incident. When Mr. Orthwein persisted in his questioning, Mrs. Bodger said she was bored with his repeated questions. Mr. Orthwein's newspaper later reported that Mrs. Bodger said she was bored with the whole incident.³³

8. On Friday, April 4, 1969, Mrs. Jerome Duggan, president of the State Library Commission, contacted Mr. O'Halloran and spoke about the adverse publicity to the State Library which Mrs. Bodger's appearances attracted.³⁴ Mr. O'Halloran told Mrs. Bodger the same day that it would be desirable for her to cancel future workshops until public reaction died down. He suggested a "cooling off" period.³⁵

9. After considering Mr. O'Halloran's advice, Mrs. Bodger decided that to curtail her activities would render her work as children's consultant ineffective. Between Friday, April 4, and Monday, April 7, she decided to resign from the State Library.³⁶ Mrs. Bodger wrote her resignation letter and made multiple copies to distribute to the staff and to submit to the news media.³⁷ Mrs. Bodger submitted her letter of resignation to Mr. O'Halloran on Monday, April 7, 1969.

10. Mr. O'Halloran felt that the State Library Commission should have the opportunity to read the letter of resignation before it appeared in the newspapers. He telephoned Mrs. Jerome Duggan and read the letter to her.³⁸ Mrs. Duggan unilaterally decided that the state librarian should not accept the resignation.³⁹ Mrs. Duggan ordered the state librarian, in his capacity as secretary of the State Library Commission, to write a letter which she dictated to him over the telephone. The letter dismissed Mrs. Bodger from the State Library.⁴⁰

Mrs. Duggan directed Mr. O'Halloran to *poll by telephone* the members of the State Library Commission on the question of Mrs. Bodger's dismissal. Following her directions, Mr. O'Halloran attempted to contact each Commission member. Judge Temple Morgett voted in favor of dismissal. One other unidentified commissioner voted in favor of dismissal. Mr. O'Halloran states that he was unable to reach the other members of the Commission.⁴¹ (Ralph Parker was not contacted and did not vote on the question.⁴²)

Mr. O'Halloran reported the results of the telephone poll to Mrs. Duggan. Mrs. Duggan decided that there was a majority in favor of dismissal.⁴³ (Mr. O'Halloran stated that Rabbi Isserman had resigned from the Commission prior to the telephone poll.⁴⁴)

11. On Tuesday, April 8, 1969, Mr. O'Halloran gave Mrs. Bodger the letter of dismissal.⁴⁵

12. On April 8, Mrs. Bodger protested her dismissal to Mr. O'Halloran and requested to speak to Mrs. Duggan. Mr. O'Halloran telephoned Mrs. Duggan and gave the telephone to Mrs. Bodger. Mrs. Bodger repeated several times to Mrs. Duggan that she had already resigned, but Mrs. Duggan refused to reply in any way. Mrs. Bodger said, approximately, "She doesn't have the guts or the courage to even speak to me."[46]

13. Mr. O'Halloran immediately announced his action to the other members of the State Library staff.[47]

14. The Missouri Library Association met in Conference on October 1–4, 1969. A printed statement, initiated by members of the Missouri Social Responsibilities Round Table, with over twenty signatures, was presented to the Missouri State Library Commission.[48]

The statement said: "We are not interested in placing blame, but only in acquiring fact. We feel that there are basic relationships between a librarian and his board of trustees involved here and it is important that they be discussed." The petition further requested that the Commission make public the minutes from its meetings concerning Mrs. Bodger because it would assist "in informing Missouri citizens of Commission policies."[49]

Mrs. Jerome Duggan asked that Dr. Parker be allowed to answer the petition.[50] In Dr. Parker's answer, he made the following statement:

The case of Joan Bodger had nothing whatsoever to do with the matters of censorship. . . . Mrs. Bodger had every right as an individual citizen to express her opinions. There was never any question of that. . . . Mrs. Bodger then drafted a letter of resignation and I'm a little confused here on the exact sequence of events; but instead of simply being willing to turn in a letter of resignation and let it go through normal channels, she felt called upon to call up Mrs. Duggan. . . . Mrs. Duggan said nothing. *But she was harangued with*

foul and filthy language the result of which was that the Commission voted not to accept her resignation, but terminated her services. . . .[51]

On April 29, 1970, Dr. Parker told the Fact-Finding Subcommittee that he was speaking on behalf of the Commission when he addressed the MLA Conference, and that his statement was impromptu.[52] Judge Temple Morgett, the current president of the Commission, contradicted Dr. Parker's statement. Judge Morgett stated that the Commission endorsed Dr. Parker's statement except for references to a phone call between Mrs. Bodger and Mrs. Duggan.[53]

Commentary on Facts

Regarding Mrs. Joan Bodger

In the opinion of the Fact-Finding Subcommittee, the letter written by Mrs. Joan Bodger to the *Columbia Tribune* clearly enunciates a responsible librarian's professional concern for the repression of and lack of accessibility to controversial materials. In making this observation, the Subcommittee is in agreement with Mr. O'Halloran and Mrs. Alexander.

On the question of Mrs. Bodger's authorization to write the letter, the facts are clear. Her act was submitted to her immediate superior, Mrs. Alexander, and to the state librarian, Mr. O'Halloran. Both approved of the letter and consented to its publication.[54]

The State Library has no policy governing the use of stationery bearing the State Library letterhead. Neither the State Library Commission nor the state librarian has ever enacted such a policy. Since the state librarian and the associate state librarian were aware that Mrs. Bodger spoke as children's consultant, it appears that they considered her use of State Library stationery to be within the scope of unwritten policy.

The State Library Commission and newspaper editorials, notably one in the Jefferson City *Post-Tribune*,[55] have stated that Mrs. Bodger's injection of the State Library into matters completely the concern and responsibility of the administration of the University of Missouri was rash, impetuous, and impertinent. Even a casual reading of Mrs. Bodger's letter to the *Tribune* makes clear that this aspect of her arguments is greatly overshadowed by the larger issues involving intellectual freedom, censorship, and the accessibility to controversial materials. It should be noted that almost all of the public responses to the letter referred to Mrs. Bodger's espousal of "obscene literature," not to the intrusion of the State Library into the affairs of the University of Missouri. The intrusion issue only became a cause of concern after the State Library Commission introduced the issue into public debate in a statement for general release after its March 20, 1969, meeting.[56]

If, in fact, Mrs. Bodger's letter constituted an intrusion of one state agency into the affairs of another, thus breaking established policy, she cleared herself of responsibility for the act by submitting the letter to the state librarian before publication.

It has also been stated that Mrs. Bodger was not dismissed because of the content of her letter to the *Tribune*, but because of objectionable criticism of the State Library Commission's policies contained in her letter of resignation, April 7, 1969. A comparison of the letter to the *Tribune* and the letter of resignation shows that the content is substantively similar.[57] Mrs. Bodger, however, did insist upon publishing her letter of resignation. The Subcommittee feels that her insistence, more than the content of the letter of resignation, may have precipitated the actions of the president of the Commission. Certainly her insistence upon publication was a major factor in Mr. O'Halloran's decision to contact Mrs. Duggan.

It has also been stated that Mrs. Bodger was dismissed because of the content of a telephone conversation between Mrs. Bodger and the past president of the Library Commission, Mrs. Jerome Duggan. Facts established by the Subcommittee clearly show that the reported conversation occurred *after* Mrs. Bodger was notified of her dismissal.[58] The testimony of Mrs. Bodger and a witness to her side of the reported telephone conversation also establishes that her statements to Mrs. Duggan were not "foul and filthy," as stated by Dr. Ralph Parker at the MLA Conference in October 1969.[59]

In assessing Mrs. Bodger's letter to the *Tribune* and the events leading to her dismissal, the Fact-Finding Subcommittee concludes that:

1. The supposed intrusion of one state agency into the affairs of another does not compare in any measure with the significant, basic issues raised by Mrs. Bodger in regard to suppression of materials.

2. If, in fact, Mrs. Bodger's act constituted an intrusion of one state agency into the affairs of another, the responsibility for the consequences of this act should not have fallen upon Mrs. Bodger, who clearly had the authorization of the state librarian to write the letter.

3. Mrs. Bodger's insistence upon publishing her letter of resignation was the probable cause of its referral to Mrs. Duggan.

4. Mrs. Bodger, in defending the issues of intellectual freedom which were under attack, took a stand which the Intellectual Freedom Committee and the American Library Association have long espoused.

Regarding Mr. Charles O'Halloran

It has been stated that Mr. O'Halloran exercised poor judgment when he approved Mrs. Bodger's letter to the *Tribune* and allowed its publication over her official title. The Fact-Finding Subcommittee does not agree that Mr. O'Halloran's approval of the letter was an incident of "poor judgment." Only if the Subcommittee viewed the "intrusion" factor as more important than the suppression of materials could it agree with the Commission.[60] Mr. O'Halloran, however, has indicated in a public statement that "her letter represented her own, and my, protest at an act of censorship. . . . It was our belief that censorship or the suppression of any publication should be challenged whenever it occurs."[61]

The Subcommittee recognizes that, perhaps, a method of protest other than publication of a letter might have been more effective and avoided adverse publicity. Alternative methods might have included direct communication, discussion, or mediation with University officials and students. The Subcommittee, however, cannot accept as fact that such a protest—whether in the form of a letter to the press or a direct communication with University officials—constitutes an intrusion of one state agency into the affairs of another.

The State Library Commission says it did not consider the censorship question.[62] Its only concern was the "intrusion" element.[63] In that respect, the Commission concluded that Mr. O'Halloran had exercised poor judgment and publicly censured him for it.[64]

Mrs. Bodger, some librarians, and the library press have charged that Mr. O'Halloran, under pressure from the Commission, withdrew his support of Mrs. Bodger. These charges, in the view of the Subcommittee, seem to arise from public misinterpretation of statements made by Mr. O'Halloran to the press and to the State Library Commission. The statement most widely misinterpreted was issued to the State Library Commission at its meeting March 20, 1969: ". . . Intrusion of the State Library into a matter completely the concern and responsi-

bility of the administration of the University of Missouri was rash, impetuous, and impertinent. As individual citizens, we may all have opinions regarding any and all of the acts of any governmental agency; as employees of one agency charged with specific duties we have no right to interfere in the affairs of another, especially in the public press."[65] This statement has been widely misquoted as referring to *Mrs. Bodger* as being rash, impetuous, and impertinent in her publication of the letter to the *Tribune*.[66] In fact, the statement refers to the "intrusion of the *State Library*," not Mrs. Bodger. Since Mr. O'Halloran is state librarian, his statement refers to himself, not to Mrs. Bodger.

Mr. O'Halloran's statement has fostered further confusion because the State Library Commission quoted the statement, out of context, in its news release.[67] The quote entirely eliminates Mr. O'Halloran's strong defense in support of Mrs. Bodger's action concerning the two intellectual freedom issues—her protest of censorship and her statement voicing the need for a library to make information, including all points of view, available to the public. In none of his public statements did Mr. O'Halloran ever fail to support either Mrs. Bodger, in this regard, or the principles of intellectual freedom.[68]

It has also been stated that Mr. O'Halloran should not have submitted Mrs. Bodger's letter of resignation to Mrs. Duggan before accepting it. In the view of the Fact-Finding Subcommittee, Mr. O'Halloran was justified in doing so because of 1) Mrs. Bodger's expressed intent to publish the letter of resignation, and 2) his knowledge of the Commission's concern about publicity and activities regarding Mrs. Bodger. However, it is also the view of the Subcommittee that Mr. O'Halloran had the authority to accept the resignation without the approval of the State Library Commission.

In assessing Mr. O'Halloran's actions in regard to Mrs. Bodger's dismissal, the Fact-Finding Subcommittee concludes that:

1. Mr. O'Halloran's approval of Mrs. Bodger's publication of her February 26 letter was not an act of "poor judgment." The Subcommittee, furthermore, cannot accept as fact that her letter constituted an intrusion of one state agency into the affairs of another.

2. Mr. O'Halloran did not withdraw support from Mrs. Bodger's defense of the principles of intellectual freedom at any time.

3. Mr. O'Halloran, considering the Commission's views, was justified in submitting Mrs. Bodger's letter of resignation to the president of the State Library Commission before accepting it.

Regarding the Missouri State Library Commission

As stated before, several members of the Missouri State Library Commission at the time of Mrs. Bodger's dismissal declined the Fact-Finding Subcommittee's invitation to appear before it.[69] Consequently, not all of the actions of the Commission in regard to Mrs. Bodger can be discussed by the Subcommittee with the detail and authority that would clarify some points of conflict and dissension involved in the controversy.

Statements received from Judge Temple Morgett, current Commission president, and from Ralph Parker, former Commission member, confirm other information which indicates that the question of Mrs. Bodger's letter to the *Tribune* came to the attention of the Commission through telephone calls and letters to Mrs. Jerome Duggan, then Commission president.

The Commission first discussed the matter in executive session on March 11, 1969. The substance of the Commission's discussion is not included in the formal minutes of the meeting.[70] Beyond stating that "the Commission has given serious consideration to many aspects of the matter before us,"[71] and announcing another session for further discussion, little official information came from the March 11 meeting.

On March 20, 1969, the Commission met again to discuss the matter. During this meeting, the Commission concluded that Mrs. Bodger had done what she should in regard to getting clearance to publish the letter.[72]

Also at this meeting the Commission discussed the State Library's acquisitions policy.[73] This policy has been described as impractical and totally inapplicable to actual, current acquisition needs and practices.[74] At least two members of the State Library professional staff stated to the Fact-Finding Subcommittee that such an acquisitions policy did not exist.[75] During the meeting of March 20, the Commission expressed some concern about not wanting to be in a position of restricting materials.[76] From the discussion of the acquisitions policy, the need for its revision, and the fear of restricting materials, the Commission, in the view of the Fact-Finding Subcommittee, did recognize that Mrs. Bodger's letter to the *Tribune* commented on serious problems involving intellectual freedom.

In addition, the Commission, at the March 20 meeting, discussed policy statements regarding extracurricular activities of State Library staff members. No specific action was taken in regard to either the acquisitions policy or the policy regarding extracurricular activities.[77]

In its discussion of Mrs. Bodger's letter, the Commission concluded that if the letter had come from Joan Bodger as a private citizen, the Commission would have had no objection to it.[78] On the face of the letter, however, it is obvious that Mrs. Bodger's letter, even if not over her official title, would have clearly identified her and

the State Library. Without this identification, the letter would have had no
strength or meaning in regard to Mrs.
Bodger's protest.

Mr. O'Halloran presented a statement to the Commission at its March
20 meeting.[79] The Commission read
Mr. O'Halloran's statement and incorporated parts of it, out of context,
in a statement which the Commission
included in its Minutes and released
to the press.[80] On the question of
Mrs. Bodger's letter, the Commission's
statement said: "The letter to the
press by a member of the library staff,
sent with the approval of the state librarian, which injected the State Library into the matter was a display of
indiscretion."[81] Comments from Mr.
O'Halloran's statement are used to
support this opinion of the Commission.[82]

The purpose of the Commission's
official statement of March 20 was to
censure Mr. O'Halloran. Two Commission members have stated that, as
far as the Commission was concerned,
the entire matter ended with the publication of the official statement.[83] In
statements to the press, Mrs. Duggan
and Dr. Parker confirmed this view.[84]

However, after the March 20 meet-
ing, the Commission president, Mrs.
Jerome Duggan, did telephone Mr.
O'Halloran in regard to pickets and
protesters at a workshop near St.
Louis where Mrs. Bodger appeared.
Though not by specific action of the
Commission, Mr. O'Halloran, on the
advice of Mrs. Duggan, requested that
Mrs. Bodger curtail her speaking
activities.[85]

This curtailment of her activities
precipitated Mrs. Bodger's letter of
resignation in which she again protested the attitude of the Commission
toward the suppression of publications.[86]

Mrs. Duggan refused to accept Mrs.
Bodger's resignation, and it was at her
unilateral initiation that the telephone
poll resulting in Mrs. Bodger's dismis-

sal was made by Mr. O'Halloran.
There is no evidence to indicate that
there was any notice that such an action would be considered or that all of
the Commission members were aware
of the action until it was actually accomplished. There is evidence that
Mr. Wheeler and Dr. Parker were not
reached by the telephone poll.[87]

The results of the telephone poll
which determined Mrs. Bodger's dismissal are not contained in the May
13, 1969, Minutes of the Commission.
Judge Morgett, the current president
of the Commission, has stated that it
is normal procedure for the numerical
results of votes on all issues of importance to be recorded in the Commission Minutes.[88] The Fact-Finding Subcommittee finds the lack of such a
record appalling because it initiates
serious doubts as to the actual existence of a majority vote in favor of
dismissal.

In regard to the total number of
Commission votes in favor of dismissing Mrs. Bodger, Mr. O'Halloran, who
made the phone calls, has stated that
he reached only Mrs. Duggan, Judge
Morgett, and Mrs. Steury.[89] Judge
Morgett has affirmed that he was
reached and voted in favor of dismissal.[90] Dr. Ralph Parker has affirmed
that he was not polled, he did not vote
for dismissal, and he had no knowledge of the vote until after the dismissal was accomplished.[91]

Mr. O'Halloran has told the Fact-
Finding Subcommittee that Rabbi
Ferdinand Isserman resigned from the
Commission prior to the vote on Mrs.
Bodger's dismissal.[92] Rabbi Isserman,
however, stated in a published interview with a reporter from *Wilson Library Bulletin* that "both as a liberal
and as a human being" he voted
against firing Mrs. Bodger.[93] Rabbi
Isserman also told *Wilson Library Bulletin* that he has since resigned from
the Commission without fanfare, in
order not to add to the effect of the
controversy on state policies.[94] The

Fact-Finding Subcommittee was unable to interview Rabbi Isserman due to his ill health and hospitalization.

The Subcommittee concludes that there is strong evidence to indicate that there were six Commission members at the time of Mrs. Bodger's dismissal. Since only three members voted in favor of dismissing Mrs. Bodger, it is probable that there was not a majority vote in favor of dismissal.

After its telephone poll vote to dismiss Mrs. Bodger, the Commission took no further action until May 13, 1969. At a meeting on that date, attended by Mrs. Duggan, Mrs. Steury, Judge Morgett, and Mr. O'Halloran, the Commission formalized its dismissal of Mrs. Bodger, effective April 8, 1969, and indicated this action in its Minutes.[95] No tally of the vote was recorded.[96]

During the period of March 21 through April 8, 1969, Mrs. Duggan and Dr. Parker made statements to the press which substantially confuse the issues in terms of the Commission's intentions and the propriety of its dismissal of Mrs. Bodger.

On March 21, 1969, the Jefferson City *Post-Tribune* (the newspaper which initially attacked Mrs. Bodger) carried the following comments on pages 1 and 5:

. . . Dr. Ralph Parker, librarian at the University of Missouri who is a member of the Commission, explained that the Commission can hire or fire a state librarian who hires his own staff. Parker said dismissals must be handled the same way. . . . Dr. Parker and Mrs. Jerome Duggan, who heads the Commission, said the final paragraph [of the attached Commission statement] *in no way meant that the dismissal* of any employee was still under consideration. . . .

On April 8, 1969, the Jefferson City *Post-Tribune* published the following comments on page 1:

. . . Mrs. Duggan said the Commission decided March 20 to "terminate" Mrs.

Bodger's employment with the Library. She said the firing was not immediate because Mrs. Bodger was working on projects which were not complete. . . .

On the same day, the *Columbia Tribune* published the following comments on pages 1 and 2:

. . . Reached at her St. Louis home this afternoon, Mrs. Duggan explained that she had, indeed, refused to talk with Mrs. Bodger. . . . "No one can argue by himself," Mrs. Duggan said. "I believe it was unnecessary to talk with her." . . . Mrs. Duggan told the *Tribune* that *she was acting on behalf of the entire Commission*, which had decided on March 20 to fire Mrs. Bodger, but only after the children's consultant had finished one of her projects. . . . Mrs. Duggan said the action was taken because Mrs. Bodger, in a letter to the editor of the *Tribune* published February 26, identified herself as a member of the State Library staff. . . . The Commission president said the action was also taken because Mrs. Bodger, by her letter to the *Tribune*, had "involved," in a way, the library and the Commission in the business of the University of Missouri. . . .

If the report of the conversations with Dr. Parker and Mrs. Duggan may be relied upon to be accurate, their statements give rise to serious questions of propriety in regard to the State Library Commission's dismissal of Mrs. Bodger. On the one hand, a Commission member states on March 21 that no further consideration will be given to terminating the members of the State Library staff involved in the incident. On the other hand, the president of the Commission publicly contradicts this statement on April 8 and goes on to give previously determined grounds and intent to dismiss Mrs. Bodger. Dr. Parker's statement clearly says that the Commission does not have the authority to dismiss Mrs. Bodger, and that such authority rests with Mr. O'Halloran. Yet, the Commission did dismiss Mrs. Bodger.

Beyond the question of the State Library Commission's authority to dismiss Mrs. Bodger is the question of the method by which she was dismissed. She was denied any opportunity to petition the Commission; the Commission and the State Library have no grievance procedure which she could implement. She was denied notice; she received a letter of dismissal effective the day of receipt, thus denying the fundamental principles of due process. She was denied any compensatory salary. Her own letter of resignation, giving thirty days notice, was summarily dismissed by the Commission. Members of the Commission have stated to the Fact-Finding Subcommittee that each of these practices was without precedent in the history of the State Library Commission.

In assessing the role of the Missouri State Library Commission in the dismissal of Mrs. Bodger, the Fact-Finding Subcommittee concludes that:

1. The State Library Commission refused to consider as important the principles of intellectual freedom expressed in Mrs. Bodger's letter or in Mr. O'Halloran's statements to the Commission.

2. The Commission failed to establish an adequate acquisitions policy for the functioning of the State Library.

3. The Commission failed to make known to the State Library staff policies and procedures in regard to the use of State Library letterhead stationery.

4. The Commission acted hastily, without precedent, without authority, and without consideration for due process when it ordered the dismissal of Mrs. Joan Bodger.

(Only the members of the Missouri State Library Commission at the time of Mrs. Bodger's dismissal are the subject of the Fact-Finding Subcommittee's assessment. These include Judge Temple Morgett, Dr. Ralph Parker, Rabbi Ferdinand Isserman, Mrs. Frank Steury, Hubert Wheeler,

and Mrs. Jerome Duggan, president. Due to the subsequent resignations from the Commission of Dr. Ralph Parker and Rabbi Ferdinand Isserman, the present composition of the Commission may include persons who had no part in the Commission's consideration of Mrs. Bodger's actions or dismissal.)

Regarding Dr. Ralph H. Parker

Dr. Ralph H. Parker, at the time of Mrs. Bodger's dismissal from the Missouri State Library, was dean of the University of Missouri School of Library and Information Science and acting director of the University of Missouri Library. As acting director of the University of Missouri Library, Dr. Parker served as an ex officio member of the State Library Commission.[97]

Because he is a prominent member of the library profession and has a strong history of defense and support of intellectual freedom, Dr. Parker's role in the Missouri State Library Commission's dismissal of Mrs. Bodger has been the source of speculation and adverse criticism among professional librarians.[98]

Specifically in regard to Mrs. Bodger's dismissal, the Subcommittee believes it is important to state that Dr. Parker was not reached in the telephone poll of the Commission conducted under Mrs. Duggan's directions. Therefore, he did not vote to dismiss Mrs. Bodger.[99] Dr. Parker was also absent from the May 13, 1969, meeting during which the Commission voted to formalize its termination of Mrs. Bodger's employment.[100]

Dr. Parker, however, acting under Mrs. Duggan's direction, addressed the MLA Conference on October 4, 1969, delivering a statement concerning Mrs. Bodger's dismissal.[101] The Fact-Finding Subcommittee, in accordance with Dr. Parker's wishes, did not question Dr. Parker concerning the address to MLA.[102] Dr. Parker volunteered to the Subcommittee that his statement was an impromptu one, and that he was directed by the Commission to make the statement.[103] All other information about the statement has come to the Subcommittee from other sources. These include the published transcript of Dr. Parker's address, which appeared in the December 1969 *ALA Bulletin*,[104] and interviews with several members of MLA and one member of the Commission who were present at the time of the address.

When he met with the Subcommittee on April 29, 1970, Judge Temple Morgett, current president of the State Library Commission, stated that the Commission now endorses Dr. Parker's statement with the exception of any reference to a phone call between Mrs. Bodger and Mrs. Duggan.[105] In effect, the Commission's failure to endorse this portion of Dr. Parker's address renders the entire address meaningless, since its purpose was to give the reasons and facts for Mrs. Bodger's dismissal.[106] The only reason given in the address was the nature of the content of the phone call. As the Subcommittee has established, the phone call occurred after the Commission had voted to reject Mrs. Bodger's resignation and fire her. Consequently, the phone call—whatever its content—could not have constituted the Commission's grounds for dismissal.

The Commission's endorsement of the rest of Dr. Parker's statement raises further questions as to the Commission's integrity because, as the Subcommittee has established, other portions of Dr. Parker's address are inaccurate. The questionable portions of Dr. Parker's statement include the following:

1. "The case of Joan Bodger had nothing whatever to do with the matters of censorship."[107]

In the view of the Subcommittee, Mrs. Bodger's letter to the *Columbia Tribune* regarding the suppression of underground newspapers clearly involves "the matters of censorship" and the broad area of intellectual freedom.

2. ". . . but instead of simply being willing to turn in a letter of resignation and let it go through the normal course, she felt called upon to call up Mrs. Duggan. . . ."[108]

Mrs. Bodger was perfectly willing to allow her letter of resignation to "go through the normal course." She submitted it to Mr. O'Halloran, her employer. Mr. O'Halloran then contacted the president of the Commission. The Commission, without consulting with Mrs. Bodger, rejected her letter of resignation and ordered her dismissal.[109] Mrs. Bodger did not feel "called upon to call up Mrs. Duggan" until after this sequence of events had occurred.

3. "There was never any question about whether the material belonged in the library. I think it should not be in a children's collection. But this is not the issue."[110]

The propriety of the Children's Examination Center collecting underground newspapers such as the *Free Press Underground* was very much a question. It was most heavily debated in the press,[111] and appears to have been of great concern to political figures in Missouri.[112] Further, the Children's Examination Center is not only or primarily a "children's collection." The Center is intended for use by adults who work with children and adolescents. Therefore, its collection ranges widely among pedagogical and popular publications for and about young people.[113] To date, the State Library does not collect underground newspapers and never has. The state librarian told the Subcommittee that there are no plans for collecting such materials in the near future.[114] The Subcommittee views the question about whether the material belonged in the State Library as one of the principal issues in the entire incident.

4. ". . . but I do know that not one

single member of the Commission was ever interrogated regarding the incident. . . ."[115]

Statements [quoted on p. 700 of this report] attributed to Dr. Parker and Mrs. Duggan, appeared in the Jefferson City *Post-Tribune* and the *Columbia Tribune* on March 21 and April 8 and were cited as coming from interviews with the two members of the Commission. *Wilson Library Bulletin*, November 1969, reported an interview with Rabbi Ferdinand Isserman, who was a member of the Commission at the time of the incident.[116] (Subsequent to Dr. Parker's address to MLA, the Fact-Finding Subcommittee invited all members of the Commission to meet with it and comment upon the Bodger incident. As stated previously, only Judge Morgett and Dr. Parker accepted the invitation.)

5. ". . . No member of the Intellectual Freedom Committee of the Missouri Library Association ever said one word or inquired of the State Library Commission regarding its activities until this petition, signed by twenty-four people, present here, was presented to the Commission this afternoon."[117]

Mrs. Helen Kreigh, past chairman of the MLA Intellectual Freedom Committee, presented to the Fact-Finding Subcommittee a copy of a proposed news release concerning the Bodger incident. The proposed release was read over the telephone to Mr. O'Halloran who requested that it not be released to the news media, either with or without his approval.[118]

The Fact-Finding Subcommittee makes no attempt to assess the sincerity or the validity of Dr. Parker's belief that the content of his statement to the MLA Conference was correct and presented a true picture of the events surrounding Mrs. Bodger's dismissal. The Subcommittee, however, must conclude that the Commission is responsible—with or without intent—for the proliferation and perpetuation of false or misleading information concerning Mrs. Bodger's dismissal. Endorsement of the address, after consideration of its text, places the Commission in a position of ignoring information within its grasp that could have corrected the confusion concerning Mrs. Bodger's dismissal.

In assessing the role of Dr. Parker in the dismissal of Mrs. Bodger, the Fact-Finding Subcommittee concludes that:

1. Dr. Parker was not reached for the telephone vote to dismiss Mrs. Bodger, and he was not present at the May 13, 1969, meeting during which the Commission formalized her termination of employment. Therefore, he did not vote to dismiss Mrs. Bodger.

2. Dr. Parker's knowledge or lack of knowledge of the misinformation contained in his address to the MLA Conference cannot be determined by the Subcommittee.

3. The Commission's "qualified" endorsement of Dr. Parker's statement reflects poor judgment on the part of the Commission in that it allows false or misleading statements to stand as fact in a serious matter.

Regarding the University of Missouri

In her Request for Action and her original letter to the *Columbia Tribune*, Mrs. Bodger charges the University of Missouri with suppression of free expression. She bases her charge on the belief that persons in the University of Missouri administration were responsible for removing salesmen for the *Free Press Underground* from the campus, and were also responsible for the arrest of the students by the county police.

As previously indicated, the question of whether the university administration did, in fact, remove *Free Press Underground* salesmen from the campus and whether the university administration called the county police and requested the arrest of the student salesmen, could not be satisfactorily answered by the Fact-Finding Subcommittee. Information received in interviews varies on this point. Newspaper coverage also varies.

The Subcommittee believes, however, that there is no question that the University of Missouri administration did remove specific issues of *New Left Notes* and *The Movement* from distribution in the student union. This point is not contested by persons interviewed or in the press.

Although the Subcommittee has no direct concern with the actions of the administration of the University of Missouri, it believes that the removal of specific issues of *New Left Notes* and *The Movement* from distribution in the student union was an act of censorship. Neither of the publications, at that time, had been judged obscene. They were removed in spite of the fact that the objectionable words were also contained in other publications which were allowed to remain on sale in the student union.

Edwin Castagna, Florence DeHart, and Alex Allain, chairman, Fact-Finding Subcommittee, Intellectual Freedom Committee.

NOTES

[1] At p. 4 of Joan Bodger's Request for Action, December 7, 1969, she states, under question #4: "This is a formal complaint against MLA, MSL, and the Commission." In Mrs. Bodger's addenda to p. 4, question #3 [labeled "Section II, #3, (4)], she states: "That the State University was abridging free expression made it all the more incumbent that the State Library should redress the balance. . . ."

[2] At p. 4 of Joan Bodger's Request for Action, December 7, 1969, under question #4, she states that she would consider a satisfactory resolution of the problem to include: ". . . A professional knuckle-rapping of Parker, et al. . . . An investigation into . . . the Commission's . . . refusal to confront me. . . . An investigation into O'Halloran's role. . . . Why did he crumple so easily? Why did he refuse outside help or publicity? Is the cause of library freedom really helped by his action? . . ."

[3] Letter to Mrs. Jerome Duggan, president, Missouri State Library Commission, January 22, 1970, from Mrs. Judith F. Krug, director, Office for Intellectual Freedom.

[4] Letters and questionnaires to Mrs. Jerome Duggan, et al, February 27, 1970, from Alex P. Allain, chairman, Investigating Committee, ALA Intellectual Freedom Committee.

[5] Notes, Meeting of IFC Subcommittee investigating the Bodger case, Monday, April 6, 1970.

[6] Letters to Mrs. Jerome Duggan, et al, April 14, 1970, from Mrs. Judith F. Krug, director, Office for Intellectual Freedom.

[7] Letter to Mrs. Judith F. Krug, April 20, 1970, from John Herbst.

[8] Statement from Doris Bolef and Elsie Freivogel, March 10, 1970, to Mr. Alex Allain, chairman, re: Missouri Association of College and Research Libraries Resolution, April 26, 1969, concerning dismissal of Joan Bodger, children's consultant, State Library, Columbia, Missouri.

[9] Transcript of Meeting with Mrs. Susanna Alexander.

[10] Transcript of Meeting with Mrs. Nina Ladof.

[11] Transcript of Meeting with Mrs. Helen Kreigh.

[12] Transcript of Meeting with Mrs. Rosetta Bullard.

[13] Transcript of Meeting with Charles O'Halloran.

[14] Transcript of Meeting with Mrs. Bernadine Hoduski.

[15] Transcript of Meeting with James Leathers.

[16] Transcript of Meeting with Mrs. Joan Goddard.

[17] Summary of Meeting with Dr. Ralph H. Parker.

[18] Transcript of Meeting with Judge Temple Morgett.

[19] Summary of Meeting with William DeJohn.

[20] The facts established by the Subcommittee concerning the incident be-

tween the Students for a Democratic Society and the administration of the University of Missouri are essentially the same as those reported in *Wilson Library Bulletin*, November 1969, p. 270. The selective description of events used by the Subcommittee in its report includes only statements which were confirmed by Dr. Ralph H. Parker and Mrs. Joan Goddard.

One major point of contention in the various reports of the incident involves the question of whether or not a member of the University of Missouri administration requested that the Columbia police arrest the student salesmen. Dr. Parker asserts that the administration did not do so. Mrs. Goddard asserts that the administration did.

21 "Banish the stargazers?" Letter to the Editor, *Columbia Tribune*, February 26, 1969.

22 Transcripts of Meeting with Mrs. Susanna Alexander, pp. 9-12; Charles O'Halloran, pp. 2, 8-9.

23 *Ibid.*

24 Summary of Meeting with Dr. Ralph H. Parker, p. 2; also various clippings from Missouri newspapers verify that letters protesting Mrs. Bodger's stand were published.

25 Missouri State Library Commission, March 11, 1969, Minutes, p. 2. Also see Transcript of Meeting with Charles O'Halloran, p. 4; Summary of Meeting with Dr. Ralph H. Parker, p. 1; and Transcript of Meeting with Judge Temple Morgett, p. 1.

26 "A Statement Regarding the Letter by Mrs. Joan Bodger," *Columbia Tribune*, Charles O'Halloran, state librarian. Also see Transcripts of meeting with Charles O'Halloran, p. 4; Summary of Meeting with Dr. Ralph H. Parker, p. 2.

27 Missouri State Library Commission, March 11, 1969, Minutes, p. 2.

28 Missouri State Library Commission, March 20, 1969, Minutes, p. 1.

29 Statement by Charles O'Halloran (given to the Commission on March 20, 1969); also see Missouri State Library Commission, March 20, 1969, Minutes, Attachment.

30 Summary of meeting with Dr. Ralph H. Parker, p. 2. Also see *ALA Bulletin*, December 1969, p. 1562, for Dr. Parker's statement to the MLA Conference.

31 Work Sheet, Joan Bodger, p. 1.

32 Transcript of Meeting with Mrs. Nina Ladof, p. 1; from typed statement presented.

33 *Ibid.*, p. 1.

34 Transcript of Meeting with Charles O'Halloran, p. 5.

35 *Ibid.*, p. 5. Also see Work Sheet, Joan Bodger, p. 3.

36 Work Sheet, Joan Bodger, pp. 3-4.

37 Work Sheet, Joan Bodger, p. 4. Also see Transcript of Meeting with Mrs. Rosetta Bullard, p. 1; from typed statement presented.

38 Transcript of Meeting with Charles O'Halloran, p. 6. Also see Work Sheet, Joan Bodger, p. 4.

39 Transcript of Meeting with Charles O'Halloran, p. 6.

40 Letter to Mrs. Joan Bodger, April 8, 1969, from Charles O'Halloran: "At the direction of the Missouri State Library Commission this is to notify you that your employment by the Missouri State Library is terminated as of 5:00 p.m. this day, April 8, 1969."

41 Transcript of Meeting with Charles O'Halloran, p. 6.

42 *Ibid.*, p. 6. Confirmed by Dr. Ralph H. Parker. See Summary of Meeting with Dr. Ralph H. Parker, pp. 2-3.

43 Transcript of Meeting with Charles O'Halloran, p. 6.

44 *Ibid.*, p. 6.

45 *Ibid.*, p. 6. Confirmed in Work Sheet, Joan Bodger, p. 4.

46 Work Sheet, Joan Bodger, p. 4. Confirmed by Mr. O'Halloran. See Transcript of Meeting with Charles O'Halloran, p. 7.

47 Transcript of Meeting with Mrs. Rosetta Bullard, p. 1; from typed statement presented.

48 *ALA Bulletin*, December 1969, p. 1561. Confirmed by Mrs. Bernadine Hoduski. See Transcript of Meeting with Mrs. Bernadine Hoduski, p. 1; from typed statement presented.

49 *ALA Bulletin*, December 1969, p. 1561.

50 *ALA Bulletin*, December 1969, p. 1561. Confirmed by Mrs. Bernadine Hoduski and Dr. Ralph H. Parker. See Transcript of Meeting with Mrs. Bernadine Hoduski, p. 1; typed statement presented; and, Summary of Meeting with Dr. Ralph H. Parker, p. 1.

51 *ALA Bulletin*, December 1969, p. 1561.

[52] Summary of Meeting with Dr. Ralph H. Parker, p. 1.

[53] Transcript of Meeting with Judge Temple Morgett, pp. 3-4.

[54] Transcripts of Meetings with Mrs. Susanna Alexander, pp. 9-12; and Charles O'Halloran, pp. 2, 8-9.

[55] "Library Commission Leaves Unanswered Questions," Jefferson City *Post-Tribune*, March 26, 1969.

[56] A comparison of newspaper articles such as the one cited at footnote #55 will show that, prior to March 20, 1969, "obscenity" was the issue. After March 20, 1969, "intrusion" became an issue.

[57] Compare A Statement of Position from Joan Bodger, Consultant, Children's Services, State Library of Missouri, April 7, 1969, to "Banish the stargazers?" Letter to the Editor, *Columbia Tribune*, February 26, 1969.

[58] See page 696 of this report.

[59] See pages 696–97 of this report.

[60] Missouri State Library Commission, March 20, 1969, Minutes, Attachment.

[61] A Statement Regarding the Letter by Mrs. Joan Bodger in the *Columbia Tribune*, Charles O'Halloran, State Librarian, p. 1.

[62] Transcript of Meeting with Judge Temple Morgett, pp. 8-10; and Summary of Meeting with Dr. Ralph Parker, p. 2.

[63] *Ibid.*, Morgett, pp. 8-10; and Parker, p. 2.

[64] Missouri State Library Commission, March 20, 1969, Minutes, Attachment.

[65] *Ibid.*

[66] A Statement of Position from Joan Bodger, etc., p. 1.

[67] Missouri State Library Commission, March 20, 1969, Minutes, Attachment.

[68] See three statements by Charles O'Halloran: #1: A Statement Regarding the Letter by Mrs. Joan Bodger . . . , #2: "There are really only three basic issues. . . .", and #3: Statement by Charles O'Halloran.

[69] See p. 695 of this report.

[70] Missouri State Library Commission, March 11, 1969, Minutes, p. 1.

[71] *Ibid.*, p. 2.

[72] Summary of Meeting with Dr. Ralph H. Parker, p. 1.

[73] *Ibid.*, p. 1.

[74] *Ibid.*, p. 1. Also see Transcripts of Meetings with Charles O'Halloran, pp. 1-2; Mrs. Susanna Alexander, pp. 4-5; and Judge Temple Morgett, p. 7.

[75] Transcript of Meeting with Mrs. Susanna Alexander, pp. 4-5. See also Letter from Joan Bodger, April 10, 1970, to Mrs. Judith F. Krug.

[76] Summary of Meeting with Dr. Ralph H. Parker, p. 1.

[77] *Ibid.*, p. 1.

[78] Missouri State Library Commission, March 20, 1969, Minutes, Attachment. See also Summary of Meeting with Dr. Ralph H. Parker, p. 2; Transcript of Meeting with Judge Temple Morgett, p. 10.

[79] Transcript of Meeting with Charles O'Halloran, pp. 10-11.

[80] Missouri State Library Commission, March 20, 1969, Minutes, Attachment.

[81] *Ibid.*

[82] Compare Mr. O'Halloran's statement with the Commission's final press release. Pertinent sections from Mr. O'Halloran's statements are incorporated, with quotation marks, into the Commission's press release.

[83] Summary of Meeting with Dr. Ralph H. Parker, p. 2; Transcript of Meeting with Judge Temple Morgett, p. 1.

This statement, although confirmed in the press by Mrs. Duggan and Dr. Parker, on March 21, 1969, was refuted by later statements to the press by Mrs. Duggan, who said that the plan was to fire Mrs. Bodger after she completed all her projects. See this report, pp. 699–700.

[84] See this report, p. 700.

[85] Transcript of Meeting with Charles O'Halloran, pp. 4-5.

[86] A Statement of Position from Joan Bodger, Consultant, Children's Services, State Library of Missouri, April 7, 1969, p. 2.

[87] Transcript of Meeting with Charles O'Halloran, p. 6; and, Summary of Meeting with Dr. Ralph H. Parker, pp. 2-3.

[88] Transcript of Meeting with Judge Temple Morgett, p. 13.

[89] Transcript of Meeting with Charles O'Halloran, p. 6.

[90] Transcript of Meeting with Judge Temple Morgett, pp. 14-15.

[91] Summary of Meeting with Dr. Ralph H. Parker, pp. 2-3.

[92] Mr. O'Halloran, at p. 6 of his Transcript, states that: "The Rabbi had, by that time, resigned from the Commission so he was no longer being counted as one of the Commission members."

Judge Morgett, at p. 4 of his Transcript, states that: "I believe that Rabbi Isserman had resigned by that time because he told us, after that last meeting in March, that his health was such that he wouldn't be able to make trips to and from Jefferson City. . . . And I don't remember whether he actually tendered it prior to this action or not. . . ."

In a letter, May 20, 1970, the Office for Intellectual Freedom requested from Mr. O'Halloran a copy of Isserman's resignation. Mr. O'Halloran responded on May 22 and enclosed a Memorandum, dated April 22, 1969 which includes this note:

"I have resigned from the Library Commission and the governor has accepted my resignation. . . . Kindest regards. F. M. Isserman." Mr. O'Halloran concludes that the rabbi's resignation was probably effective sometime around April 1, 1969.

The OIF also contacted Rabbi Isserman to confirm the date of resignation, but received no response. Consequently, the question remains unanswered.

93 *Wilson Library Bulletin*, November 1969, p. 266. Confirmed in telephone conversation with William Eshelman, editor, *Wilson Library Bulletin*, May 20, 1970.

94 *Ibid.*

95 Missouri State Library Commission, May 13, 1969, Minutes. Confirmed by Dr. Parker and Judge Temple Morgett.

96 Missouri State Library Commission, May 13, 1969, Minutes. See Transcript of Meeting with Judge Temple Morgett, p. 13, for confirmation of lack of tally.

97 *ALA Bulletin*, December 1969, p. 1561.

98 *Wilson Library Bulletin*, November 1969, p. 274: "Ralph H. Parker . . . failed to take any action to defend the students' right of free speech on campus. As a member of the State Library Commission, there is no evidence to indicate that he voted in favor of retaining Mrs. Bodger. . . ."

Library Journal, December 15, 1969, p. 4469: " 'The Hayakawa Award for Functional Semantics' to Ralph H. Parker, for his statement at the Missouri Library Association that 'the case of Joan Bodger had nothing to do with the matter of censorship . . . but that

Bodger was fired for her language during a telephone call that occurred after she had been terminated from the Missouri State Library."

99 Summary of Meeting with Dr. Ralph H. Parker, pp. 2-3. Confirmed by Charles O'Halloran. See Transcript of Meeting with Charles O'Halloran, p. 6.

100 Summary of Meeting with Dr. Ralph H. Parker, p. 6. Confirmed by Missouri State Library Commission, May 13, 1969, Minutes, p. 1.

101 Summary of Meeting with Dr. Ralph H. Parker, p. 1. See statement delivered to MLA Conference by Dr. Parker in *ALA Bulletin*, December 1969, p. 1561+.

102 Dr. Parker requested this agreement in a Letter, April 3, 1970, to Alex Allain, chairman of the Fact-Finding Subcommittee. Mr. Allain agreed to the request in a Letter, April 16, 1970, to Dr. Ralph H. Parker.

103 Summary of Meeting with Dr. Ralph H. Parker, p. 1.

104 See footnote #101 for citation.

105 Transcript of Meeting with Judge Temple Morgett, pp. 2-4.

106 *ALA Bulletin*, December 1969, p. 1561.

107 *Ibid.*

108 *Ibid.*, p. 1562.

109 Transcript of Meeting with Mr. O'Halloran, p. 6.

110 *ALA Bulletin*, December 1969, p. 1562.

111 Various press clippings confirm the newspaper coverage of the Bodger incident.

112 Transcript of Meeting with Charles O'Halloran, p. 8; Summary of Meeting with Dr. Ralph H. Parker, pp. 1, 3-4.

113 Transcripts of Meetings with Mrs. Susanna Alexander, pp. 1-2; and Charles O'Halloran, pp. 1-2.

114 Transcript of Meeting with Charles O'Halloran, pp. 16-18.

115 *ALA Bulletin*, December 1969, p. 1562.

116 Articles from the press.

117 *ALA Bulletin*, December 1969, p. 1562.

118 Transcript of Meeting with Mrs. Helen Kreigh, p. 1; from typed statement presented.

Action

The ALA Executive Board approved the following actions on June 29, 1970:

1. That "Findings" and "Commentary on the Facts" of the Bodger Report, with relevant documentation, be distributed to Mrs. Joan Bodger, Mr. Charles O'Halloran, Dr. Ralph H. Parker, Judge Temple Morgett (in his capacity as president of the Missouri State Library Commission), and Mr. James Leathers (in his capacity as president of the Missouri Library Association).

2. That "Findings" and "Commentary on the Facts" be published in the July-August issue of *American Libraries*.

B Free Press and Free Trial: Statements of Ethical Principles

Canon Twenty of the Canons of Ethics
of the American Bar Association

Newspaper publications by a lawyer as to pending or anticipated litigation may interfere with a fair trial in the Courts and otherwise prejudice the due administration of justice. Generally they are to be condemned. If the extreme circumstances of a particular case justify a statement to the public, it is unprofessional to make it anonymously. An *ex parte* reference to the facts should not go beyond quotation from the records and papers on file in the court; but even in extreme cases it is better to avoid any *ex parte* statement.

The statements comprising this appendix originally appeared as appendixes to an Occasional Paper on the Free Society, *Free Trial vs. A Free Press* (Santa Barbara, Calif.: Center for the Study of Democratic Institutions of The Fund for the Republic, 1965). Adapted and reproduced with permission.

Oregon Bar–Press–Broadcasters Joint
Statement of Principles

Oregon's Bill of Rights provides both for fair trials
and for freedom of the press. These rights are basic
and unqualified. They are not ends in themselves but
are necessary guarantors of freedom for the individual and the public's rights to be informed. The necessity of preserving both the right to a fair trial and the
freedom to disseminate the news is of concern to responsible members of the legal and journalistic professions and is of equal concern to the public. At
times these two rights appear to be in conflict with
each other.

In an effort to mitigate this conflict, the Oregon
State Bar, the Oregon Newspaper Publishers Association and the Oregon Association of Broadcasters
have adopted the following statement of principles to
keep the public fully informed without violating the
rights of any individual.

1. The news media have the right and the responsibility to print and to broadcast the truth.

2. However, the demands of accuracy and objectivity in news reporting should be balanced with the
demands of fair play. The public has a right to be
informed. The accused has the right to be judged in
an atmosphere free from undue prejudice.

3. Good taste should prevail in the selection,
printing and broadcasting of the news. Morbid or
sensational details of criminal behavior should not
be exploited.

4. The right of decision about the news rests with
the editor or news director. In the exercise of judgment he should consider that: *a)* an accused person
is presumed innocent until proved guilty; *b)* readers

and listeners are potential jurors; *c)* no person's reputation should be injured needlessly.

5. The public is entitled to know how justice is being administered. However, it is unprofessional for any lawyer to exploit any medium of public information to enhance his side of a pending case. It follows that the public prosecutor should avoid taking unfair advantage of his position as an important source of news; this shall not be construed to limit his obligation to make available information to which the public is entitled.

In recognition of these principles, the undersigned hereby testify to their continuing desire to achieve the best possible accommodation of the rights of the individual and the rights of the public when these two fundamental precepts appear to be in conflict in the administration of justice.

Massachusetts Guide for the Bar and News Media

In an attempt to reconcile long-standing divergence of opinion as to the relative rights of the press and that of the individual to a fair trial, a special Massachusetts Bar-Press Committee was established in the fall of 1960. After two and a half years of study and discussion, the Committee, with the aid of observers from the judiciary, drafted a Guide which was approved by the Committee. Subsequently ratified by the sponsoring groups, the Guide was adopted by 26 daily and 31 weekly newspapers in this State. The Broadcasting Guide was also adopted by the Massachusetts Broadcasters Association. The text reads:

1. GUIDE FOR PRESS

PREAMBLE

1. To promote closer understanding between the bar and the press, especially in their efforts to reconcile the constitutional guarantee of freedom of the press and the right to a fair, impartial trial, the following mutual and voluntary statement of principles is recommended to all members of both professions.

2. Both professions, recognizing that freedom of the press is one of the fundamental liberties guaranteed by the First Amendment to the United States Constitution, agree that this fundamental freedom must be zealously preserved and responsibly exercised subject only to those restrictions designed to safeguard equally fundamental rights of the individual.

3. It is likewise agreed that both the press and the bar are obliged to preserve the principle of the presumption of innocence for those accused of wrongdoing pending a finding of guilty.

4. The press and the bar concur on the importance of the natural right of the members of an organized society to acquire and impart information about their common interests.

5. It is further agreed, however, that the inherent right of society's members to impart and acquire information should be exercised with discretion at those times when public disclosures would jeopardize the ends of justice, public security and other rights of individuals.

6. The press and the bar recognize that there may arise circumstances in which disclosures of names of individuals involved in matters coming to the atten-

tion of the general public would result in personal danger, harm to the reputation of a person or persons or notoriety to an innocent third party.

7. Consistent with the principles of this preamble, it is the responsibility of the bar, no less than that of the press, to support the free flow of information.

FOR THE PRESS

Newspapers in publishing accounts of crime should keep in mind that the accused may be tried in a court of law.

To preserve the individual's right to a fair trial, news stories of crime should contain only a factual statement of the arrest and attending circumstances.

The following should be avoided:

1. Publication of interviews with subpoenaed witnesses after an indictment is returned.

2. Publication of the criminal record or discreditable acts of the accused after an indictment is returned or during the trial unless made part of the evidence in the court record. The defendant is being tried on the charge for which he is accused and not on his record. (Publication of a criminal record could be grounds for a libel suit.)

3. Publication of confessions after an indictment is returned unless made a part of the evidence in the court record.

4. Publication of testimony stricken by the court, unless reported as having been stricken.

5. Editorial comment preceding or during trial, tending to influence judge or jury.

6. Publication of names of juveniles involved in juvenile proceedings unless the names are released by the judge.

7. The publication of any "leaks," statements or conclusions as to the innocence or guilt, implied or expressed, by the police or prosecuting authorities or defense counsel.

2. GUIDE FOR BROADCASTING INDUSTRY

PREAMBLE

1. To promote closer understanding between the bar and the broadcast news media, especially in their efforts to reconcile the constitutional guarantee of freedom of the press and the right to a fair, impartial trial, the following mutual and voluntary statement of principles is recommended to all members of both professions.

2. Both professions, recognizing that freedom of the press is one of the fundamental liberties guaranteed by the First Amendment to the United States Constitution, agree that this fundamental freedom must be zealously preserved and responsibly exercised subject only to those restrictions designated to safeguard equally fundamental rights of the individual.

3. It is likewise agreed that both the broadcast news media and the bar are obliged to preserve the principle of the presumption of innocence for those accused of wrongdoing pending a finding of guilty.

4. The broadcast news media and the bar concur on the importance of the natural right of the members of an organized society to acquire and impart information about their common interests.

5. It is further agreed, however, that the inherent right of society's members to impart and acquire in-

formation should be exercised with discretion at those times when public disclosures would jeopardize the ends of justice, public security and other rights of individuals.

6. The broadcast news media and the bar recognize that there may arise circumstances in which disclosures of names of individuals involved in matters coming to the attention of the general public would result in personal danger, harm to the reputation of a person or persons or notoriety to an innocent third party.

7. Consistent with the principles of this preamble, it is the responsibility of the bar, no less than that of the broadcast news media, to support the free flow of information.

FOR THE BROADCAST NEWS MEDIA

The broadcast news media in news stories originated by them concerning a crime should keep in mind that the accused may be tried in a court of law.

To preserve the individual's rights to a fair trial, news stories of crime should contain only a factual statement of the arrest and attending circumstances.

The following should be avoided:

1. Broadcasting of interviews with subpoenaed witnesses after an indictment is returned.

2. Broadcasting of the criminal record or discreditable acts of the accused after an indictment is returned or during the trial unless made part of the evidence in the court record. The defendant is being tried on the charge for which he is accused and not on his record. (Broadcasting of a criminal record could be grounds for a libel suit.)

3. Broadcasting of confessions after an indictment is returned unless made a part of the evidence in the court record.

4. Broadcasting of testimony stricken by the court unless reported as having been stricken.

5. Editorial comment preceding or during trial, tending to influence judge or jury.

6. Broadcasting of names of juveniles involved in juvenile proceedings unless the names are released by the judge.

7. The broadcasting of any "leaks," statements or conclusions as to the innocence or guilt, implied or expressed, by the police or prosecuting authorities or defense counsel.

3. GUIDE FOR THE BAR

To preserve the individual's rights to a fair trial in a court of law the following guide lines are prescribed for the Bar.

1. A factual statement of the arrest and circumstances and incidents thereof of a person charged with a crime is permissible, but the following should be avoided: A) Statements or conclusions as to the innocence or guilt, implied or expressed, by the prosecuting authorities or defense counsel.   B) Out-of-court statements by prosecutors or defense attorneys to news media in advance of or during trial, stating what they expect to prove, whom they propose to call as witnesses or public criticism of either judge or jury.   C) Issuance by the prosecuting authorities, counsel for the defense or any person having official connection with the case of any statements relative to the conduct of the accused, statements, "confessions" or admissions made by the accused or other matters

bearing on the issue to be tried.   D) Any other statement or press release to the news media in which the source of the statement remains undisclosed.

2. At the same time, in the interest of fair and accurate reporting, news media have a right to expect the cooperation of the authorities in facilitating adequate coverage of the law enforcement process.

Notes

Chapter 1

1. Norbert Wiener, "Grand Privilege, A Scholar's Appreciation," *The Saturday Review* 43:54 (Mar. 5, 1960).

2. Currin V. Shields, in his editor's introduction to John Stuart Mill's *On Liberty* (New York: Liberal Arts Press, 1956), p. xvi.

3. This quotation is from a statement sent by Clifford Johnston for the Christian Science Committee on Publication to the American Civil Liberties Union, New York State Affiliate, for their meeting in New York Cty, Monday, Feb. 4, 1952. At the time I was a member of the New York Civil Liberties Union Board of Directors, and also a member of its committee appointed to draft a position paper for this board.

After a meeting with Mr. Johnson and Mr. Roff at the office of the Christian Science Committee on Publication, the "Statement" of this point of view was considered by the New York Civil Liberties Union Board, which concluded that the law and the directive for its implementation were harmful to intellectual freedom and should be opposed. The full Board of Directors of the NYCLU took the position:

> The statute in question must be considered in the light of present day conditions—in the context of the current attempts to destroy free public education by banning or labelling books and barring controversial subjects from the class-room. We are cognizant that Christian Scientists, notable for their liberal views, have not a conscious part in and probably abhor and oppose such attempts. Yet unwittingly the law which they proposed opens the door to bigoted opponents of free education to weaken further the public schools. . . .
>
> To permit any group to hinder free public education by declaring those ideas it considers objectionable "matters of faith" would destroy any possibility of effective public education. . . .
>
> We urge that the New York Civil Liberties Union work for the repeal of the Hammond-Morgan Amendment to the Education Law.

Comment: As with the banning of the *Nation,* this case illustrates the fact that most people, even "liberals," hold attitudes on some subjects where the threshold of pain resulting from fully free expression may become intolerable, causing them to act as censors.—DKB.

167

4. On this subject the folowing readings are suggested:

Edward Crankshaw, "Soviet Censorship in Action," *The Progressive* 18:22–23 (May 1954); Michael Keresztesi, "Hungary, Thought Control in Communist Libraries," *Wilson Library Bulletin* 35:439–43 (Feb. 1961); Jay Stein, "Soviet Librarian," *Library Journal* 77:164 (Feb. 1, 1952).

5. Harry Golden, "Tarzan and Jane," in Martin Levin, ed., "The Phoenix Nest," *Saturday Review* 45:6 (17 Feb. 1962).

6. Chapter 7 is an essay on this particular threat to intellectual freedom in libraries. Although it may appear to be a new threat, Ralph Shaw sent me a letter on March 3, 1950, which shows that some librarians perceived a similar danger to intellectual freedom at that time. At that date Edward B. Stanford was chairman of the ALA Board on Administration and Tenure, and I was chairman of the ALA Committee on Intellectual Freedom, and we were proposing a position for ALA regarding loyalty oaths. Shaw wrote:

> Dear Mr. Berninghausen:
> In accordance with Mr. Stanford's request of February 23, I am noting below my opinion on the matter of the A.L.A. action on loyalty oaths.
> In the first place, I question very seriously the wisdom of having A.L.A. take positions on general social and political issues which are not particularly library issues. As you recall, I pointed out that the A.L.A. almost passed a resolution recommending that all librarians be exempted from the draft, and it was clear that the Council considered at this later date that that would have been a pretty silly resolution. We did not pass it, and the world did not come to an end. But at the time it was presented it was considered very seriously and probably would have been passed if I had not presented the worm's-eye view of it. Now we are doing something which is just as unjustifiable in going out of our proper province— the provision of reading matter to people—into the field of general political and social issues. Each member of the A.L.A. is free to vote any way he likes, but that does not mean that the A.L.A. as an organization of librarians should take stands on all political issues, speaking for all librarians on those issues. I think we would do much better to concentrate our weak efforts on issues which are strictly library issues, and would be on sounder ground if we did. . . .
> [Reproduced with permission of Mary M. Shaw, Executrix of the estate of Ralph R. Shaw.]

7. H. H. Remmers and D. H. Radler, "Teenage Attitudes," *Scientific American* 198:26 (June 1958).

Chapter 2

1. Walter Lippman, *Public Opinion* (New York: Macmillan, 1922). p. 1. [Quoted with permission of The Macmillan Company.]

2. R. H. Day, *Human Perception* (Sydney: Wiley, 1969), p. 1.

3. J. S. Bruner and Leo Postman, "On the Perception of Incongruity: A Paradigm," *Journal of Personality* 18:206 (Sept. 1949).

4. David Krech and Richard S. Crutchfield, "Perceiving the World," in Wilbur

Schramm's *The Process and Effects of Mass Communication* (Urbana: Univ. of Illinois Pr., 1954), p. 121.

5. Ibid., p. 122.

6. George Santayana, *Scepticism and Animal Faith* (New York: Scribner's, 1923), p. 71.

7. Alfred Korzybski, *Science and Sanity* (3d ed.; Lakeville, Conn.: Institute of General Semantics, 1948), p. 386 ff.

8. Wilbur Schramm, "How Communication Works," originally published in the *Shimbun Kenkyu* of Tokyo, and later in Schramm's *The Process and Effects of Mass Communication* (Urbana: Univ. of Illinois Pr., 1954), p. 4. [Reprinted with permission of the publishers.]

9. Wendell Johnson, *People in Quandaries* (New York: Harper, 1946), fig. 17, p. 472. [Reprinted with permission of Harper & Row, Publishers, Inc.]

10. Paul Henle, ed., *Language, Thought and Culture,* by Roger W. Brown et al (Ann Arbor, Mich.: Univ. of Michigan Pr., 1958), p. 7.

11. Dorothy Lee, "Conceptual Implications of an Indian Language," *Philosophy of Science* 5:90 (1938).

12. Henle, *Language, Thought and Culture,* p. 18.

13. John Hospers, *An Introduction to Philosophical Analysis* (2d ed.; Englewood Cliffs, N.J.: Prentice-Hall, 1967), p. 114–15.

Chapter 3

1. Anatol Rapoport, "What Is Semantics?" in S. I. Hayakawa, ed., *Language, Meaning and Maturity* (New York: Harper, 1954), p. 15.

2. Adam Ulam, *The Fall of the American University* (Freeport, N.Y.: Library Press, 1972).

3. Orin Kramer, "The Death of the American Ethic," *The Yale Review* 61:73 (Oct. 1971).

4. Norman Podhoretz, "The New Inquisitors," *Commentary* 55:8 (Apr. 1973).

5. Daniel P. Moynihan, "An Address to the Entering Class at Harvard College, 1972," *Commentary* 54:60 (Dec. 1972).

6. Margaret Chase Smith, "Declaration of Conscience—20 Years Later," *Congressional Record* 116, pt. 13:17683 (June 1, 1970).

7. Theodore H. White, *The Making of the President, 1972* (New York: Atheneum, 1973), p. 56.

8. Seymour Lipset and Earl Raab, "The Election and the National Mood," *Commentary* 55:48–50 (Jan. 1973).

Chapter 4

1. Judith F. Krug and James A. Harvey, "ALA and Intellectual Freedom: A Historical Overview," in *Intellectual Freedom Manual,* compiled by the Office for Intellectual Freedom (Chicago: American Library Assn., 1974), pp. xi–xxx.

2. James A. Harvey, "Acting for the Children," *School Library Journal* 98:602 (Feb. 15, 1973).

3. *See* the editorial, "Who's in Charge Here?" in *School Library Journal* 98:581 (Feb. 15, 1973).

4. *See* Office for Intellectual Freedom, comp., *Intellectual Freedom Manual* (Chicago: American Library Assn., 1974), p. 16–17.

5. California Library Committee on Intellectual Freedom, "The Right to Find Out: An Analysis of the Criticisms of *Building America*" [distrib. by ALA Intellectual Freedom Committee; printed June 1948], p. 4.

6. Ibid., p. 6.

7. For further reading on the subject of censorship, *see* Alan H. Levine, " 'Impressionable Minds,' . . . 'Forbidden Subjects': A Case in Point," *School Library Journal* 98:595 (Feb. 15, 1973) *and* Robert M. O'Neil, "Libraries, Liberties and the First Amendment," *University of Cincinnati Law Review* 42, no. 2:209–52 (1973).

8. American Library Association, Office of Library Film Advisor, "ALA Film Newsletter, Special Edition on Censorship of Film Collections," Sept. 15, 1950, p. 3.

9. This statement was received directly from Xenophon Smith by this author, at the time Librarian at Cooper Union and Chairman of the ALA Committee on Intellectual Freedom.

10. There are many articles and books about McCarthyism. For one quick reference that evokes the climate of opinion in which Mr. Smith was working, I suggest Norman Cousin's "Peoria," published in the *Saturday Review* 35:24–25 (May 3, 1952).

11. This essay was originally published in *The American Scholar* 19:44–55 (Winter 1949) and copyrighted by the author, David K. Berninghausen, then Head of the Cooper Union Libraries and professor on the academic staff, teaching philosophy in the humanities department of the Cooper Union Engineering School and, as well, chairman of the ALA Committee on Intellectual Freedom.

12. This letter is reproduced with permission of Helen R. Sattley.

13. Reproduced with permission of Helen R. Sattley.

14. *See* frontispiece.

15. H. L. Mencken, *Minority Report* (New York: Knopf, 1956), p. 65.

16. Dean of the Law School, University of Minnesota at the time.

17. Statement sent to all members of Congress on March 3, 1971 (from the files of the ALA Office of Intellectual Freedom).

Chapter 5

1. Morris Cohen, *The Faith of a Liberal* (New York: Holt, 1946), p. 2. [Reprinted with permission of Harry N. Rosenfield, Administrator, Estate of Morris R. Cohen.]

2. James Q. Wilson, "Liberalism versus Liberal Education," *Commentary* 53:51 (June 1972).

3. H. J. Eysenck, "The Dangers of the New Zealots," *Encounter* 39:82 (Dec. 1972).

4. Ibid., p. 89.

5. Wilson, "Liberalism versus Liberal Education," p. 54.

6. David R. Goddard and Linda Koons, "Intellectual Freedom and the University," *Science* 145:608 (Aug. 13, 1971). [Reprinted with permission of the authors and of *Science,* published and copyright 1971 by the American Association for the Advancement of Science.]

7. Louis Joughin, ed., *Academic Freedom and Tenure* (Madison: Univ. of Wisconsin Pr. for the American Assn. of University Professors, 1967), pp. 35–36.

8. *See* the discussion of Margaret Chase Smith's speech in the U.S. Senate in chapter 3 of this work.

9. *Students and Society,* An Occasional Paper of the Center for the Study of Democratic Institutions (Santa Barbara, Calif.: The Center, 1967), p. 43.

10. Ibid., p. 41.

11. Wayne Booth, *Now Don't Try to Reason with Me* (Chicago, Univ. of Chicago Pr.: 1970), p. 214.

12. Faculty activism is discussed at some length in *Priorities for Action: Final Report of the Carnegie Commission on Higher Education* (New York: McGraw-Hill, 1973), pp. 54–62.

13. "Uninterrupted Teaching," *School and Society* 99:135 (Mar. 1971).

14. Arthur Melton, "APA and Public Policy," *American Psychologist* 225:ix (July 1970).

15. Patrick Young, "The Lessons of History Take on a Radical Hue," *National Observer,* 9, no. 39:22 (Sept. 28, 1970).

16. Karl Nyren, "Muzzles and Tin Cans," *Library Journal* 98:717 (Mar. 15, 1974).

17. Margaret Chase Smith. For excerpts from this speech in the U.S. Senate, June 1, 1970, *see* chapter 3 of this work.

18. William J. Fulbright, "What Students Can Do for Peace," *The Progressive* 34, no. 6:16 (June 1970).

19. Kingman Brewster, "If Not Reason, What?" *American Scholar* 39:246–47 (Spring 1970).

20. Theodore Caplow and Reece J. McGee, *The Academic Marketplace* (New York: Basic Books, 1958), p. 93. (In a different decade and another context, these authors also note that evaluations of professors are based upon performance, rather than personal biases as to viewpoint. They conclude that judgments as to appointment and tenure are made on professional bases.)

21. Kingman Brewster, "If Not Reason, What?" *American Scholar* 39:251–52 [Reprinted from the *American Scholar,* copyright 1970, by the United Chapters of Phi Beta Kappa. By permission of the publishers.]

Chapter 6

1. Wilbur Schramm, "The Nature of News," *Journalism Quarterly* 24:259 (Sep. 1949). [Reprinted with permission of *Journalism Quarterly.*]

2. Eugene Lyons, "Stifled Laughter," *Harper's* 152:559 (Apr. 1935).

3. Wilbur Schramm, "The Soviet Communist Theory of the Press," in *Four Theories of the Press,* by Fred S. Siebert, Theodore Peterson, and Wilbur Schramm (Urbana: Univ. of Illinois Pr., 1956), p. 107.

4. Arthur Koestler, *The God That Failed,* ed. by Richard Crossman (New York: Harper, 1959), p. 34.

5. The Beria story is informative to librarians as to the nature of reference librarianship in a totalitarian society. It is basic to an understanding of Soviet librarianship, as well as of Soviet journalism, that the Marxist-Leninist point of view is the only truth, hence all other views must be rejected as false, evil, or corrupt. News media and libraries are instruments to "educate" the people.

6. William Ernest Hocking, *Freedom of the Press* (Chicago, Univ. of Chicago Pr., 1947), p. 23.

7. Ibid., p. 23.

8. Arlene Lum, "A Bookworm Could Starve in China," *Honolulu Star Bulletin,* Nov. 11, 1971, p. D24.

9. Alfred North Whitehead, *Science and the Modern World* (New York: Macmillan, 1948), p. ix.

10. The Minneapolis *Star,* September 1, 1972, p. 6A.

11. The Commission on Freedom of the Press was chaired by Robert M. Hutchins, Chancellor, The University of Chicago, and was financed by Time Inc., and by *Encyclopedia Britannica.* Its members included Archibald MacLeish, Harold Lasswell, Reinhold Niebuhr, George N. Schuster, Arthur M. Schlesinger, Beardsley Ruml, Robert Redfield, Zechariah Chafee, Charles E. Merriam, John M. Dickinson, and William E. Hocking.

Robert D. Leigh was the Director of the staff, which included Ruth A. Inglis, Llewellyn White, and Milton D. Stewart.

The commission's publications on freedom of the press are among the most significant ever published, yet the reader of the *Chicago Tribune* would have been misled into believing that it was some kind of a subversive conspiracy formed with the aim of controlling the press.

12. Milton Mayer, "How to Read the Chicago *Tribune,*" *Harper's Magazine* 198: 24–35 (Apr. 1949).

13. Donald M. Schwarz, "General Semantics and the Reporter's Job," in *Language, Meaning and Maturity,* edited by S. I. Hayakawa (New York, Harper, 1954), p. 148.

14. Librarians, scholars, and journalists interested in the complex problems of free press versus fair trial can also find good illustrations of the conflict between these two principles in Donald Gillmor's book, *Free Press and Fair Trial* (Washington, D.C.: Public Affairs Pr., 1966), and in the aforementioned occasional paper published by the Center for the Study of Democratic Institutions (Santa Barbara, Calif.: The Center, 1965). This paper quotes, in reference to President Kennedy's assasination, *The Report of the Warren Commission . . .* (New York: McGraw-Hill, 1964), chapter 5:

> Neither the press nor the public had a right to be contemporaneously informed by the police or prosecuting authorities of the details of the evidence being accumulated against Oswald. Undoubtedly the public was interested in these disclosures but its curiosity should not have been satisfied at the expense of the accused's right to a trial by an impartial jury. The courtroom, not the newspaper or the television screen, is the appropriate forum in our system for the trial of a man accused of a crime.

15. John Tebbel, "The Old New Journalism," *Saturday Review* 54: 96–97 (Mar. 13, 1970).

16. Hocking, *Freedom of the Press,* p. 37.

17. Herbert Brucker, "Can Printed News Save a Free Society?" *Saturday Review* 53: 55 (Oct. 10, 1970).

18. Daniel Bell, "Columbia and the New Left," *The Public Interest* No. 13: 85–87 (Fall, 1968). Quoted by Leo Rosten in *A Trumpet for Reason* (Garden City, N.Y.: Doubleday, 1970), p. 19.

19. Mitchell V. Charnley, *Reporting* (New York: Holt, 1966), p. 291–92.

20. From the *New York Times Literary Supplement,* Sept. 15, 1972, p. 1–3.

21. John Chancellor, "A Bias Toward Reason," Minneapolis *Tribune,* Nov. 15, 1970, p. 11.

22. Siebert, Peterson, Schramm, *Four Theories of the Press* (Urbana: Univ. of Illinois Pr., 1956, 1972), p. 7.

23. Theodore Peterson, "The Social Responsibility Theory of the Press," in *Four Theories of the Press,* p. 74.

Chapter 7

1. *ALA Handbook of Organization 1973–74* (Chicago, American Library Assn., 1973), p. 58.

2. David K. Berninghausen, "The Librarian's Commitment to the Library Bill of Rights," *Library Trends* 19:27 (July 1970).

3. American Library Association. Activities Committee on New Directions for ALA, Subcommittee on Social Responsibility, *Final Report* (Chicago: ALA, 1970), pp. 29–30.

4. Ibid., p. 30.

5. John Berry, (Editorial) *Library Journal* 98:11 (Jan. 1, 1973).

6. John Berry, "Council Cop-out," *Library Journal* 96:918 (Mar. 15, 1971).

7. Ibid., p. 921.

8. *American Libraries* 2:248 (March, 1971).

9. Ibid., p. 263.

10. Ibid., p. 251.

11. William Eshelman, "Social Responsibility and the Library Press," *Wilson Library Bulletin* 46:805–6 (May 1972).

The constant reader of the "opinion coverage" of ALA affairs is probably already aware that the library press seldom gives its readers straight news reports of what happened at ALA conferences. He may also have realized how rarely has there been a challenge to the social responsibility concept of libraries and the ALA as partisan advocates. Of course, the above items are examples, and the reader must remember that whenever passages are quoted out of context some distortion is likely to occur, even when it is not intended. Therefore, the reader is urged to read and judge for himself the full text of each example cited.

12. William Gilman, *Science USA* (New York: Viking, 1965), p. 23.

13. *Atlantic Monthly* 228:43 (Sept. 1971). [Copyright© 1971, by the Atlantic Monthly Co., Boston, Mass. Reprinted with permission.]

14. Judith Krug and James Harvey, "An Ox of a Different Color," *American Libraries* 2, no. 1:533 (May 1971).

15. Morris Philipson, "What Is a University Press Worth?", *University of Chicago Magazine,* p. 17 (Sept./Oct., 1972).

16. Lincoln Barnett, *The Universe and Dr. Einstein* (New York: Sloane, 1948), pp. 81–82.

Chapter 8

1. Louis Joughin, *Academic Freedom and Tenure* (Madison: Univ. of Wisconsin Pr., 1967), p. 36.

2. Bertram Davis, "Principles and Cases, the Mediative Work of the AAUP," *AAUP Bulletin* 56:169–73 (Summer 1970).

3. In Joughin's *Academic Freedom and Tenure,* p. 6, is an elaboration of due process:

> Another essential protection for the freedom of academic persons is a system of announced, orderly procedures governing internal institutional business. This protection is particularly necessary for the adjudication of charges which, if sustained, would lead to the termination of a tenure appointment or a nontenure appointment before the expiration of its limit. "Due Process" in termination proceedings should provide safeguards generally similar to those afforded by due process in legal proceedings: for example, there should be right to assistance by counsel or other advisor, confrontation of adverse evidence and witnesses, appropriate opportunity to cross-examine, to present evidence, and to submit argument, the making of a record, and decision by an unprejudiced tribunal. "Academic due process" adds to the mandatory procedural minima those further characteristically academic procedures, especially participation by faculty members in decisions, which hopefully will provide an informed and just adjudication of academic controversy.
>
> Academic freedom, tenure, and academic due process thus form a triad which brings together the deep regard of the civilized world for knowledge and the practical forms of protection needed by academic workers. . . .

4. The Program of Action for Mediation, Arbitration and Inquiry, adopted by ALA Council, June 25, 1971, defines the scope of responsibility of SCMAI as follows:

> The Committee is hereby assigned responsibility for mediation, arbitration, and inquiry, relating to tenure, status, fair employment practices, due process, ethical practices, and the principles of intellectual freedom as set forth in policies adopted by the Council of the American Library Association.
>
> The Committee shall have full authority to interpret all pertinent ALA approved policies in implementing this PROGRAM OF ACTION FOR MEDIATION, ARBITRATION AND INQUIRY and conducting activities to meet its committee responsibilities.
>
> Nothing in this PROGRAM OF ACTION FOR MEDIATION, ARBITRATION AND INQUIRY nor in the authority assigned to the Committee shall be understood, implied, or interpreted as granting or vesting in the Committee any policy-making function for any unit of the American Library Association. Nothing in this limitation, however, shall preclude the Committee from referring to any appropriate unit the need for ALA policy.

Regarding complaints, this *Program of Action* also states:

> A.   All complaints of alleged violations received at ALA Headquarters, regardless of the unit or individual receiving such, shall be forthwith transmitted to the Committee. No complaint of any alleged violation shall be considered unless it is made by a party directly involved in the alleged violation.

1. When a complaint is received, whether oral or written, the Committee shall supply a standard form, to be called Request for Action. The form is to be completed and signed, and returned to the Committee by the complainant.
2. Until a completed and signed Request for Action is received by the Committee, no formal action will be taken. (Formal action means mediation, arbitration, filing of a brief, or inquiry.)

5. "St. Peter's Teacher Wins an Extension," New York *Times,* July 17, 1969, p. 54.